P9-CCO-656

Sociological Approaches to Law

Sociological Approaches to Law

Edited by Adam Podgórecki and
Christopher J. Whelan

ST. MARTIN'S PRESS NEW YORK

© 1981 Adam Podgórecki and Christopher J. Whelan
All rights reserved. For information write:
St. Martin's Press, Inc., 175 Fifth Avenue, New York, N.Y. 10010
Printed in Great Britain
First published in the United States of America in 1981

Library of Congress Cataloging in Publication Data
Main entry under title:

Sociological Approaches to Law.

Chiefly papers presented at a conference held at
Corpus Christi College, Oxford, England, Oct. 2-4, 1978.
Bibliography: p.
Includes indexes.
1. Sociological jurisprudence — Congresses.
I. Podgórecki, Adam. II. Whelan, Christopher J.
K367.S6 340'.115 81-5311
ISBN 0-312-73962-1 AACR2

LIBRARY
LAKEWOOD COMMUNITY COLLEGE

Contents

Acknowledgements

The editors would like to thank their colleagues, Keith Hawkins and Doreen McBarnet, for valuable comments on the Introduction. We would like also to express grateful thanks to the 'team' of typists without whose co-operation the task before us would have been too great. They were Jenny Dix, Noel Harris, Carolyn Hartley, Beverly Roger, Jeanne Bliss and Rosemary Stallan. We would also like to thank Martha Davis for her help in compiling the index. We would also like to express gratitude to the Centre for Socio-Legal Studies, Wolfson College, Oxford and its Directors, Donald Harris and Max Hartwell, for the opportunity of preparing this volume.

Introduction

> In 1968 Renato Treves and J.F. Glastra van Loon edited *Norms and Actions*, a book of essays by indigenous scholars describing 'law and society' research in their countries. No account of work in Britain was included, probably because there was so little activity in the field at that time. Yet only eight years later, remarkable changes seem to have occurred.

This state of affairs was reported in an article in *Law and Society Review* by Campbell and Wiles in 1976. One notable exception to the lack of activity in this field in Britain which was not referred to by Campbell and Wiles was the work of Sir Otto Kahn-Freund.[1] For several decades, Sir Otto was a major contributor to the study of 'law and society'. His studies placed family law and labour law in their social context. His use of sociology, unprecedented from an academic lawyer in Britain, placed him in a virtually unique position. The explanation for this stems largely from his upbringing in Germany and from his informal but intensive contact with a group of younger lawyers and sociologists there, some of whom were especially influenced and inspired by the writing and teaching of Hugo Sinzheimer in Frankfurt, including his *Task of the Sociology of Law* (Sinzheimer, 1935). In addition, the influence of Marx and of Weber, and also of jurists such as the Austrian Eugen Ehrlich, whose methodology had sociological leanings, can be seen in Sir Otto's introduction to Karl Renner (1949). His role as a founding father of socio-legal studies in Britain will be outlined later.

Although Campbell and Wiles did stress important factors, such as the development of social sciences in general, the real achievement of British criminology and a well established anthropology of law, they seemed unable to find a satisfactory or comprehensive explanation of the rapid and unexpected development of the 'sociological' study of law in Britain. In this introduction we shall attempt to point out some of these underlying causes, to outline some distinctive features of British studies, and to locate the place of this volume in the development of the sociological study of law in Britain.

Traditional Legal Science

Without doubt, the theoretical study of law in Britain has been underdeveloped. Although jurisprudence (especially analytical jurisprudence) has achieved a good deal by way of semantic clarification, it has never really *explained* law. Beyond 'armchair theorising' jurisprudence has little to say about the nature of real, existing legal systems, it has no methodological bases upon which to explain law or legal phenomena.

The sociological approach to studying law is quite different. While the sources of analysis for lawyers are the taken-for-granted indicators of legal rules, such as legislation and formal court decision, for the sociologist major issues might include, amongst other things, the role of law in achieving social order, social control, social organisation or social change.

The completely negative attitude of the English legal profession, and of many academic lawyers towards socio-legal studies (including a widespread distrust of criminology and penology), as well as the changes during the last ten years or so must both be explained on two levels: first, from the particular structure of the law and the profession in this country, and secondly, from causes not specific to this country but in the nature of legal practice in general. The specifically English causes are linked with Weber's insight into the 'guild' nature of the common law, and the link between guild origin and a process which encourages, indeed demands, thinking by way of case law (casuistic thinking). Law is an art or a craft, transmitted from master to apprentice; any other way is suspected as destructive — hence, the continued and continuing resistance to changes in legal education. It is taught at undergraduate level, whereas on the Continent, in contrast, the study of law at universities is aimed at teaching civil servants rather than guild members. In this country, law has developed piecemeal: current principles are derived largely from past precedents; the structure and form of English law differs markedly therefore from Civil Law jurisdictions, where codes of law are the main resource, and where reliance on pragmatism therefore is far less marked.

The absence of social theory in the training of English lawyers has thus been very apparent. One major reason for this may be the traditional English attitude to social science which (at least in the past) has itself been marked by pragmatism, and also by a preference for empiricism over theorising. Thus, there have been few, if any, major English theorists upon which lawyers could draw. Moreover, sociologists had themselves, until recently, neglected the study of law and legal institutions.

The result is that until recently, in English law faculties, there has rarely been any reference to the 'law in context', to the relationships of law to society. Instead, law has been studied in little boxes: in terms of offer and acceptance, negligence and divorce, rather than non-contractual relations between businessmen (Macauley, 1963), insurance (Ross, 1970) and family breakdown (Eekelaar, 1971). As a result, few English law students (who, in comparison with their Continental counterparts, have studied in very small law schools) have entered careers other than the traditional legal profession. This is not surprising; since law is not regarded as a general career training they are ill-equipped to tackle public administration, labour-management relations, industry or government.[2]

More generally, lawyers are conditioned by the nature of their work (even if it is drafting legislation) to think in the marginal, the exceptional or the abnormal situations. While this may also be the concern of the empirical social scientist, the routine and typical situation is for him also an important topic of study. While the lawyer may extract a rule to handle routine situations and problems, his data base is built up by accretion from cases which are by definition abnormal. The lawyer is rarely interested in the general, only in the individual case. Hence, his lack of understanding of empirical research and of any statistical, quantitative approach to law. He also views with distrust qualitative or interpretive research which may rely on observation.

The general distrust which persists is exemplified by the response to the study by Baldwin and McConville (1977) on plea bargaining in Birmingham. It was greeted by a public debate of bitter intensity, including criticism by the Bar Council and by Sir David Napley, former President of the Law Society. While 'remarkable changes' have occurred, in that such studies are now being done, the process of change in a more fundamental, structural sense is much slower and more resisted.

A further factor which may have increased lawyers' distrust was their suspicion of explanations couched in terms of social causation. The lawyer and the empirical social scientist may operate with different concepts of 'cause' or 'causation'. The lawyer does not see law as a social phenomenon caused by and in turn causing other social phenomena, but something which is self-sufficient in itself. And as regards the conduct of individuals, the question, what caused this conduct, is often overshadowed by the question of subjective fault or of guilt which puts a limit to any more general causal argument, and again makes it, to some extent, suspect.

Rapid Development of the Sociological Approach to Law

From the standpoint of the practising lawyer, considerable changes have occurred since the Second World War, and the tempo of change has recently accelerated. First, the profession (particularly solicitors) is getting involved in law concerning the many rather than the few (for example, through legal aid) and secondly, the law for the many is contained mainly in statute, and the study of statutes, or codes, presupposes a new, more systematic and broadly-based technique, which must go behind and beyond the words of the statute, for example, to the context in which it was framed. Increasingly, therefore, lawyers have been faced with a new set of questions which demand a sort of analysis different from the traditional approach. The creation of new rights for specific sections of the community, laws relating to labour and race relations, to consumers and to families, together with increased state intervention in the regulation of lives, have all led to a growing awareness amongst lawyers (to varying degrees) of the deficiencies of traditional legal services. A major manifestation of this has been the institutionalisation of law reform, and law reformers, in particular the Law Commission, have had a very active and positive attitude towards developments in socio-legal studies, especially in family law, since it was founded in 1965. This too may have contributed towards the gradual growth of a new mentality, caused by the changing structure of the sources of law, and of the needs of the new 'consumers' of law.

Pressures for legal reform, for greater 'access to justice' and for the 'delegalisation' of the judicial process have led to attempts to improve legal representation, the proliferation of tribunals, legal advice centres and so on, while lawyers have more often been faced with problems that go beyond the minutiae of legal analysis. Thus, over-specialisation in the 'black-letter' approach and in the pragmatic, individualistic, case-by-case attitude is being continually threatened by the growing recognition that a complete understanding of the law cannot be obtained within traditional legal science. Specialists from several legal sub-disciplines — labour law, (for example, Wedderburn, 1971), race relations (for example, Hepple, 1970), family law (for example, Eekelaar, 1971) — began attempts to explore the potential of the empirical approach as a possible remedy for their frustrations with unresolved problems.

A useful recent example of the sorts of questions which are now being asked can be found in a study of law and consumer agencies by Cranston (1979, p. 171):

> An examination of the regulatory process of consumer agencies raises the question of whether it is successful. Do we conclude that consumer protection is a myth; that consumer law is modified in its implementation in favour of those being regulated; that consumer agencies and businesses have evolved an accommodation which harms neither; and that the occasional prosecution for a breach of consumer law is ritual with little practical significance? Is consumer protection actually favourable to the business community because it falsely deludes the public into believing that something is being achieved, and permits businesses to continue their traditional practices while surrounded with an aura of social responsibility?

To answer these questions, theoretical studies in law based on an empirical approach have become recognised by legal scholars as complementary and indispensable contributions to the understanding of the operations of law. A reliable answer is not available within traditional legal science; indeed, to formulate these questions a theoretical perspective is necessary.

The value of such studies increases when the changes which law schools introduce into the curriculum are in response to demands made from outside. Industrial innovations, political pressures and social needs force law schools to redesign their training to meet newly emerging expectations. Theoretical studies in law based on empirical research are also consistent with the new idea (prominent in North America) of the university and its relationship to the broadly understood environment; no longer are universities such ivory towers, existing independently of the rest of society.

Finally, theoretical studies in law based on empirical research tend also to criticise the 'establishment' for its quite often hidden, but oppressive, functions. Sociology is a sceptical discipline, it unmasks as opposed merely to describing or even to eulogising the law.

Invisible Colleges

The roots of the 'remarkable changes' referred to by Campbell and Wiles, then, of the rapid development of theoretical studies based on empirical research in the law in Britain can be ascribed to the disenchantment with the explanatory potential of jurisprudence and as a reaction against its stronghold academically. Their analysis of the remarkable changes also suffered from a paradigmatic limitation, probably fashioned by the traditional respect for academically elaborated results, such as studies presented in the form of articles, books, monographs and so on.

But, in fact, the flow of new ideas in social sciences, at least in some branches of them, has recently taken a different form. Our guess is that the rapid development of empirically oriented studies of law is also connected with the activities of so-called 'invisible colleges'. In certain areas of social sciences, novel or non-conformist thoughts, for various reasons, have to discover forms of expression which differ from those already established. In social sciences, this may occur if ideas are 'frozen' by existing organisational schemes; or if basic assumptions appear to be unquestionable or taken for granted as obvious; or if existing ideas are treated as more or less sacred dogmas. The more or less informal groups which discuss these non-conformist thoughts, exchange copies of unpublished papers, hold almost private party meetings and so on, can be viewed as 'invisible colleges' (Crane, 1972). They may or may not anticipate academic achievements that are later fully recognised, for while many ideas try to find expression, only some are able to survive. Indeed, those ideas that are not able to withstand attacks from other academic establishments, to defend themselves against constant tests of methodological scrutiny, or to generate enough attention tend to disappear. In any case, all these processes of discussions, tests, trials and intellectual challenges require a proper milieu. In many cases, 'invisible colleges' can create this.

It seems quite plausible that the 'invisible colleges' established through the activities of members of the Research Committee of the Sociology of Law of the International Sociological Association (RCSL — ISA), played this role in the development of sociological studies of law in Britain. A characteristic of this committee is that it spreads its ideas mainly through conferences held every year since its inception in Washington in 1962. (The book edited by Treves and van Loon (1968) on the sociology of law in different countries was the product of a conference organised by this committee.) It also seems plausible that the conference organised by Jean Floud, Philip Lewis and Roy Stuart at Nuffield College, Oxford in 1971, funded by the Nuffield Foundation, had exactly the same character. Moreover, this conference attracted several members of the RCSL — ISA, including Torstein Eckoff, Pauline Morris, Phillippe Nonet, Adam Podgórecki, Philip Selznick and Richard White. In addition, the rise of critical criminology, for example, through the National Deviancy Conference in the 1960s and 1970s, led, through both a political and theoretical stance, from the study of crime to a study of the criminal law itself. This also opened the way towards the development of a sociology of law in Britain.

In 1972, a 'socio-legal panel', set up by the SSRC, recommended the establishment of the Centre for Socio-Legal Studies. A new SSRC committee, on Social Sciences and the Law, was established shortly after. Sir Otto Kahn-Freund, one of the leading figures in initiating the panel and on the panel itself, and a member of the Social Sciences and the Law Committee, was made the first chairman of the Centre's standing committee, a sign of the 'special relationship' between the two.

Campbell and Wiles claim that the precise reason for establishing the SSRC Social Sciences and the Law Committee 'remains somewhat obscure' (1976, p. 570). In fact, establishment was part and parcel of these developments; in particular, it was a response to fears that the Centre might come to monopolise funds and personnel in the field.

The general proposition that theoretical studies based on empirical research in the law were encouraged in Britain through the activities of an 'invisible college or colleges' is supported by the influence of another conference, organised by Pauline Morris for the RCSL — ISA at Girton College, Cambridge in 1973. The dominance of international figures in the sociology of law was not accidental. Indeed, ten out of the twelve papers were delivered by foreigners.

Although sociology of law may lead 'a somewhat precarious existence predominantly located on the fringes of law departments and faculties' (Hunt, 1978, pp. 1-2), its position in Britain appears to be more secure and growing in strength. More and more law schools offer options in the sociology of law, while some make it compulsory. A number of post-graduate degrees in socio-legal studies are now available. The *British Journal of Law and Society* has now been joined by the *International Journal for the Sociology of Law* which began publication (as such) in 1979; the theme for the 1979 British Sociological Assocation's annual conference was 'Law and Society'.

Meanwhile, the Socio-Legal Group has held fairly regular meetings at Manchester and Sheffield. Further signs of the broader nature of legal education can be found also in the creation of two other British-based journals, the *International Review of Law and Economics* (which reflects a slow but steady introduction of economic techniques to legal problems) and the *Oxford Journal of Legal Studies*.

Purpose and Structure of this Volume

With these developments in mind, a conference organised by Adam Podgórecki and the Centre for Socio-Legal Studies and held at Corpus Christi College, Oxford (2-4 October, 1978) was intended to analyse and consider the following points:

(a) to recall the important notion that sociological techniques and methods of inquiry have cognitive value only if they are based on recognised theoretical assumptions. Although such techniques and methods may be used in an attempt to discover the extent to which they are suitable in the analysis of a given problem, in order to find new perspectives or results, they should serve as a means of testing advance *a priori* theoretical expectations. While much excitement has been caused by the use (and misuse) of sociological research, this principle quite often has been neglected. As a result, many studies have appeared which, without a theoretical framework, have been fragmented and oriented in different directions and have added little or nothing;

(b) to show that approaches which are fashionable are not necessarily the most appropriate ones. The intrusion of sociological perspectives into the study of law is also a recent development. It is probably accidental that it is those theoretical perspectives which were at hand and in circulation that have been selected. But these accidental choices do not necessarily coincide with the intrinsic needs of theoretically and empirically oriented studies of the law;

(c) to indicate that the comprehensive understanding of a given legal system and its multiple connections with the corresponding social system needs to have access to a multi-dimensional theoretical perspective, that is 'The totality of sociological theories and nothing less can satisfy a sociology of law' (Schiff, 1976, p. 295). For students, in particular, a variety of theoretical perspectives should be provided in the context of different social questions and problems rather than a one-dimensional view.

The discussion at the conference showed quite clearly that many lawyers recognised the need to enlarge the spectrum of theoretical perspectives which might be useful to them. Consequently, taking into account the conference discussions, some of the papers presented at the conference have been 'translated' in this volume to meet a different, possibly less ambitious, task — to link together the current approaches in the social sciences (especially sociology) with the selected problems of the study of law. This book, which includes other contributions, should be regarded as the result of this endeavour.

Notes

1. For a valuable insight into the early German writings and career of Kahn-Freund, see R. Lewis and J. Clark (eds.), *Labour Law and Politics in the Weimar Republic: Selected German Writings of Otto Kahn-Freund* (Blackwell, Oxford, 1981).
2. Legal training in the UK is discussed in detail in the *Final Report of the Royal Commission on Legal Services* (Cmnd. 7648 HMSO, London, 1979), vol. 1.

Bibliography

Baldwin, J. and McConville, M., *Negotiated Justice: Pressures to Plead Guilty* (Martin Robertson, London, 1977)

Campbell, C. and Wiles, P., 'The Study of Law in Society in Britain'. *Law and Society Review*, vol. 10, no. 4 (1976), pp. 574-8

Crane, D. *Invisible Colleges* (Chicago University Press, Chicago, 1972)

Cranston, R. *Regulating Business: Law and Consumer Agencies* (Macmillan, London, 1979)

Eekelaar, J. *Family Security and Family Breakdown* (Penguin, Harmondsworth, 1971)

Hepple, B. *Race, Jobs and the Law in Britain*, 2nd edn (Penguin, Harmondsworth, 1970)

Hunt, A. *The Sociological Movement in Law* (Macmillan, London, 1978)

Macauley, S. 'Non-Contractual Relations in Business', *American Sociological Review*, vol. 28 (1963), pp. 55-69

Renner, K. *The Institutions of Private Law and their Social Function* (Routledge and Kegan Paul, London, 1949; edited and introduced by O. Kahn-Freund)

Ross H.L. *Settled Out of Court* (Aldine, Chicago, 1970)

Schiff, D.N. 'Socio-Legal Theory: Social Structure and Law', *Modern Law Review*, vol. 39, no. 3 (1976), pp. 287-310

Sinzheimer, H. *The Task of the Sociology of Law* (in German, H.D. Tjeenk, Willink and Zoon, N.V., Haarlem, 1935)

Treves, R. and G. van Loon *Norms and Actions: National Reports on the Sociology of Law* (Martinus Nijhoff, The Hague, 1968)

Wedderburn, K.W. *The Worker and the Law*, 2nd edn (Penguin, Harmondsworth, 1971)

1 Fundamentals of Structuralist Theory

Edmund Leach

Definition of Structuralism

With a bit of journalistic licence the term structuralism can be made to mean almost anything. Quite apart from structuralist linguistics and structuralist social anthropology, where the jargon seems to have started out, we have structuralist literary critics, structuralist psychoanalysts, structuralist historians, structuralist philosophers, structuralist Marxists and so on and so forth. It had not occurred to me until I was asked to give this paper that there might even be a form of structuralist legal study; but why not?

I do not intend to explore all these avenues nor am I going to chase after great names by trying to distinguish the structuralism of Lévi-Strauss from the structuralism of Chomsky or of Lacan or of Foucault or whatever. I shall simply try to give some account, in the limited space available, of some of the basic ideas that seem to be involved.

The most basic idea of all is that the phenomena of culture — our houses, our clothes, our meals, our social conventions at all levels — embody messages which convey information to those who participate in these conventions. Structuralists claim to be able to break the codes of the various kinds of cryptography in which this hidden language is supposed to be expressed. Ordinary spoken language is itself one such system of social conventions. In this case we take it for granted that linguistic expressions convey information. But how does this come about? If we fully understood the language of words, we might be able to understand the language of clothes.

So let me start with the notion of a word. At an empirical level in the world out there, a word is a segment of sound pattern imposed on the breath; as such, it is evanescent, but the variations in air pressure can be picked up by the diaphragm of a microphone when they can be transformed into electrical impulses and then recorded in permanent form, such as a patterned trace of residual magnetism on a tape. A word can also be given empirical form in the world out there by tracing a pattern on a piece of paper, or hitting the keys of a typewriter in a particular order, or programming a computer to generate the word in response to certain predetermined patterned instructions. Notice that what is common to the various forms in which the word may be manifested or stored away is a structured pattern. The possibility of making a transformation from one manifest form into another manifest form depends upon pattern recognition, either on the part of a human agent or on the part of a specially programmed machine. Notice also that in the whole of this argument so far there has been no reference to 'meaning'; I have simply been talking about a word as a segment of sound pattern.

But most segments of sound pattern are not words; the noise of a passing car is not a word. Sound patterns only become words when they are generated by human brains. From here on I shall cease to be strictly empiricist and start talking about concepts and images 'in the mind'. Let me admit that I do not really know what the word mind means and neither do you, but provided you do not quibble too much I think you ought to be able to understand what I am saying.

A sound pattern such as 'boo' can exist in the world out there and it can be picked up by the diaphragm of my ear after the fashion of a microphone. But I can also 'think' of the sound 'boo' without there being any actual noise generated anywhere. I shall refer to such mental constructs as sound images. But here again a sound image is not necessarily associated with a meaning: it is not in itself a concept. But a sound image might be a concept. If I replace the b of 'boo' with a p we are still (as English-speakers) left with a meaningless pattern . . . 'poo'; but if the shift is to d or t then suddenly the patterns become words. Rather odd, dissociated words in this particular case: 'do', 'to', 'two', 'too'; but if we then move down the alphabet we quite quickly come to 'loo', which is a noun with a whole clutter of associations. Notice that while the sound pattern 'too' may evoke in the mind the twoness of two, the concept of 'twoness' certainly has nothing to do with the sound image; on the other hand, the historical etymology whereby the word 'loo' came to be used as a euphemism for 'water closet', on the analogy of Waterloo, has now worked right round in a circle with the construction of a 'superloo' in Waterloo station!

The object of these remarks is to bring out the point that the relational structure, which ties together empirical objects in the world out there with denotative names, considered as words out there, with word images in the mind, is really very loose so that all sorts of transformations are possible between one end of the chain and the other. As we move along such chains from object to sound pattern to sound image to concept or backwards in the reverse direction the links in the chain consist of patterned structures.

Let me explain that by a musical analogy which was first used by Bertrand Russell (Russell, 1948, p. 270). A musical composition is first generated by operations in the mind of the composer. The first form in which it is likely to exist in the external world is as a notation on a sheet of paper. Later, through the mental operations of performers and orchestral conductor and the movements of the performers' fingers, lips and so forth it is generated as a pattern of sound imposed on the air. From this state it may be recorded and converted into grooves on a gramophone record or patterns of magnetism on a tape. In all these transformations where do we locate the music? Clearly the music is just as much *on* the gramophone record as it is *on* the composer's original sheet of music. What is common to the various transformations is ordered pattern — a very specific ordered pattern which makes the music what it is and not something else. It is not the sound that is the music it is something much more abstract which can equally well be an attribute of human brain process (or mind) and the surface of a gramophone record.

Let me take another example. Here is a passage from James Joyce's *Finnegans Wake:* 'In the name of Annah the Allmaziful, the Everliving, the Bringer of Plurabilities, haloed be her eve, her singtime sung, her rill be run, unhemmed as it is uneven!' (Joyce, 1946, p. 104). As you can easily recognise this is a complicated dream-like transformation of bits of the Lord's Prayer, a Muslim invocation to Allah, various heresies about the status of the Virgin Mary, and sundry other things all designed to be recited with an Irish accent. But it is not the words which tell us this. Indeed, most of the words are made-up words which would not ordinarily appear in any lexicon. The meaning of the passage is in the patterned structure, in the grammatical construction. Or, to put it slightly differently, it is the total set of words, together with other sets of words, of which these words are echoes, which provide the 'meaning'. The words taken one by one, or even sets of words taken in groups do not really convey any information. It is the total system, what we observe consciously plus what we recognise unconsciously, which tells us what it is all about. And of course we shall each of us individually give rather different meanings to this totality depending upon our respective religious backgrounds, our acquaintance with James

Joyce's other writings, our familiarity with the processes of free association and so on.

And another point: in interpreting Joyce's nonsense language we make two kinds of association. We treat the words 'as if' they formed an ordinary sentence; that is we consider the passage as a sequence of separable units and we draw significance from the fact that some units are contiguous with other units. This relationship by contiguity is what structuralists are talking about when they refer to 'syntagmatic chains' and to 'metonymy'. In making sense out of Joyce's nonsense all speakers of English will recognise the same syntagmatic chains since they derive from the syntax of genuine English. But we also rely on quite a different kind of association — that of metaphor or paradigm — and in this case the 'message' will vary from individual to individual. 'Annah the Allmaziful' will be the shared metaphor for 'Allah the All Merciful' for a great many people, but the scores of other harmonic echoes which this phrase may suggest will vary according to the reader's private experience. The coupled oppositions: syntagmatic chain/paradigmatic association, metonymy/metaphor, melody/harmony are not quite identical but they are very similar and their use is fundamental in all varieties of structuralist decoding procedures.

What I have just been saying about how, up to a point, we may come to understand what is being said in a passage from *Finnegans Wake* is very similar to Lévi-Strauss's theories about how we should understand what is being said in a myth recorded among the Bororo Indians of Amazonia (Lévi-Strauss, 1964-71). Lévi-Strauss insists first of all that myths exist as sets and not just as isolated items; so that we can only understand any particular myth by reference to its similarity and contrast with other myths in the set. But also, even beyond that, the myths which are consciously known to exist and which can be recorded on a tape by a diligent field-working anthropologist, echo at an unconscious level other myths which have been generated by other human minds in quite different cultural contexts, so that the meaning which is embodied in the shared structure of a corpus of myth should ultimately be regarded as an attribute of a total collectivity, the human mind itself.

Cultural Phenomena

This is all very grand and it is much easier to think in this grandiose way if you are a Frenchman or a German than if you are English. For in

French the word *esprit* and in German the word *Geist* have a very wide spread of meaning which includes both mind and spirit whereas the empiricist English carefully distinguish metaphysical spiritual essences of the ghost, soul type from abstractions such as mind which, for all its vagueness, they like to tie down to the operation of specific material brains.

However, structuralism of the sort that I am trying to expound is not an uncompromisingly idealist philosophy. The facts that the structuralists are trying to understand are facts in the world out there, cultural phenomena, the distortions which human beings, in their human activities, have imposed upon Nature — meaning by Nature the world that would be there anyway even if there had never been any human beings around to push it about. Structuralists hope to understand the patterns that can be discerned in such hard material things as groups of buildings and networks of roads; they are not exclusively concerned with the operations of metaphysical minds. But I have to admit that the roots of the argument do seem very metaphysical.

One of the most basic and most misunderstood features of structuralist argument is the use that is made of binary oppositions. Since most of the practitioners of the art have not understood the complexity of what is involved it is very difficult to give a lucid summary.

The first step is already implicit in the Saussurian argument which I have already presented (Saussure, 1916). If I am reading a text and my eyes pick up the sequence of letters g-o-o-d in the form of a complex pattern of marks on a piece of paper, this will generate in my mind the sound image good and the sound image will in turn generate a concept 'goodness'. In de Saussure's terminology the sound image and the concept, both of which, be it noted, only exist as abstractions 'in the mind', together constitute a sign. The sign has two component but inseparable parts — the *signifié* (the signified), that is to say the concept, and the *signifiant* (the signifying), that is to say the sound image.

We can thus write the sign as: S/s where S is the signifying or signifier and s is the signified. The key element in de Saussure's argument at this point is that the relationship between S and s which is denoted by the solidus is arbitrary. It happens that in English the sound pattern generated by the letter sequence g-o-o-d corresponds to the concept of goodness, but the same or some very similar concept is generated in other languages by other sound patterns, for example, French b-o-n.

There is nothing intrinsically good about the English sound pattern; the sound pattern as such could stand for anything. Now some of the latter-day structuralists have chewed on this part of the argument until it is completely unrecognisable but the guts of the matter are that in the totality of the two-part Saussurian sign which we write S/s there are really three elements: the signifier, the signified and the relationship between them, and it is the relationship, not the signifier nor the signified, which carries the hidden part of the 'meaning', and it is the relationship that we really want to understand.

The next step follows directly. Any concept can be defined by specifying the negation of its opposite. Goodness is that which is not 'not goodness' and, vice versa, badness is that which is not 'not badness'. Or, if you like, the opposition 'good/bad' can also be written 'good/not good'. And here again the argument is that the meaning is not in the word 'good' nor in its opposite 'not-good' but in the relationship between the two halves of the binary pair. But the first step of the argument led to the conclusion that the two halves of the binary pair are themselves relationships. So when structuralists concern themselves with binary oppositions they are, from their point of view, showing a preoccupation with relationships between relationships and this is indeed the guts of what structuralism is all about.

Structuralists maintain that social reality consists of abstract networks of relationships-between-relationships and that cultural phenomena in the world out there represent conscious and unconscious attempts by men to objectify these networks. Just as there is no necessary one-to-one correlation between a sound image and the concept it evokes in the mind, so there is no one-to-one correlation between cultural expression and what it is that is expressed. The cultural behaviour of South American Indians and of Oxford undergraduates are about as far apart as it is possible to get yet they might still be expressing the 'same thing'. But the sameness, if it exists, is at the abstract level of relations-between-relations and not at the superificial level of symbolic association, where A stands for B.

My problem, of course, is to demonstrate that such a very abstract form of argument might, at some point, begin to connect up with empirical reality, and the difficulty is that if I do try to give you examples in a context of this sort the result is bound to seem completely trivial. This is because it is an essential part of the structuralist thesis that the networks of related relationships which generate meaning are highly complex and that all short cuts are bound to trivialise the whole enterprise. The four volumes of Lévi-Strauss *Mythologiques* are all, formally at least, concerned with the analysis of a single Bororo myth which takes up less than two pages of text. But let me see what I can do.

As must be obvious the structuralist thesis is highly transformational. Cultural phenomena take many different forms. Some are material; some are institutional. Sometimes, but not always, the material forms and the institutional forms are closely integrated. Thus the word 'church' may stand for a building of a particular and easily recognisable type or for the organisation which owns and uses the building; this is likewise true of the word 'university'. For tourist visitors Oxford University is a collection of buildings; for the readers of this volume it is something quite other; though just what it is would be difficult to say.

This ambivalence of meaning reflects the fairly obvious fact that although there is a functional interdependence between the internal arrangements of the buildings and their institutional use this interdependence is a good deal more complicated than might at first appear.

For example, in the case of the Christian Church, which has a history of sectarian factionalism which extends over nearly 2,000 years, the organisation of the church considered as an institution has varied between very large-scale authoritarian hierarchy — as, for example, in the case of the Papacy — to locally organised pentecostal congregationalism with an extreme egalitarian bias. Doctrine varies accordingly — with the orthodox dyophysite theory of the Trinity at one extreme, and versions of the Aryan and monophysite heresies at the other. The use of church buildings has varied too. In the contexts of hierarchy the altar is separated from the congregation by a sequence of spaces, admission to which is reserved for the choir and the priesthood and which are themselves separated from each other by steps, screens, rails and names. Thus a typical church in the hierarchically-organised Church of England now has separate sections named nave, chancel, sanctuary, altar but at periods of liturgical history when the hierarchy of priestly authority is being played down the altar has been brought right forward into the nave (Leach, 1973).

It does not require a structural analysis to appreciate that in circumstances such as these the internal arrangements of buildings, the categories of doctrine, the hierarchy of roles and offices within the institution and the patterning of liturgical practice are all transformations of the same structure, but this example does give you some idea of what structuralists may be talking about under the label 'transformation'. However, an actual structuralist analysis of a set of buildings and their internal and external ordering would proceed at a much more abstract level; perhaps somewhat on the following lines.

A village church is not a building by itself, it is a building among other buildings that we need to look at. The buildings as a total set can be distinguished from one another in all sorts of ways — by their size, their permanence, their style of construction, their major use and so on. Here too there have been many changes in the course of history but it is still likely to be the case that the church, which is doctrinally 'the House of God', is the largest and most permanent structure in the village, that most other buildings will be houses for human habitation, and that the buildings which are allocated for animal habitation are less permanent, though not necessarily less elaborate, than those intended for human beings.

The spaces in such buildings can be distinguished as private and public. The distinction is that a private space is set apart from a public space by some barrier — a door, a step, a rail, a stretch of empty ground — and that access to the private space at any one time is reserved for particular persons. In a church the sanctuary area around the altar is private in this sense; in a domestic building, privies and the bedroom occupied by the householder are likewise private. In the language of anthropology they are separated from public space by barriers of taboo.

The point of making such comparisons is that it leads us to think seriously about the otherwise fanciful idea propounded by the late Lord Raglan (Raglan, 1964) that domestic dwellings originated as family temples rather than shelters from the weather. No doubt this is somewhat far-fetched but we may learn quite a lot about the postulated relationship between God and Man by first seeing that there is an explicit analogue between two other relationships, namely: (i) Man/Man's dwelling place ('the house of Man'), and (ii) God/God's dwelling place ('the house of God'). Or, to go on from there, we shall only begin to appreciate the theological significance of religious architecture if we keep reminding ourselves at every step that 'the house of God' is a 'transformation' of 'the house of Man'. This has nothing to do with legal studies but it is close to the core of the anthropologist's interests.

My argument about church/house has turned on the distinction between 'private' spaces and 'public' spaces. At the beginning of this century Durkheim developed the thesis that a category opposition of this kind, which he called 'sacred'/'profane', exists *a priori* as a basic characteristic of human thought and his whole analysis in the *The*

Elementary Forms of the Religious Life (Durkheim, 1912) is built up from this axiom. But when one looks into it one finds that Durkheim's assumptions about the relationship between the profane and the sacred were very much on a par with the assumptions which de Saussure was making at the same time about the relationship between signified concepts and their signifying sound images. The dichotomy sacred/profane constitutes a binary opposition and what is really 'significant' is the relationship, which we write as —/—, not the sacredness nor the profanity as such. So too in my present example, the significant point is that privies and householder's bedrooms and high altars are set apart, not that they are private or sacred.

But why are they set apart? In looking at things in this relatively abstract fashion we are also moving from the particular to the general. Privies and bedrooms are set apart because they are places for the performance of bodily excretion and sexual intercourse and it is almost universal throughout human society that these physical acts are subject to taboos of just this kind. Except in very special circumstances of religious ritual these are private acts performed in private places. Why? The structuralist answer is again very general. Man in society, the argument goes, is everywhere concerned to prove to himself and to his fellows that he is other than a beast. The humanity of mankind is precisely that which is human rather than animal, cultural rather than natural. But of course we are in fact animals and, in particular, the acts of excretion and sexual intercourse are animal actions; therefore such actions must be kept apart; out of sight, out of public display.

Many peoples, including in the recent past the rural British, emphasise this point by having their farm animals live in buildings immediately adjacent to the human dwellings but compelling them to wallow in their own mire. Men are not pigs because men have privies and pigs live in filthy pig-sties. And if you want to be particularly contemptuous of the life-style of your neighbours you accuse them of living like pigs. The fact that the pig, if left to itself in open space, has notably sanitary habits is beside the point!

Another marker of being a human being is that whereas animals eat all their food raw, human beings eat most of their food cooked. The structure of culinary practices and the significance that is to be attached to such differences as raw versus cooked, roast versus boiled, smoked versus rotted has been the subject of a number of impressive structuralist essays both by Lévi-Strauss himself and his imitators. They do not all carry 100 per cent conviction but there is certainly something in it. We do not just eat; we eat in accordance with very elaborate conventions which determine when we shall eat, with whom we shall eat, what we shall eat at what time of day and on what kind of occasion, and even the sequence in which different dishes shall appear on the table. The more elaborate these conventions become the less animal we feel ourselves to be. The banquet feast is everywhere felt to be prototypical of civilised man.

The point I am making here is rather like the point I made about dwelling houses. Common sense tells us that the 'purpose' of a dwelling house is to provide shelter, but if we look into it we see that dwelling houses are, in fact, used to convey all kinds of messages about the mutual social statuses of those who enter them. So too common sense tells us that we eat to satisfy our hunger; yet the way we eat provides a whole lexicon of messages about the relative status of those who eat together and of their collective attitudes towards those who eat elsewhere. This switching of emphasis from the functional utility of customary behaviour to the message-bearing coding of that behaviour is highly characteristic of structuralist procedures.

But let me go back to my village buildings. Cooking needs fire. One of the first questions that a structuralist who is investigating the grouping and lay-out of a set of buildings will want to ask is: where are the fireplaces and what is the fire used for? Just as the design of dwelling houses and the design of meals and mealtimes can serve many other purposes besides those of providing shelter from the weather or the satisfaction of hunger, so fire does many other things besides keeping us warm. The Greeks in their myth of Prometheus suggested that the control of fire was the primary marker that relates Man to the Gods and distinguishes him from the beasts. Fireplaces, like privies and bedrooms, are very special localities. The position of the cooking hearth is especially important. Eating as such is, like excretion and sexual intercourse, an act of animal nature. But by cooking our food, which animals can never do, we can imagine that the fire, in indirect or direct fashion, converts the impure food of animals into the pure food of gods. By eating only food which has been prepared in a special way, usually by cooking, and eating it only at special times in special places we convert the action of eating from a biological into a prototypical cultural act. In such a framework the location of the cooking hearth marks the boundary between the natural world of animal life and the cultural world of human life.

In this connection it is worth noticing that in the Christian convention the food which is eaten in church is not cooked in the church and the only manifest fire is that used to generate light from candles and smoke from the burning of incense. But if we trace the Christian pattern back to its biblical model (which is provided by the description of the mythical Jewish tabernacle) we shall realise that the screen barriers which separate the nave from the chancel and the chancel from the sanctuary have replaced sacrificial fires of which the smoking incense in Catholic ritual is a reminder.

The transformation seems fairly clear:-

(a) as we move from the outside world towards the seat of God we pass through a sequence of barriers. As we pass each barrier we move into a space which is 'more sacred' than the last. We are 'purified' as by a fire.

(b) as raw food is brought into the house from the outside world and we move towards the marriage bed, which is the shrine of the house, the food passes through a sequence of conditions each 'more sacred' than the last. The food is purified by the fire and then we ourselves are purified by the act of consuming the purified food in 'ritual' circumstances. As Robertson Smith (Smith, 1889) long ago recognised, the fact that the Eucharist, the central ritual of Christianity, is built around the myth of the Last Supper in itself immediately declares a direct equivalence between what goes on at the altar rails of a church in the performance of the Mass and what goes on around the dining table of a domestic family meal.

The Potential of Structuralism

Those of you who are not already familiar with the sort of thing that structuralists do are likely to react to what I have been saying in one of two ways. Either you will say: 'How trivial and obvious!' or you will say: 'How fanciful and far-fetched!' Both comments are perfectly justifiable but my difficulty is that I have very little space to expound a set of rather complicated ideas. Structuralist procedures, when applied systematically by practitioners who know what they are up to, do throw new light on cultural phenomena; but to do the job properly takes up a lot of space. At the end of the day, you are still liable to say: 'Well yes, but I knew that already'. Because, after all, that is the whole point of the exercise. The structuralists are saying that the patterning of cultural phenomena in the world out there conveys 'hidden' information; it conveys the information at a semi-conscious level. All that structuralist analysis can do is to make what is perceived semiconsciously fully conscious; if structuralist analysis were ever to reveal something which you did not, in a certain sense, know already, then the analysis would be in error.

How can any of this be relevant for socio-legal studies? Quite frankly I simply do not know. It is, however, very obvious that the concept of criminality has a binary relationship with its opposite, that of normal respectable legality. It is also very obvious that the various things that we do to criminals, such as shutting them up in prison, are very much on a par with what we do to other kinds of sacred abnormal persons such as the sick, the mad and the sanctified — we put them into isolated institutional buildings, away from society and out of sight. It is also obvious that criminality, like religious heresy, is generated by its binary counterpart; the more rigidly defined the canons of orthodoxy, the more varied will be the forms of heresy and the greater the number of heretics, and the busier the Inquisition will be with their task of purifying the world by fire. But since orthodoxy and heresy are simply binary opposites, the issue of what is orthodox and what is heretical is ultimately simply a matter of politics, as became very clear in the England of the sixteenth century. When Protestants were in power, Catholics were heretics; when Catholics were in power, Protestants were heretics. And the same surely applies to criminality. The terrorists of our age are simply standing 'normal' values on their heads. We think that we are virtuous and they are villainous; they think just the reverse — they are virtuous, we are villainous. The question of which side is right is again simply a matter of politics: those who have the power will decide who is right and who is wrong.

There is nothing particularly structuralist about this relativist point of view. But structuralists take it for granted that any particular pattern of beliefs, values and cultural practices that happens to exist in any particular region at any particular point in history is just one of many possibilities and that if you can understand how any particular pattern fits together and then 'reverse all the signs' you will be back where you started — the relations between the relations will be the same as before.

In capitalist society the prototype criminal is the robber, the murderer, the rapist — someone who fails to respect the personal rights of the property-owning individual. But in communist countries the worst kind of criminal is precisely the man who would assert the personal rights of the individual as against the collective rights of the state. In some societies the 'worst' criminals are those who commit treason, in others 'heresy' and so on. In any particular case a careful study of just how different categories of offence are distinguished and evaluated in comparison with each other would, by inversion, tell us quite a lot about the positive valuations current in the society in question. Likewise the *obiter dicta* that judges and magistrates are prone to deliver when pronouncing sentence could often with advantage be read as if they were passages from *Finnegans Wake.* They tell us many things that are not manifestly in the words and, in particular, they tell us a great deal about both the formal and informal structure of English social class and about the inverse presuppositions of (a) those who have a vested interest in the system as it is and (b) those who do not.

But would this game of looking at society backwards, as in a mirror, tell us anything that we did not know already? I simply have no idea.

Perhaps one has to have a slight leaning towards mathematics to appreciate all this. A universe of negative matter in which time flows backwards is not possible to contemplate except as the inverse of what we know and experience, but this does not mean that exercises of the imagination of that sort are a complete waste of time. After all, the attributes of God are impossible to contemplate except as the inverse of what human beings know about — man is mortal, impotent, ignorant: God is immortal, omnipotent, omniscient. But if God is a fiction, it is a fiction which clearly plays an important part in human affairs. All that the structuralists are really saying is that there exist in the field of culture a great many other fictions which are generated in the first place as the binary opposites of what we already know, but that the patterning of these fictions affects, in a very radical way, the way we organise and exploit our man-made world. Therefore such patterning deserves careful study and analysis.

Bibliography

Durkheim, E. *Les formes élémentaires de la vie religieuse. Le system totemique en Australie* (Alcan, Paris, 1912)

Joyce, J. *Finnegans Wake* (Faber and Faber, London, 1946)

Leach, E. 'Melchisedech and the emperor: icons of subversion and orothodoxy', *Proceedings of the Royal Anthropological Institute of Great Britain and Ireland for 1972* (1973), pp. 5-14

Lévi-Strauss, C. *Mythologiques* (4 vols., Plon, Paris, 1964-71)

Raglan, Lord *The Temple and the House* (Routledge and Kegan Paul, London, 1964)

Russell, B. *Human Knowledge: Its Scope and Limitations* (George Allen and Unwin, London, 1948)

Saussure, F. de *Cours de Linguistique Générale* (Geneva, 1916). Edited posthumously by C. Bally, A. Sechehaye, and A. Riedlinger (C. Bally and L. Gauthier, Paris, 1921). The

text is based on lectures given in Geneva between 1906 and 1911
Smith, W. Robertson *Lectures on the Religion of the Semites: The Fundamental Institutions* (A. and C. Black, London, 1889) (3rd edn, edited by S.A. Cook, 1927)

2 A Structuralist Theory of Law: An Agnostic View

J.W. Harris

> If, as we believe to be the case, the unconscious activity of the mind consists in imposing forms upon content, and if these forms are fundamentally the same for all minds — ancient or modern, primitive or civilised (as the study of the symbolic function, as expressed in language, so strikingly indicates) — it is necessary and sufficient to grasp the unconscious structure underlying each institution and each custom in order to obtain a principle of interpretation valid for other institutions and other customs, provided, of course, that the analysis is carried far enough. (Lévi-Strauss, 1963, p. 21)

In the preceding essay, Dr Leach expresses uncertainty as to whether structuralism is of value to legal studies. There have been a few attempts to apply the methodology of the structuralists to specific areas of law. In the United States George Fletcher has studied the development of the Common Law of larceny in terms of two underlying structural principles, those of possessorial 'immunity' and 'objective criminality' (Fletcher, 1976); and Donald Hermann has examined certain areas of modern case law in the light of posited binary oppositions and transformations — for example, the progression from tort liability only for inherently dangerous products to a general manufacturer's liability based on reasonable foresight of harm, expounded in terms of the opposition between 'self' and 'environment' (Hermann, 1975). In the United Kingdom, Paul Robertshaw (1975) has examined a single decision of the House of Lords,[1] declaring *ultra vires* conditions imposed by a local authority on the grant of a licence to a caravan-site operator, in the light of the opposition between movables and immovables and their attendant statuses. It is this opposition, he suggests, which explains why their lordships considered it 'unreasonable' for the authority to insist on security of tenure provisions (appropriate to land) in the case of movable objects like caravans.[2] The explanatory value of such approaches to specific areas of law can only be assessed by comparing them with conventional historical or functional discussions of the same materials. What I should like to attempt here is something which, so far as I know, has not yet been tried, namely, a sketch of what a structuralist theory of law as a whole might look like.

Functionalists, whether their subject-matter is social anthropology, linguistics, cognitive psychology or whatever, require us to relate the innate qualities of the mind to cultural products. The latter may vary enormously. The former are always the same. The 'mind' contains a set of binary oppositions which are imposed on nature. These binary oppositions are physiologically based. They got there through evolution by natural selection of the human species and — given the slowness of biological evolution — they cannot have changed during the mere ten thousand years or so in which there have been cultural products of the sort in which legal researchers are interested. Whereas other social theorists have endeavoured to explain the evolution and present panoply of legal systems in terms of political and economic external pressures, on the one hand, or individual and group consciousness or ideologies, on the other hand, or combinations of both, the structuralist would tell us that all that has been produced had to fit into evolved slots in the subconscious mind. He would not dispute that external and internal forces drove man along the road to legal institutions. He would insist, however, that the parameters of what happened (and of what could have happened) were set by innate binary oppositions which man had evolved before the law process began. This means that any plausible candidates for relevant binary oppositions which man had evolved before the law process began. kind before there was any law, although they later shaped those cultural products which we now call 'law'. The binary oppositions were applied, before there was law, to non-law things; but they were susceptible, through transformations of the things they paired, of being applied to legal phenomena. A structuralist theory of law must assume that the human mind itself contains what we might call 'law-slots'.

How should a structuralist legal theorist set about finding the law-slots? Some of the writers cited above have started with legal materials. But, from the point of view of a general structuralist theory of law, this is to put the cart before the horse. We are looking for those innate binary oppositions which shaped law as a cultural product. They preexisted any particular bifurcations which various legal systems contain, though they might be related to them. Dr Leach tells us that the sort of structure in which structuralists are interested consists of relations between relations. A concept like 'cooked' is related to its opposite 'raw', but each side of this relationship is itself a relation between a signifier and what is signified. Strictly speaking, then, binary oppositions in the subconscious have no content at all. They are a sort of 'umph' in the mind which connects the auditory noise 'cooked' (or any equivalent auditory noise or other equivalent stimulus) with the idea 'cooked'; and this 'umph' is in turn related by a higher-order 'umph' to the 'umph' represented by the relation between 'raw' (as a noise' and 'raw' (as an idea). Thus, it can be posited that the binary opposition, the higher-order 'umph', is a universal feature of the human mind, whatever linguistic conventions or other symbols are used to stand for the signifiers which are involved in the lower-order 'umphs'.

It does seem to be a question of positing. Take a pair of opposed ideas like cooked/raw, darkness/light and so forth. Provided it is likely to have had tangible references for man in his most primitive conditions, you have a plausible candidate for a binary opposition. You then have to show how, through substituting for the concrete things originally paired by the opposition some more culturally significant artefacts, light can be shed on the institutions you are theorising about. Even though the binary oppositions may be in principle contentless, we shall have to use words to stand for them — English words if we are writing in English. We do not thereby commit ourselves to the view that exact equivalents are present in other languages for the paired words. The true binary opposition is the underlying, second-order 'umph'.

What are Legal Phenomena?

So much for the innate side of the structuralist equation. A structuralist theory of law would inevitably have problems with the other side of the equation which the big names in structuralism have not had. Just what is the 'law' which the binary oppositions are supposed to have shaped? Lévi Strauss's cultural products were myths and totems; Chomsky (1957) was explaining language; and Piaget's subject-matter was the linguistic performances of children. What are the 'legal phenomena' with which the sociology of law is concerned?

This is a question as to which legal theorists are notoriously divided. As we have to start somewhere, I shall stipulate that these phenomena are of three basic kinds. First, there are the typical sets of institutions which centre on courts, including legislatures, police forces, prisons, legal professions, legal departments of governments, corporations and trade unions, legal aid committees, legal advice centres and so on. Secondly, there are written collections of maxims which serve as the source of legal doctrine in adjudicating disputes. Thirdly, there are rules ('norms') produced by legislatures and courts, with or without the help of legal doctrine, and systematised in descriptions of the law. I have elsewhere suggested that these three phenomena represent different senses of what is meant by a 'legal system'. They are, respectively, institutional legal systems, historic legal systems (like the Common Law or Islamic Law), and momentary legal systems (like 'the law as at 1st January 1979') (Harris, 1979). Parasitic on these three basic types of legal phenomena are a wide range of attitudinal and behavioural phenomena. These include the patterns of behaviour evinced in the role-play of those who staff institutions, and their methodological and ideological presuppositions; the attitude of citizens towards the role-players, their deferential or defiant behaviour patterns; and the attitudes people have, correlating or not correlating with legal maxims and legal rules.

These are the legal phenomena of the modern industrialised state. The innate mind, however — as the quotation from Lévi-Strauss at the beginning of this chapter makes clear — was the same in pre-industrialised and in non-state tribal societies, as it is now. Yet such societies had quite different 'legal phenomena'. It is a matter of dispute amongst anthropologists as to whether we should apply our modern categories to small-scale, tribal societies at all. Should we look in them for analogues of courts and legislatures, dispositively adjudging disputes, or consciously laying down rules? Are there, indeed, in such societies any standards to which the distinctive label 'legal' (as against 'moral' or 'religious') can usefully be applied? There are arguments either way. The 'consciousness' of the members of such societies towards associates and standards was no doubt different from anything the modern legal sociologist might call 'legal consciousness'. But then if we are going to contrast and compare at all, we need some scheme of terms to do it with — we could call what they had 'law' even if they did not.

The structuralist legal theorist might respond in one of three ways to the problem of evolution in legal phenomena. First, he might claim that what he was seeking to explain in terms of the innate subconscious was only 'law' as that institution is understood in modern states. Therefore, although the primitive mind had the same law-slots as the modern mind, they were never triggered by cultural pressures into producing law until some comparatively recent date. Of course, it will be necessary to posit binary oppositions which had evolutionary utility before the march to law began; but such positing is common to any structuralist approach. Such a response seems unattractive, because it might be thought to imply that transformations within the binary oppositions occurring during the pre-law stage of 'primitive law' are uninteresting or unimportant. Secondly, he might claim that the same basic binary oppositions filtered the emergence of cultural products throughout social evolution, and for that very reason these products, widely different though they might be, should all be called 'law'. I shall suggest that this response is also the wrong one, because some of the binary oppositions which now circumscribe the intellectual operations of legal science had no institutional pay-off whatever in some earlier stages of man's development. The third and, I believe, the most fruitful response would be to look for plausible candidates for binary oppositions, and then observe how first some, and eventually all, of them (in varying combinations) were related to law-like cultural products.

A Structuralist Story

I shall now tell a story, which purports to be a structuralist theory of law. Some ten thousands years ago, *Homo sapiens* was a creature living in small-scale, tribal units. He had language, but no writing. His brain was physiologically what it is now. In its astonishing evolution from the brains of the common anthropoid stock, the brain of *Homo sapiens* had acquired certain innate binary oppositions. They directed men to impose certain bifurcations upon brute experience, as they still do. But the content of either half of any pair produced by the binary opposition was ready to be changed, given the right material or cultural triggers. Many of these binary oppositions — like light/darkness, cooked/raw — play no part in our particular story, which is one about 'law'. The ones that do play a part were five in number: sanctified/unsanctified, inside/outside, above/below, living/dead, present/absent.

In these small-scale communities, the inside/outside opposition had many cultural transformations. It was applied to observations of the physical world. It was also applied in social interactions to distinguish members of the community from strangers, and in-kin from out-kin. There was also sufficient of that typically language-dependent and specifically human practice of abstraction for it to be applied, in education and exhortation, to behavioural patterns — 'what we do'/'what we do not do'. In other words, there was custom. Not, of course, that anyone made a profession of formulating abstract propositions and attaching 'ought' to some and 'is' to others. That was to come later. The sanctified/unsanctified opposition attached to a wide variety of things — animals, places, people, ritual actions. It too produced 'normative' conceptions, probably of a pretty concrete kind. Then, though this may be at a later stage, the above/below opposition came to be applied to individuals — leaders in hunts, chiefs — whose transient orders occupied some cranny in normative life. The living/dead and the present/absent oppositions had plenty to do with cultural products, and may well have interacted on the level of content with customary and religious norms and executive orders; but their supreme role in modern legal science was yet to come.

Next, we come to the age of literacy and empire. The legal-cultural products of ancient Mesopotamia, Egypt, India, China and the Graeco-Roman world differ enormously, but they differ precisely in the varying ways they filled the pairs in our binary oppositions. In India and Mesopotamia, the opposition sanctified/unsanctified became firmly attached to written texts, and the progeny of this dichotomy in Mesopotamia was the sacred law of Israel, Islam and Christian canon law. In all of them, the opposition above/below had increased scope for norm-filtering, with the increase in princely power and the need for promulgation throughout a polity which was no longer a face-to-face community. The inside/outside opposition was still going strong, and in some instances the contrast between law as custom and law as code was recognised. In China, it was the basic of the conflict between the Confucianists and the legalists. Where feudal structures emerged, the opposition above/below was applied, not merely to individuals, but to ranks. In some of these empires, at some stages, the same opposition would be applied discriminately to lawgiver/subject, and to judge/supplicant.

Out of this process emerged legal science. It was not the same kind of intellectual activity in all cases — it is not clear that it happened at all in ancient Egypt; and only in classical Rome did it become anything like its modern counterpart. But for it to emerge at all, two new correlations between innate binary oppositions and cultural products were needed.

LAKEWOOD COMMUNITY COLLEGE LIBRARY

First, the oppositions inside/outside and above/below had to become attached to abstract normative propositions. Secondly, the oppositions living/dead and present/absent had to be brought into play.

A normative proposition is assumed by modern legal science either to be inside or outside a particular system of law. The innate cerebral feature, which led primitive man to force the continua of physical nature into a useful dichotomy, and which was in due course applied by him within crucial relationships to distinguish the stranger from the in-group member and the out-kin from the in-kin, is now applied to objects generated by the mind itself. It distinguishes rules as legal or non-legal; and it also distinguishes them as within the legal system under description or without it. The binary opposition itself is biologically based. The transformations are culturally contingent. 'All car-drivers must give way to traffic coming from the right' is a normative proposition. Nothing in nature requires a yes/no response to it. From a non-legal. scientific stance, we can view it along a continuum of, say, more or less useful, or greater or less conformity. The lawyer, however, insists that it is a rule of law, a member of a particular system of law, or it is not. He presupposes that there are criteria for identifying rules as within the system he describes or outside it. This binary opposition, inside/outside, is thus the structuralist explanation of the principle of the logic of legal science which I have called 'the principle of exclusion' (Harris 1979).

The above/below binary opposition, in modern legal science, is applied, not merely to role-players, but to reified prescriptive ideas, The lawyer identifies the bye-laws of a local authority as 'law' by subsuming them under some authorising statute. Above/below (of natural objects or ranks) becomes authorising/authorised. Because of the transformation within the binary opposition, the predicates *'intra vires'*/*'ultra vires'*, or 'constitutional'/'unconstitutional', are not seen as continua. In countries with written constitutions, the courts do not rule that a statute was fairly constitutional. This binary opposition above/below is, then, the structuralist explanation of the legal-science logical principle of subsumption.

The living/dead binary opposition was not applied directly to 'law' in small-scale communities whose relationships were governed by custom and by assumptions about the sanctified. That what was required of man could be suddenly annulled was a notion which, at most, would have had scope only in trivial matters governed by transient orders of leaders. In contrast, modern legal science speaks

31565

happily of dead or repealed law. Such and such a rule is not part of the law now, because it cannot stand with a later proposition flowing from a higher source. This binary opposition thus provides the structuralist account of the legal-science logical principle of derogation.

The present/absent binary opposition is the structuralist explanation of the logical principle of non-contradiction. Why on earth should we assume that it cannot be true both that X is the case and also that X is not the case? Because the human brain has evolved a trackway of a certain kind. It was useful to approach survival endeavours with the assumption, say, that either there was a lion in the cave or there was not. Primitive man, of course, did not transform the binary pair into abstract propositions. But eventually this was done, and eventually legal science began to apply the principle of non-contradiction to propositions about the law.

Among legal theorists of this century, Hans Kelsen has been the most famous exponent of the idea that legal science comes to legal phenomena armed with presuppositions. He encapsulated these presuppositions in a 'basic norm' which, he said, 'really exists in the juristic consciousness' (Kelsen, 1961, p. 116). He drew an analogy between the basic norm and the categories of Kant's epistemology. But the idea that something could somehow exist in the subsconscious was disturbing to his anti-metaphysical soul. In his last years, he rejected the propriety of the principles of derogation and non-contradiction (Kelsen, 1973, p. 274); and he described the basic norm as a 'typical case of a fiction in the sense of Vaihinger's *Philosophie des Als-ob*' (Kelsen, 1966, p. 6).

The structuralist could have poured balm on Kelsen's disquietude. The basic norm or (as I have called it) 'the basic legal science fiat' (Harris, 1979), is a representation of the relations between the binary oppositions which, through a series of transformations, have come to be applied by lawyers to the subject-matter of their descriptions. Its ontological status is thus physiological. It reads:

> Legal duties exist only if imposed (and not excepted), by rules originating in the following sources . . . or by rules subsumable under such rules. Provided that any contradiction between rules originating in different sources shall be resolved according to the following ranking amongst the sources . . . And provided that no other contradition shall be admitted to exist.

In this formulation, the word 'only' indicates the structural significance of the inside/outside binary opposition when applied to duty-imposing rules — the principle of exclusion. The above/below binary opposition is part of the mental equipment of the legal-scientific mind. It stands ready to have inserted within its pairing some constitutional source-rule inserted in the first blank of the fiat and some other rule originating in an inferior source — the principle of subsumption. The living/dead binary opposition is that part of the structure of the mind which accounts for derogation, the relation between paired rules being determined by the ranking which any particular legal system requires to be inserted in the second blank. The final proviso exhibits the application to legal rules of the binary opposition, present/absent — the principle of non-contradiction.

So far our structuralist account of modern law has dealt only with what I referred to as the third basic kind of legal phenomena, namely rules systematised as 'the present valid law' of a particular community. What about the other two basic kinds of legal phenomena, that is, legal institutions and legal doctrine? No analogue of Kelsen's basic norm will help here.

In the case of legal phenomena of both these types, the binary opposition sanctified/unsanctified continues to have some of the filtering effect on law-culture that it did in earlier forms of law. So far as systems of doctrine are concerned, this is most apparent for legal systems which still centre about religious texts — such as the Jewish, Islamic and Hindu legal systems. For other historical systems, such as 'Common Law' or 'Equity', the opposition has, at times, also rung true. So far as institutional systems are concerned, the decisions of legislatures and courts are sometimes distinguished from the same decisions made by other bodies by reference to a sanctified/unsanctified opposition. In the case of institutional hierarchies, the application of the above/below opposition is clear enough.

Evaluating the Story

Well, that is the story, a purported structuralist theory of law. What are we to make of it? An obvious objection may be that the story must be wrong because it has the wrong ending. I have begun with my own controversial characterisation of legal phenomena, and told a story to fit this preconceived end. So I have. Someone taking a different view of what legal phenomena today are like is at liberty to begin with different binary oppositions, or to argue that different transformations have taken place within the same binary oppositions. For example, one who takes the view that legal and moral phenomena are systematically interconnected, as Professor R.M. Dworkin does (Dworkin, 1978), might insist that the binary opposition, present/absent, has come to be applied to rights, and deny that the inside/outside opposition is applied as between legal and moral rights. The much more important question for the purposes of this essay is: can any general structuralist account of legal phenomena be of value?

In the title to this essay, I indicated that mine was an 'agnostic view'. I have tried to make the story as plausible as possible, although I have no doubt that someone steeped in the structuralists' terminology could make it much more so. In my own account of law and legal science, I placed no reliance on arguments about the innate human mind as the basis for the legal-science logical principles of exclusion, subsumption, derogation and non-contradiction. The most I allowed myself was a passing reference to 'deep structure', borrowing that metaphor from the transformational grammarians. I founded these principles, not in the innate, but in the contingent political role-values of legality and constitutionality. Judges and other important occupants of official roles in modern states purport to describe and apply law; and it is the political motivation supplied by their roles which guides them to reduce the multifarious products of legislative processes into systematic form. Legal science, being an intellectual activity parasitic on the performance of these official roles, therefore also systemises the law it describes. I believe that that is sufficient to explain the structure presupposed for law by lawyers.

However, if the structure could also be seen to have some biological base, well and good. If it did, this would not mean that our present institutions had some more permanent status than otherwise they would have. As was stressed earlier, the binary oppositions in the subconscious are themselves contentless. If social and economic forces were to produce such radical changes in institutions that it became no longer useful to provide guidance for conduct by means of systemised rules, the binary oppositions would simply no longer be applied to rules. Or if legal reasoning as at present practised was given up, the sanctified/unsanctified opposition would not be applied to doctrine. Or again, given the replacement of our social structures by ones without any kind of official hierarchy, the above/below binary opposition would move away from a sphere to which it at present applies. It may be also that the binary oppositions, though innate, can be consciously suppressed, like other innate characteristics; or even, I suppose, that the biological evolution of the human brain is an ongoing process.

If the binary oppositions I have posited exist in the human subconscious, they provide a level of explanation for legal phenomena which adds to, but does not subtract from, functional and historical explanations. But do they exist? How could one prove it? It is not possible to have a re-run of quasi-human evolution with these features masked out, to see whether something other than what we understand by 'law' would have resulted. Lévi-Strauss, in the quotation at the beginning of this essay, states: 'If, as we believe to be the case, the unconscious activity of the mind consists in imposing forms upon content . . .' It is a big 'if'. Dr Leach hints that there may be something metaphysical in the structuralist conception of mind, but goes on to suggest that structures formulated in terms of it may still have explanatory power. Where other satisfactory levels of explanations are available — as I believe they are in the case of legal phenomena — it seems to me that one can be no more than agnostic about structuralist claims.

Notes

1. *Chertsey Urban District Council* v. *Mixham's Properties Limited* [1965] A.C. 735.
2. My attention to the essays by Fletcher, Hermann and Robertshaw was drawn by a paper delivered by Bernard Jackson at the meeting in April 1979, of the British section of the Association for Legal and Social Philosophy, entitled 'Structuralism and Legal Theory'. Dr Jackson departs from the usual structuralist approach to cultural phenomena through binary oppositions. Instead, he believes, we should seek to understand law along various continua.

Bibliography

Chomsky, N. *Syntactic Structures* (Mouton, The Hague, 1957)
Dworkin, R.M. *Taking Rights Seriously* (Duckworth, London, 1978)
Fletcher, G. 'The Metamorphosis of Larceny', *Harvard Law Review*, vol. 89 (1976) pp. 469-530
Harris, J.W. *Law and Legal Science* (Clarendon Press, Oxford, 1979)
Hermann, D. 'A Structuralist Approach to Legal Reasoning', *Southern California Law Review*, vol. 48 (1975) pp. 1131-94
Kelsen, H. *General Theory of Law and State* (Russell and Russell, New York, 1961)
_____ 'On the Pure Theory of Law', *Israel Law Review*, vol. 1 (1966), pp. 1-7
_____ *Essays in Legal and Moral Philosphy* (D. Reidel, Dordrecht and Boston, 1973)
Lévi-Strauss, C. *Structural Anthropology* (Basic Books, New York, 1963)
Robertshaw, P. 'Unreasonableness and Judicial Control of Administrative Discretion: the Geology of the Chertsey Caravans Case', *Public Law* (1975), pp. 113-36

3 Understanding, Action and Law in Max Weber

S.L. Andreski

What are we to Understand by 'Understanding'?

The expression 'understanding sociology' (*'verstehende soziologie'*) was perhaps the least commendable of Weber's innovations. If taken as any of the commonly accepted meanings of the word 'understanding', it is superfluous, presumptuous and misleading because (since everybody agrees that the aim of sociology is to understand how societies work) affixing to it the label 'understanding' is like speaking of 'watery water', 'human women', 'ongoing process' or 'popular democracy' (that is 'people's people's rule'). A good pragmatic rule for finding out whether a predicate adds any information is to look for its negative and (if it has one) for its opposite. Applying this test we can at once see that the expression *'verstehende soziologie'* makes no better sense in German than it does in English. Its dismissal, however, should not deter us from trying to figure out what Weber was getting at; for, though often careless and sometimes seriously misleading in his choice of words, he was a great thinker who was far above trying to impress the audience with empty verbiage. Furthermore, although the unhappy expression might be construed as evidence that he was attempting to monopolise the label 'understanding', he nowhere claims that only his brand of sociology merits it. On the contrary, it is perfectly clear from his discussion that he is concerned with the fundamental difference between the study of nature and the study of society or culture. In the former field — according to his famous phrase — we 'explain' while in the latter we 'understand'. There is a contradiction between what he says in the text and the implications of the label, which appears completely pleonastic in the light of his own words because if in all the branches of the study of culture and society we are trying to 'understand' then how can sociology, let alone any particular school thereof, be distinguished from the others by 'understanding'?

The greatest difficulty in discussing this problem is the question of what do we understand by 'understanding'? As with trying to define any other fundamental category of thought, it is very difficult here to escape from going round in circles. Take, for example, Wittgenstein's famous dictum (with which I have a great deal of sympathy): 'Whatever can be said, can be said clearly; what cannot be said, must be left in silence.' The trouble here is that Wittgenstein does not make clear what he means by 'clearly': he does not succeed in providing an unambiguous criterion by which we could always judge whether a statement is clear or not. Consequently, he breaks his rule by uttering it. Likewise, Weber does not explain what he means by 'understanding'. His characterisation of the difference between the study of nature and the study of culture makes no sense if we accept the meaning which the words 'to explain' and 'to understand' have in the natural sciences, where our ability to explain is said to constitute the fundamental measure of the extent of our understanding. To introduce some clarity into this matter, we must realise that Weber had in mind something much more specific than 'understanding' in its general sense. The nature of the latter has provided the philosophers with their chief problems which are 'how do we know that we know?' or 'what do we understand when we say that we understand something?' As Weber made no contributions to pure philosophy, I shall try to avoid entering this field too deeply and I shall only say that I subscribe to the view that our ability to explain is the best criterion of our understanding in the sense of the possession of adequate knowledge. However, to express our knowledge (let alone to test its adequacy) we must have words (or some other signs) and be able to understand them in the sense of knowing what they mean. A meaning is said to be a connection between a sign (a pattern of sounds or shapes) and something else: either other signs or something that has happened, is happening or will happen. 'Understanding' of the meaning of a word does not presuppose the possession of adequate knowledge in the sense of the ability to explain and predict the behaviour of the phenomenon to which this word refers. To avoid confusion, I shall speak of 'comprehension' rather than 'understanding' to describe the knowledge of the meaning of a word, which need not be accompanied by the 'understanding' or adequate knowledge of the behaviour of the thing to which this word refers. I may comprehend the word 'tide'; that is know to what it can be applied, without knowing why there are tides, let alone be able to predict when and where they will come and go.

Now, it is true that our comprehension of words which describe human traits and actions relies on the assumption that other people's minds are sufficiently like ours to permit inferences about their feelings and thoughts on the basis of our own experiences. Up to a point we do that even with inanimate nature when we speak of 'the angry sea' and 'a gentle wind', and the primitive interpretation of nature was mostly along these lines. The development of science, however, was closely connected with the elimination of anthropomorphism, and expressions like those above are now treated only as metaphoric. Aristotle wrote that 'nature abhors vacuum' but no modern physicist would attribute to gases or liquids the capacity to feel abhorrence. Modern physics consists of equations which subsume, explain and permit the prediction of various kinds of measurements. But when physicists communicate their formulae they assume the existence of other minds like theirs in whom these formulae will evoke mental representations similar to theirs, although the terms contained in these formulae refer only to observations which can be confirmed by many observers. Many people can verify that I am 183 cm tall, but no one can confirm my feelings.

There is no prospect that we could eliminate from the social sciences words which refer to human feelings and thought. All the names for actions contain implications about volitions. Actually, the latter sentence is true by definition because 'action' is commonly defined as voluntary behaviour which is contrasted with reflexes and involuntary activities, which might be conscious like sneezing or unconscious like winking or the movements of the intestines. We do not need to dwell on behaviour which is particularly laden with emotions, because even if we take something so impersonal as business correspondence we see that it is full of words like 'intend', 'agree', 'expect', 'undertake', 'demand' and such like, which cannot be comprehended except in the light of our own mental experiences. There is no need to emphasise that the same applies to 'trying', 'ambition', 'angry', 'punishment', 'love', 'cheating', 'conquest' and countless other words of this kind. Many of these carry presuppositions not only about the state of mind of the doer but also about the expectations and feelings of the passive objects of actions, as is the case with the words 'to torment', 'to please' and suchlike.

Despite their strenuous attempts to produce a replica of physics, even mathematical economists keep talking about 'expectations', 'profit', 'exchange' — all of which carry implications about thought — especially intentions.

I propose to call 'empathic comprehension' the kind of comprehension which relies on the assumption of analogy between our mental experiences and those of other people, and which results in attributing to other people the thoughts and feelings which we would experience in similar conditions. Weber was certainly not the first to notice that our ability to understand other people's behaviour is based on this process. In the *Theory of Moral Sentiments,* Adam Smith (1854) says: 'As we have no immediate experience of what other men feel, we can form no idea of the manner in which they are affected, but by conceiving what we ourselves should feel in the like situation.'

There is no way in which the words which describe feelings, thoughts and sensations could be translated into descriptions of physical states. Reading a chemical formula of a substance will not give you an idea of its taste, except in so far as you might guess that it might taste like something else which you have tasted and which it resembles chemically. We can no better imagine the dog's world of smells than he can understand mathematics.

As a philosophical digression, I must add that the assumption that there are other minds like ours is a true *a priori* axiom which can neither be refuted nor proven because any attempt to convince anyone of its truth or falsity presupposes the belief in the interlocutor's existence and that he possesses a mind in which we can evoke certain representations by uttering appropriate words. Meaning is the capacity of words and other signs to evoke representations in minds. The so-called verification theory of meaning can be accepted as a body of rules which enable us to distinguish concepts which lead to reliable knowledge from those which do not. It is wrong, however, to equate meaning with conditions of verifiability because you cannot verify a sentence unless you already know its meaning.

We can perceive only the overt behaviour of others, and we can make sense of it only through empathic comprehension — 'putting ourselves into other people's shoes' — the correctness of which can never be directly verified. Further, in hindsight we often discover that our assumptions about other people's thought and feelings were wrong. How do we know that they ever are right? The proof that empathic understanding must be more often correct than wrong is furnished by the existence of society. Any social order would disintegrate totally within seconds if the people enmeshed in it ceased to be able to predict each other's behaviour. In other words, since there can be no society without co-operation, which requires the ability to communicate and to predict other people's behaviour, the existence of a society proves that these necessary abilities also exist; and consequently, that empathic comprehension functions with the necessary (though evidently imperfect) efficacy.

It may be worth remarking on the margin that, looking from this angle, we can also solve the much-debated question of whether there are any objective criteria of madness or whether it is simply a label for those who deviate from the beliefs of the majority. Those who accept the latter view see no difference between madness, heresy and innovation, between enforced hospitalisation of the insane and incarceration of dissenters and innovators, or between our inability to understand schizophrenics and our inability to understand a foreign language or a branch of mathematics which we have not learned. Now, I do not deny that there are many shading off and mixed cases where it is difficult to draw the line; and it is equally true that a belief or a manner of behaving may be common in one culture but regarded as a symptom of insanity in another. Thus someone who believes in witches riding on broomsticks will be regarded in our society as a lunatic but would be treated as a man of sound judgement in the sixteenth century. None the less, there is a fundamental difference between the two distinctions; foreigners, believers in other religions, heretics and mathematicians understand one another and co-operate — indeed heterodox and persecuted minorities often display a much higher solidarity than does the majority — whereas lunatics can communicate (let alone co-operate) with one another even less than they can with the nurses and psychiatrists. No society consisting of lunatics could survive for a moment. The inability to co-operate with anyone is the objective test of madness which distinguishes it fundamentally from dissent, opposition or crime.

It remains to be added that empathic comprehension is essential not only in co-operation but also in conflict where much effort is often put into figuring out the opponent's goals, assessing his character and knowledge, and forecasting his moves.

Being the foundation of all social life and all communication, empathic comprehension cannot be expunged from the social sciences, and Weber was clearly right in stressing that this is a fundamental difference between them and the natural sciences.

His shortcoming was that he did not clearly see — or at least did not make it clear in his methodological writings — that sociology (or any other branch of learning aspiring to study mankind or its works scientifically) begins where empathic comprehension no longer suffices. In other words, whereas the practical common-sense understanding of human behaviour relies mainly (or at least largely) on empathic comprehension, the scientific method is needed for going beyond the knowledge thus attainable.

The everyday understanding of people's action through empathic comprehension mostly relies on goal-and-means schemes. To a question 'why is he doing it?' we normally get (and are satisfied with) a reply indicating his goal or the steps needed to achieve it. If I ask: 'why is he digging up his lawn?', I shall feel that my understanding has advanced when I am told that he wants to grow tomatoes there — my tacit assumptions being that he believes that digging up the lawn is necessary for growing tomatoes there, and that this belief is correct. If I did not make the latter assumption, I would also want to know why he believes this. In cases normally dealt with in books on history the goal-and-the-means schemes are usually much more complicated and much of the effort of the historian is spent on reconstructing the circumstances to piece together evidence which can be arranged as a goal-and-the-means-scheme. If you ask why did Hitler's army's main thrust into France go through southern Belgium, the answer will have to include the information about the geography of France and Belgium, the composition, tactics, armament and the spirit of the armies involved, the political set-up and so on. Weber's analysis of historical understanding on the example of the battle of Marathon is of the same kind. Such knowledge is valuable but it is pre-scientific in the sense of requiring no theoretical formulations about causal relationships which go beyond what was known to the participants. Such formulations are needed when we try to explain cumulative and unintended consequences of actions.

The simplest example of a collective phenomenon which is there, despite being desired by nobody, is a market price. All the buyers would like it to be lower, while all the sellers would like it to be higher. Most movements of prices can be explained without assuming any changes in the dealers' eagerness to buy cheap and to sell dear. Nor would empathic comprehension (or '*verstehen*') carry us very far in trying to explain inflation, unemployment, overpopulation or changes in fashions and moral values. The same applies to beliefs. If someone tells us that he believes because he wants to believe, we can infer that his belief is shaky. A true believer cannot help believing. To ascertain what he believes we have to resort to empathic comprehension, but this faculty is of no use when we try to explain why he believes what he does or why the number of people who share his beliefs is decreasing or increasing.

Even in dealing with strictly individual characteristics, we can extend our knowledge beyond common sense only when we go beyond the explanations in terms of intentions. When we see somebody walking towards a wash-basin, turning on the tap and putting soap on his palms, we do not need a psychologist to tell us that this man is doing this because he wants to wash his hands. But if he washes his hands several hundred times every day, although his work does not require it, we shall not be able to explain his behaviour by using our faculty of empathic comprehension. Only through systematic research can we find common features in the antecedents or traits of character of people suffering from this incapacitating compulsion, and this knowledge may enable us to discover causal relationships which might explain their behaviour. So even in psychology, science begins where empathic comprehension no longer suffices.

Despite toying with the label *'die verstehende soziologie'*, Max Weber did not allow it to constrain his studies. Like everybody else he used empathic comprehension to understand texts describing actions and beliefs, but he did not rely on it when he tried to explain how social structures and systems of beliefs persist or change. For this purpose he embarked on comparative historical studies and used inductive reasoning. His method was not very rigorous but decidedly inductive. To regard the *'verstehen'* as the distinguishing mark of his approach is to misunderstand completely the nature of his contribution to knowledge.

In his substantive studies, to repeat, Weber was very much an inductivist who built his generalisations on a comparative study of history, albeit his formulations were far from rigorous. He certainly never said that sociological inquiry ought to confine itself within the bounds of empathic comprehension. None the less, his failure to make clear the issues connected with the various meanings of *'verstehen'* has recently provided an encouragement to a trend which advocated a retreat from the fundamental principles of scientific method and panders to the obscurantisist and parasitic proclivities of sub-standard academics. One of the sources of this trend was perfectly respectable intellectually: namely the book by Peter Winch, *The Idea of a Social Science* (1958), where he argued that in interpreting and describing a social set-up it is illegitimate to use concepts other than those which the observed people use themselves. He refers to the anthropological studies of Evans-Pritchard (1937) who repeatedly stresses that there are no English words which adequately translate to the magical and religious notions of the Nuer and the Azande. It is true, of course, that the difficulty of translation grows with the cultural and linguistic remoteness, and that no interpretation, description or analysis can be perfectly reliable, accurate or comprehensive. It does not follow, however, that all such works must be totally misleading and worthless, which would be the case if Winch's arguments were valid.

It is particularly anomalous that such arguments should be advanced by linguistic philosophers because linguistics has been much more successful than anthropology or sociology in discovering rules which the speakers obey without knowing them. It is a notorious fact that only very few (if any) among the people who speak their language correctly know its grammar, whereas a linguistician who has discovered and formulated the rules of the given language may not be able to speak in accordance with them. Likewise when Radcliffe-Brown discovered the general rules which govern (or underlay) the marriage custom of the Australian aborigines he did not do it by simply writing down what he was told by them, but by drawing inferences from what he saw and heard. His informants knew who ought or ought not to marry whom, but were not able to formulate any general principles or even to conceive of their customs as forming a system. This kind of work, as well as economics and demography, would have to be abandoned if the limitation in question were to be enforced. Nay, an anthropologist who has studied a people who can only count up to five would not be permitted to tell us how many of them there are.

The only sensible conclusion to the question raised by Weber concerning *'verstehen'* is that the raw materials of the social sciences — the meanings of words referring to individual actions, thoughts and feelings — can be comprehended only with the aid of empathy, which has no place in the study of nature; but that science begins only where it goes beyond empathic comprehension (and therefore common sense) and discovers facts, theories and explanations which could not be known without systematic collection and verification of empirical data and inductive inference.

Social Action and Methodological Individualism

One of the most absurd misconceptions about Weber's contribution to knowledge is to see in it something called a theory of social action. According to some versions of this view, this 'theory' consists of the 'discovery' that sociology studies social actions . . . as if anyone sane could ever doubt it. Everyone agrees that sociology is supposed to study the social life of mankind; and since life is a chain of actions, there is nothing else that sociology could study. All structures are patterns of recurrent action. This is true even of solid material objects which, as physics teaches us, consist of packets of energy circulating in the void. A material structure is a pattern of recurrent movements of particles. A social structure and its components — such as laws, organisations, customs, kinship and so on — is an arrangement of recurrent patterns of human interaction. Weber did not put it like this, but his remarks about social actions clearly appear to be designed to counter the common tendency to reify sociological concepts.

Weber had no theory of social action in any acceptable sense of the word 'theory'. Apart from some remarks about mutual comprehension being a prerequisite of interaction, he offered a classification of social actions into four categories: emotional, traditional, goal-rational and value-rational. In itself a classification explains nothing, and amounts to no more than a mere cataloguing, unless it permits a discovery and formulation of true general propositions. The aforementioned classification fails by this criterion, as neither Weber nor anyone else was able to formulate with its aid any general propositions, with explanatory or predictive power. This is not surprising because the classification itself is defective, as it sins against the elementary logical requirements specified already by Aristotle: namely it has no single principle of division, the classes do not collectively exhaust the field and they are not mutually exclusive.

The distinction between 'goal-rational' and 'value-rational' is useless because Weber does not tell us what is the difference between a goal and a value; and, as generally used in philosophical discourse, these words are treated either as interchangeable or at least as having a very large overlap. We must therefore discard this subdivision and amalgamate the two 'kinds' of rational actions, taking them to be actions based on a correct decision (in the light of available knowledge) of the means for a given goal. The first question which now arises is: can there be actions which are rational as well as traditional or emotional, or are these types mutually exclusive? The second question is: are there social actions which do not fall under any of these headings?

A choice of correct course towards a goal — that is, a rational decision — involves scrutinising the available knowledge, surveying various possibilities, forecasting their outcomes, evaluating benefits and disadvantages (costs). As thus conceived, a rational action is a premeditated and planned action. But what about, say, a driver who swerves to avoid hitting a child who suddenly runs across the road? It is not a premeditated action, yet it is rational in the sense of serving the purpose which we have at the back of our minds: we do not want to run over children. And what about actions which are carefully calculated but on wrong premises . . . perhaps insane delusions: for example a paranoiac who carefully plans elaborate precautions to avoid persecution which nobody has the slightest intention of carrying out? So we have at least three types of action here: planned actions based on rational decisions, planned actions based on irrational decisions, and unpremeditated or even automatic actions which do serve our purposes. And we also have automatic actions which produce the opposite effect from that which we desire.

If by 'emotional' action we mean actions accompanied by emotion, then this attribute neither presupposes nor excludes rationality. A prisoner attempting an escape which he has been planning and preparing for months will experience an extremely strong emotion but his action may be rational or irrational according to the circumstances. The same can be said about all kinds of other actions where big stakes are at issue. So we see that this criterion is independent of that of irrationality. However, German *affektuel* can also be translated as 'impulsive' which excludes deliberation.

If by 'rational' we mean based on considered decision, then no impulsive action can be rational; but if by 'rational' we mean adapted to our goal then an impulsive action may be either rational or irrational, according to the circumstances. A man who lost his temper and hit or insulted someone, but gained nothing thereby, while having had to endure the ignominy of appearing before a court, may feel that he has acted irrationally; whereas if he shot a lunatic who was about to murder his child, he would feel that his act was very rational despite all the trouble with the police and the coroner which it occasioned.

Making a distinction between 'traditional' and 'rational' action, Weber seems to have in mind the difference between a peasant who goes on tilling the soil in the way his ancestors did, without ever even considering that it might be done in a different way, and a businessman who thinks of many alternatives and weighs their advantages and disadvantages, and ends by introducing a radical innovation. The latter does more calculation and figuring out, but it does not follow that he acts more rationally than the peasant because their environments (especially the knowledge available to each) are so different. Assuming that the most important goal is to survive, sticking to the old and proven ways may be the most rational course in primeval conditions. Traditional methods are usually a product of a long process of trial and error. Experimentation offers a prospect of success only if it is based on accumulated knowledge which enables one to envisage various possibilities and to forecast with some confidence their outcomes. When knowledge is exiguous, while the safety margin is very small on the level of mere subsistence, the most rational course may be to stick to the ways which have been found to be compatible with survival in the past.

The term 'traditional' is inappropriate as a contrast to 'calculated' or 'planned' because many traditional crafts involve a great deal of thinking out and deciding. Furthermore, this term confuses the antiquity of a pattern of behaviour with the question of whether it does or does not involve much ratiocination. Following a new fashion is in no sense more rational than following an ancient custom. The proper word here is 'habitual', but (as we saw earlier in the example of driving) habitual ('unthought out') behaviour may or may not be adapted to the purpose or purposes which the doer has. A habitual reaction of a seasoned driver may be more 'rational' in this sense than the deliberate efforts of a learner.

The conclusion of all this is that, if we want to have a classification of social actions which is better than common sense, we must start anew and we will not get much help from Weber. His historical and comparative analyses, fortunately, do not depend on this classification. So, by discarding it and putting some of his statements into a clearer language, we can enhance the value of his insights.

I have made no comments so far about Weber's general concept of social action because little needs to be said about it, as it boils down to an underlining that social action is interaction between individuals which entails communication and therefore mutual comprehension. One can think of certain exceptions to this: when one is coshed from behind in a dark alley and robbed while unconscious, the social action is unilateral and there is neither interaction nor communication. Such situations, however, are marginal, as even in a case of a hold-up there is plenty of communication (or, if you prefer, of symbolic interaction) involving mutual comprehension. So, although what Weber says about the nature of action is true, it is certainly not new, as all this was made perfectly clear much earlier by David Hume (1874) and Adam Smith (1854). Much more useful was Weber's stress on the need to define sociological concepts in terms of actions of individuals. This line of thought is pushed to the extreme by the so-called ontological nominalists who maintain that only individuals 'really' exist whereas groups do not. As I have shown in *Social Sciences as Sorcery* (1974), this is an untenable view, which involves dubious assumptions about what is meant by 'existence'. Weber did not deny the existence of groups; and much more in line with his thought is the methodological (as opposed to ontological) individualism which refrains from making ontological judgements (that is judgements about the nature of 'reality' or 'existence') and confines itself to advocating a methodological rule. The following quotation from its leading exponent conveys the essential points:

> This principle states that social processes and events should be explained by being deduced from (a) principles governing the behaviour of participating individuals and (b) descriptions of their situations. Whereas physical things can exist unperceived, social 'things' like laws, prices, prime ministers and ration-books, are created by personal attitudes. But if social objects are formed by individuals' attitudes, an explanation of their formation must be an individualistic explanation.
>
> The social scientist and the historian have no 'direct access' to the overall structure and behaviour of a system of interacting individuals (in the sense that a chemist does have 'direct access' to such overall properties of a gas as its volume and pressure and temperature, which he can measure and relate without any knowledge of gas-molecules). But the social scientist and the historian can often arrive at fairly reliable opinions about the dispositions and the situations of individuals. These two facts suggest that a theoretical understanding of an abstract social structure should be derived from more empirical beliefs about concrete individuals. (Watkins, 1952)

There can be little doubt that methodological individualism is right in its positive recommendations: the only way of guarding against reification of concepts which denote collective phenomena, and their degeneration into empty sounds, is to indicate individual actions which they entail. Words like democracy, capitalism, liberty, socialism, imperialism or fascism are so useful for propaganda because more people react to them by mindless approval or disapproval instead of thinking about who does, did or will do what, when and how, under the circumstances to which these big words vaguely refer. Unfortunately, although the idea of scientific study of society implies by definition a careful scrutiny of the concepts, many people who are supposed to be practising it are just as gullible as the man in the street.

Indeed, in many ways they are even worse, as they manufacture vague generalities which obscure and distort their perception of the world. So Weber and the methodological individualists are perfectly right in insisting that whenever we use a sociological concept we must think of the typical actions which it covers. Actually in everyday life everybody does it when they think of the meaning of names of social positions or roles. When you have to explain to a child or a newcomer what a quality controller, a chairman of the board of directors, or a tax inspector is there is no other way of doing it but to tell him what such people do and how other people react to their actions. Dealing with names for positions or roles, people usually keep quite well in touch with reality. It is when they employ big and more abstract words, like class or freedom, that they tend to remain on the level of vague generalities.

Despite having initiated this line of thought, Weber was less one-sided than the exponents of methodological individualism, who treat it as the fundamental principle, because he did not deny the legitimacy of the opposite procedure — which Watkins (1952) calls 'holist' — where the traits of an individual are explained by the nature of the group to which he belongs. If you ask why Bill is so touchy, you may be told that he belongs to an ethnic or religious minority which has been demeaned for generations, or that he is the second youngest son in a large family. The very meaning of the words for individual traits — such as kind, clever, cruel, lazy — entails a reference to a mean for the population or to a moral norm whether generally accepted or merely postulated. A reference to the structure of a group and its norms is even clearer in statements like 'Edward is a good husband but a bad manager', where many tacit assumptions are made about the duties, responsibilities and qualifications with which the behaviour of the individual in question is compared. The methodological individualist will say that the structural attributes of a group rest upon the dispositions of the individuals who constitute it — which is true enough — but it is equally true that these dispositions are there because the individuals who have them are members of the given group. It is true that there would be no Hungarian language if no one had ever spoken it; but it is equally true that no one would be speaking it, if the set of phonetic patterns known as Hungarian did not exist. To regard either group or the individual as more fundamental than the other is analogous to giving a simple answer to the chicken-and-egg question. Not even the evolution of the purely anatomical features of mankind can be explained without taking into account the patterns of co-operation and the accumulation of knowledge without which our species could not have survived.

It seems that methodological individualism was conceived by analogy with physicalism which is the view that ultimately all knowledge can be 'reduced' to the laws of physics and the statements about the movements of physical bodies. 'Reduced' means here 'deduced from'. I gather that chemistry has been 'reduced' to physics in the sense that the laws of chemical composition can now be deduced from the laws of atomic physics. Deducibility permits a replacement of the statements about units of the given level (here the chemical substances and their properties) by the statements about the units which compose them (here atoms) and their relationships. The debate between the vitalists and mechanists in biology hinges on the question of whether all the structures and functions of an organism can be 'reduced' to statements about the entities dealt with by chemistry and physics.

In an aside in *Social Sciences as Sorcery* (1974), I have mentioned the arguments which invalidate physicalism as an ontological doctrine. None the less physicalism is a more tenable doctrine than methodological individualism because it proposes the reduction of the statements about structure of the higher order to statements about their components whose characteristics do not depend on their inclusion in or exclusion from these structures. Thus the properties of an atom of oxygen remain the same when it combines with hydrogen to form water or with carbon to form carbon dioxide. We must also note that steps towards a 'reduction' of biology to chemistry and physics (which are being made by all biologists, including those who do not believe in physicalism as a philosophical doctrine) involves a replacement of statements about organic processes by statements about units which do not change in consequence of being involved in these processes: that is the chemical elements and their volumes, velocities and masses. If the mechanists in biology advocated a reduction of statements about organisms to statements about cells, they would get into the same kind of circularity as the methodological individualists because the properties of a cell depend on the nature of the organism of which it forms a part. No cell in a differentiated organism can retain its characteristics after its separation from the rest. A reduction makes sense only when it proceeds to the level where the units are invariant.

The choice between individualism and holism is a false dilemma as neither is acceptable as the fundamental or final reduction. Both procedures are equally valid and indeed necessary. In explaining collective phenomena we must take into account individual dispositions and the other way round. This means that sociology and psychology are inseparable, that there can be no clear frontier between them and neither can claim priority over the other. Weber paid no attention to demarcation disputes. When he learned about Freud, he expressed reservation about the correctness of his theories but thought that they were potentially of fundamental importance to sociology. The lesson we can retain from Weber is that any term denoting a collective process or structure must be so construed that the question of whether it does or does not apply to a given situation can be resolved by observing actions of individuals. In other words, for every sociological concept we must have observational criteria of its applicability.

To end this section I must say a few words about how we can reconcile the above-mentioned principle with Durkheim's dictum (1949) that 'social facts are things'. Here again we must figure out what he was getting at rather than accept at its face value this dubious pronouncement. Taken literally, Durkheim's dictum either amounts to an empty confirmation that, loosely speaking, everything is 'a thing', or to a nonsensical assertion that a marriage or a law is a thing like a chair or a house. Taking into account the way in which he conducted his inductive studies (especially of suicide) we can interpret his dictum less literally as a call for objectivity and the application of scientific method to the study of social phenomena, and a reminder about how durable and massive these phenomena are.

Weber's attitude to sociological concepts can also be reconciled with Durkheim's definition of social facts in terms of constraint exercised upon the individual. This definition cuts out certain actions which Weber and most of us would call social because they affect other people — like choosing a friend or setting up a club. None the less all large-scale social phenomena appear to an individual as compelling and unalterable. The apparent contradiction, however, dissolves when we think about how the constraints operate: they do not come from outer space but result from human actions. Each single individual is constrained collectively by all the others. The cumulative effect of the attitudes of the others puts on every one of us a constraint which is more unalterable and inescapable than a prison wall.

Though not quite of the same stature as Weber, Durkheim was an original and outstanding thinker. Neither of them ever indulged in empty verbiage, but they were tackling great problems without the benefit of clarifications which the philosophy of science has achieved since their times. Consequently their formulations appear defective and mutually contradictory if taken too literally. But with a bit of chiselling their contributions can be made to fit together very well.

Max Weber's Sociology of Law and his Concept of Rationality

Weber's sociology of law — which appears as a chapter in the first edition of *Wirtschaft und Gesellschaft* but constitutes a separate volume in the English translation — inspires awe by the breadth of the learning on which it rests. He began as a legal historian, wrote a thesis on the beginning of company law in the Middle Ages (chiefly in Italy) and a book on the impact of private law on the agrarian history of Rome. By the time he came to write his main treatise he had studied not only the legal history of the chief nations of Western Europe but also the codes of Russia (in Russian) and of India and China (in translations). The subtitle — *The Economy and the Law* — indicates his focus; and, as elsewhere, the recurrent 'leitmotif' is the search for an explanation of the rise of the modern form of capitalism in the West: here by examining how this process was affected by the peculiarities of the legal system.

Traditionally the study of law was concerned with what Weber calls 'dogmatics' and exegesis — that is the determination of the meaning of the statutes, drawing subsidiary rules from them and the discussion of the sources of their validity. Sociology of law is supposed to look at the laws like a botanist looks at plants; classifying the legal systems, explaining why they are what they are, and examining their consequences for other aspects of social life. The first difficulty is how to draw the line between the entities which are supposed to be interacting: in the present context the economy and the law? The concept of 'the economy' includes the property relations, which are more or less identical with the law of property; and therefore it overlaps with the concept of 'the law'. We must be able to separate the variables before we can study their interaction. To make a rigorous sociology of law possible much analysis and clarification is still needed; so we cannot criticise Weber for not having provided a solution to this fundamental question. Intuitively, however, he seems to sense the trap and talks about general aspects of the legal systems — such as regularity versus arbitrariness of the procedures — rather than about provisions of the law which could be regarded as a part of the structure of the economy.

As laws are rules made and applied by people, there is no *a priori* reason why they should not be adapted instantaneously to the changing circumstances. On the other hand, it has been observed that the laws often persist through a kind of inertia. It is very difficult to judge what weight to attach to this variant of cultural inertia in an explanatory analysis.

Although he did not supply neat answers to such baffling questions, Weber's merit resides in having revealed the immense complexity of the interaction between the law and other social circumstances. In relation to how this subject was treated before him, his achievement fits the role of a synthesis in Hegelian dialectics. As the initial thesis we can consider the old jurisprudence which treated the law (as in the main jurisprudence still does) as something so to speak disembodied or superhuman, and confined itself to discussions about the normative validity of various interpretations without inquiring into the social effects of the laws or attempting to explain changes therein. Marx and Engels formulated the antithesis, declaring the law to be a mere epiphenomenon — a reflection of the economic interests dominant in a given society. Possibily under their influence, Max Weber (already in his first book) went beyond the limits of the jurisprudence and legal history on which he was brought up as a student, but he also knew that it was sheer dogma to assert that the economic circumstances determine the laws rather than the other way round. His synthesis consisted of the study of the interaction of the two factors without any monistic preconceptions.

Many of his explanations of various turns in legal history refer to the play of economic interests. Weber, however, improved upon Marx and Engels by discarding the oversimplified dualistic vision of society which has condemned the writing of so many of their followers to sterility. Actually, in his better moments — when he writes as a historian rather than a preacher — Marx himself takes into account the separate economic interests of the clergy, the officialdom and the landed nobility as distinct from the capitalists and the workers. Of special relevance to sociology of law is Weber's interest in the economic interests of the legal profession — not as a mere appendage of the capitalists but as an independent and cohesive group with considerable power and very specific interests. For example, he attributes the non-codification of the English law to the lawyers' pecuniary interest in keeping it incomprehensible to the layman.

The second notable feature in Weber's sociology of law is his recognition of the importance of the technical element. A new concept or procedure will not come from extraterrestrial sources but somebody must invent it. Without the invention of the concept of limited liability the joint-stock company — that corner-stone of modern capitalism — could not have come into existence. But should we view such an invention as an independent factor, or can we assume that the demand would call forth a needed invention? We are treading here on a very difficult ground full of insoluble counterfactual questions: there is no way of knowing about inventions which could have been made and would have been applied, had they been made, but in fact have not been made. In science and technology we certainly cannot explain the sequence of inventions simply by the need. Did not the Romans need the gun? Do we not need a cure for cancer? It might be argued that because the legal concepts are simpler than those of science or technology they are less subject to intrinsic concatenation (or immanent dynamics, if you like) and can be brought forth more readily in response to the demand. Weber assumed that new legal ideas are also difficult to invent, and that the ingenuity (or the lack thereof) of the lawyers must be treated in historical explanation as an independent (or at least partly independent) factor.

Weber's ideas do not add up to a system ... which is all to the good. When he comes nearest to offering a master key, he is most open to criticism. As in other parts of his writings, the culprit is the word 'rational' with its derivatives, although in contrast to other contexts, in his sociology of law he does explain what he means by it by defining its opposite. On page 395 of the first edition of *Wirtschaft und Gesellschaft* he says (the translation is mine and not word by word which would be incomprehensible):

> Legislation and adjudication can be either rational or irrational. They are formally irrational when the decisions are based on methods other than reasoning, such as oracles or their equivalents. They are materially irrational when the decisions are based not on general rules but on ethical, sentimental or political evaluation of individual cases.

Here at least we can see what he is getting at, but the proper word for the opposite of what he describes is not 'rational' but 'regular'. Furthermore, the concept of 'materially rational' law is pleonastic. If individual cases are decided according to their 'sentimental or political evaluation' rather than with reference to a general rule, then either there is no relevant law or it is disregarded. In other words we have either the absence or a breach of the law. A 'materially irrational' law

— that is a law which is not a general rule — is a self-contradictory notion. Weber himself comes near to recognising the pleonastic character of his explication when he adds 'Every formulated law is (at least relatively) formally rational'. This is a bit like 'every flower is (at least relatively) flowery'. Furthermore, the rule that an oracle must decide is just as general and definite (materially formal in his terminology) as one which says that the Court of Appeals must decide. True, you might say that it is irrational to believe in oracles, but here you are passing a judgement not on the law but on religious beliefs; because if you assume that God speaks through the oracles, then it is perfectly rational to consult them. If you regard the disbelief in this matter as 'rational' you are using this term not in Weber's sense but in the sense in which it was and is used by people who call themselves rationalists and consider reason and sense perception as the sole sources of knowledge, and dismiss all claims of communication with superhuman beings. If we take the enforcement of the laws (as they are) as the goal in relation to which we shall judge the rationality of the procedures, then the recourse to oracles in African tribal courts seems much more effective (and therefore rational) than the taking of statements sworn 'by Almighty God' in Britain in 1981 when the opinion surveys have shown that most people are not at all afraid of God's punishment.

It may not be meaningless to debate whether the present French or the British penal procedure is more rational in relation to the goals proclaimed by the legislators or the values accepted by the public, because these are not very different in the two countries nowadays. But it makes no sense whatsoever to say that the customary laws of the Barotse or the Zulus are irrational whereas the laws in Britain, France or the USA are rational. Actually a strong case could be made for the view that the laws of the Barotse were more rational in relation to the goal of preserving the values of their culture than is the case in any Western country today. In a forthcoming little popular book called *Post-Marital Bondage* I maintain that, as judged by the criterion of compatibility with the ethical standards accepted by the majority of the population or with the goals and values proclaimed by the legislators who have passed these laws, the present British divorce law is singularly irrational; and that no irrationality of this degree can be detected in the rules which regulate matrimonial affairs in any of the number of African tribes with whose customs I am acquainted. Actually, only in relation to the goal of maximising the solicitors' income (taken as the sole criterion) can the present British divorce law be regarded as rational.

Once we replace 'rational' by 'regular and predictable', Weber's argument becomes valid in principle though erroneous on a number of points of fact. He is perfectly right in insisting that the market economy (or, if you prefer, capitalism) can flourish only where the consequences of legal transactions can be foreseen with near certainty, as without the security of property and unfailing enforcement of contracts neither the profits nor the costs can be foreseen. If legal obligations can be set aside at somebody's whim, business becomes a sheer gamble. Banks cannot function where the recovery of debts depends on a verdict of an oracle or a trial by battle. But societies, where the courts resort to such methods of settling disputes, are also too primitive in other aspects of culture (such as technology, literacy, or the enforcement of internal peace) for an elaborate division of labour and intensive exchange. It would be, therefore, just as gratuitous to attribute the non-development of capitalism among the Barotse to the 'irrationality' of their law, as to say that the reason why a baby cannot drive a car is because it cannot sit up. A comparison relevant to the question of the rise of capitalism is between Europe in the sixteenth, seventeeth and eighteenth centuries and the great civilisations of Asia and Antiquity.

Dealing with China, Weber underestimates the regularity with which the laws were administered during the great epochs of the empire. This is perfectly understandable because, lacking other sources of information, he relied on the judgements of nineteeth-century Europeans about the empire rapidly sinking into chaos. True, various laws hampered business enterprise in China and not only arrested but reversed the rise of the merchant class which reached the zenith of its importance around 1000 AD. These laws, however, were made (as rationally as any laws anywhere) for this purpose.

Weber also underestimates on this score the Islamic law which affords good protection to property and trade. Very broadly speaking, it is true that after the great period of the Islamic civilisation, which ended in the thirteenth century, but especially since the eighteenth century, the administration of the law was less regular and predictable in the Islamic lands than in the countries of Western Christendom, but this was due not to the content of the laws but to their disregard stemming from despotism, unlawful exactions by satraps and soldiers and the venality of the judges and officials, not to speak of the depredations by invaders. Weber knew very well about all this and he was undoubtedly right in seeing in juridical irregularity a crucial impediment to the development of the market economy in the Near

East. He clearly did not feel, however, that the former set of circumstances sufficed to account for the latter, and resorted to unwarranted grading of the legal systems on the scale of rationality.

If we felt that we must apply this scale to the legal systems, then the only proper way of going about it would be first to discover whether there is a single purpose which most of the laws appear to serve, and then to find out whether they are adapted to this purpose. If this is the case, we can say that the legal system in question is rationalised in the sense that a business firm is said to be rationalised when all its procedures are adapted to the purpose of maximising the profits. An application of this criterion leads us to a conclusion which is the opposite of Weber's: namely that the most 'rational' legal codes appear to be those promulgated by clever despots. After Ivan the Cruel and Ivan the Terrible — and even more under Peter I — the laws of Russia were very rational in the sense of being well adapted to the single purpose of maximising the Tzar's internal and external power. The laws of the Ottoman Empire at its zenith could also be called rational (or rationalised) in this sense. The laws of England were much more rationalised under William the Conqueror than under Queen Victoria or now. Rationalisation of this kind was, in fact, inversely related to the development of the industrial market economy (or capitalism, if you prefer this word) which occurred only in societies where neither a single individual nor a tightly knit oligarchy was strong enough to subjugate entirely the rest of the population and to shape all (or at least most of) the laws to serve his or their single purpose.

When Weber talks about the legal requirements of capitalism we can often replace his 'rational' and 'rationality' by 'the rule of law' or 'juridical security' — that is freedom from arbitrary interference by the wielders of power with the application of the laws. As Montesquieu discovered more than a century earlier, such a condition depends on the division of power. The latter rules out 'rationalisation' (in the sense of subordination to a single purpose) except at rare occasions of universal consent.

Bibliography

Andreski, S. *Social Sciences as Sorcery* (André Deutsch, London, 1972)

Durkheim, E. *The Rules of Sociological Method,* translated by S.A. Solovay and J.H. Mueller (Chicago University Press, Chicago, 1949)

Evans-Pritchard, E.E. *Witchcraft, Oracles and Magic among the Azanda* (Clarendon Press, Oxford, 1937)

Hume, D. *A Treatise on Human Nature* in T.H. Green and T.H. Grose, *The Philosophical Works of David Hume* (Longman Green, London, 1874)
Smith, A. *Theory of Moral Sentiments* (Richard Griffin, Glasgow, 1854, new ed)
Watkins, D.N.G. 'Methodological Individualism', *British Journal of Philosophy of Science,* vol. A (1952)
Weber, M. *Gesammelte Schrifter zur Wissenschaftslehre* (J.C.B. Mohr, Tubingen, 1922)
——— *The Methodology of the Social Sciences,* translated by E.A. Shils and H.A. Finch (Free Press of Glencoe, Glencoe, Illinois, 1949)
——— *Basic Concepts in Sociology* (P. Owen, London, 1962)
——— *Wirtschaft und Gesellschaft* (Studienausgabe Kiepenguew & Witsch, Köln-Berlin, 1964)
Winch, P. *The Idea of a Social Science and its Relation to Philosophy* (Routledge and Kegan Paul, London, 1958)

4 The Potential of Functionalism for the Sociological Analysis of Law

Philip J. Wilkinson

This chapter aims to provide a technical specification of the constituents of functionalism and an appreciation of how functionalism so understood may provide for an understanding of legal phenomena.

The discussion will steer clear of iconoclasm but must be prefaced by an admonition to sociologists in general. The sociology of law is but a sub-discipline of sociology and, as such, aims at the understanding of that discipline's particular subject-matter. Sociology studies regularities in social phenomena composed of social actions in some manner meaningful to participants. Functionalism aims at an objective analysis of social action through the investigation of social systems constituted by patterns of meaningful activity. A naive functionalism unencumbered with a base in social action cannot claim to itself the logical support of functionalism as a social theory, for it is in the concept of social action that the functionalist method of analysis, as contemporarily understood, has its origin. It is the interest in normative phenomena and the interrelationship between norms, roles and institutions which marks functionalism as a structural mode of analysis and it is within this structural mode that the concept of social action and reference to subjective motivation has to be accommodated. Much of this chapter will be taken up by a consideration of the technical meaning of 'function' and the problems such a meaning imparts to empirical studies carried out under its auspices. The terminology of functions is itself fraught with ambiguity given both technical usages in social science as well as lay connotations.

The functionalism that is to be discussed here as a technically refined social theory can be introduced by reference to its property as an analysis of social systems. Not far below the surface of functionalism and undoubtedly of historical significance has been the biological analogy of social systems as organisms. Organisms as bounded entities composed of interdependent parts can be analysed for the contribution each part plays in the maintenance of the whole. Interdependence and differentiation are the key points of reference involving three related types of questions. First, in what way are the parts related; second, how is this interdependence effected; and, thirdly, what are the causes of the origins and persistence of these interrelations.

If we pursue the biological analogy[1] we can see that in the understanding of biological organisms we can either look at an organism as it is, how it works, of what parts it is composed and so forth, at one moment in time therefore producing a structural analysis or we can look at the origin of the organism in terms of Darwinian evolution and Mendelian genetics thereby producing a causal analysis. Functionalism as a systems analysis is structural although, as we shall see, such an analysis of the interrelationships composing a society has also been as of causal significance. To begin with, however, we will assert the distinction between 'functionalism' and 'causation', we will liken functionalism to a non-evolutionary biology of organisms and note that, unlike biology, functionalism has been bedevilled by the lack of any causal machinery for explaining the origins of social forms.

The chapter will progress by way of a discussion of certain authors, stopping at suitable places to make technical refinements of our understanding of functionalism.

Durkheim

Durkheim posited three interrelated axioms for social theory: treat social facts as things; explain the form of solidarity holding society together by a positive analysis of social facts; eschew metaphysics. Social facts could be either normal or pathological. Society could be healthy, like an organism, by having the optimum arrangement of its parts contributing to the whole. The whole as a form of social order could be analysed by atemporal correlations. Since both normality and pathology, as social categories, were based upon the degree of generality of the appearance of particular social items the study of social order was to be achieved by the comparative method, investigating social facts of sufficient generality to be accounted as normal. Explanation was to be both causal, in regard to the origins of social facts, and functional, as regards their contribution to the whole.

Cause had to be efficient cause or that which brought about through traceable prior processes the effect. Functions came after the items which provided those functions or contemporaneously with such items. To analyse the function as the cause of the item is to provide an analysis of final not efficient causes and this Durkheim claimed to be an unwarranted metaphysic for the concept of 'cause' and, further, an introduction of unknowable 'needs' by which to explain the existence of a given social item.

The concept of system needs is worth dwelling on for a moment even at the expense of departing somewhat from a consideration of Durkheim. The logic of the difficulties with a proposition involving system needs is easy to state. If we take functionalism to state that 't' explains X as being the contribution of X to Y ('t' is the function X fulfils in system Y; or X maintains the system Y through effecting 't') this only works as a logical final cause of X (a) if Y can be held to need 't'; (b) if the continued existence of Y is given; and (c) if the continued existence of Y can be held dependent not only on 't' but also on 't' being provided by X rather than by some other process. These are all metaphysical props to what should be an empirical logic of discovery. Not only is antecedent cause replaced by system need but system need is equated with satisfaction of that need.

Since Durkheim's preoccupation was with the relation of the individual to society his substantive analyses in this regard were concentrated upon the requirement for complementarity amongst the acts of depersonalised individuals. Ways of acting had to be consistent for the stability of the social ordering and had to be objectively specified for the purposes of Durkheim's method. Law met both criteria and as, in Durkheim's words, 'law reproduces the principal forms of social solidarity, we have only to classify the different types of law to find . . . the types of social solidarity which correspond to it' (Durkheim, 1933, p. 6). This Durkheim proceeded to do, the study of law thereby being provided with the characteristic atemporal analysis which marks Durkheim as a progenitor of functionalism.

The study of law began with law as a symbol of the interdependencies of social systems. The correlates of the investigation into types of law by reference to type of sanction, however, provided an evolutionary scheme of social development. Both mechanical and organic solidarity are relationships of interdependence and therefore, although Durkheim's analysis is based upon the functional unity of the social whole, his analysis is one of functional *alternatives*. The need for orders of solidarity can be provided in different ways but, at any one moment in time, given states a . . . y of society, state z is both functionally required and required to be provided in a particular way. This element of Durkheim is implicit in his 'Two Laws of Penal Evolution' (Durkheim, 1969). That study begins on a functional plane. Crime is normal on the evidence of comparative analysts. It occurs as a form of leakage from an otherwise healthily functioning system. But societies, unlike biological organisms, are self-defined wholes not materially identifiable. The boundaries of society have to be maintained and identified and it is for this function that the normality of crime provides. But if crimes are normal why do they shock the conscience commune? In Durkheim the answer is readily provided, for they do not shock because they are crimes and so the normality of the latter is not at issue. They are crimes because they shock the conscience commune, the community of shared sentiment or, in other words, the social solidarity of the society as a whole. Penal law as an expression of this reaction of the conscience commune reflects a social solidarity based upon resemblances. Social cohesion is founded on conformity. The individual is directly linked with society. Punishment functions to maintain the solidarity by enforcing similarities. Here lies the basis for the comparative analysis of social solidarities for 'in determining what fraction of the judicial system penal law represents we at the same time measure the relative importance of this solidarity' (Durkheim, 1933, p. 109). As de Espinosa observes, however, there is a dualism here between law as a symbol of functional interdependencies and law as a causative factor in the operation and maintenance of the particular solidarity obtaining (de Espinosa, 1980).

The fate of Durkheim's analysis need not detain us, given both its empirical insufficiency and conceptual barriers to proof or disproof, but the structure of the analysis is worth recounting. Durkheim began with a category of subject-matter defined by necessary constraints of positive science. Social action could not be handled through the individual psychology of actions. Actions had to have ends set for them by external constraints and these ends had to have system properties. It was open to use a comparative analysis to discover the significant constituents of functioning social systems and then to analyse by way of atemporal correlations the role of the constituent parts in maintaining the system as a whole. As a systems analyst Durkheim shows one of the values of functionalism, its ability of forcing one to open up an otherwise myopic study of particular legal phenomena. Law and legal phenomena are not to be viewed simply and as such as social facts *sui generis,* but by reference to their normality and their symbiotic relation to the social whole of which it is the purpose of social theory to fathom. Although the analogy of symbiosis is close to functionalism it is unfair to hoist such an albatross round the neck of Durkheim without a word of caution. Durkheim, while undoubtedly establishing functionalism as a respected social theory, himself eschewed functionalism in the sense of a causal theory of social phenomena. Although it is hard not to read Durkheim as saying that co-operative law as a reproduction of complementary relations developed because of the requirements of social order in an era of increased competition for scarce resources, he did explicitly disjoin functional from causal analyses. This then may be a convenient place to stop and make some technical refinements to our understanding of functionalism through this issue. The issue is of two parts. First, what is the relationship of talk of functions with talk of causes, and, secondly, depending on the answer to that question, how can analysis of social wholes be functional without positing some metaphysical proposition concerning system needs? The first question will be tackled here, the second is more adequately placed in a general discussion of Parsons.

Function and Cause

Durkheim rejected functionalism because he rejected the idea that the cause of a social item could be located in its effects on other items, and the part it played in sustaining their social existence. Causes, for Durkheim, came before effects and were not to be confused with functions. More contemporary functionalists have not been so reticent. What, then, is the difficulty of holding to a teleological form of explanation? We may begin by refining the basic concept of function. Function as a technical sociological term references those effects of social items objectively discoverable which, through a finite and specifiable process, maintain the system of which the item is a part. As such then there is no reference to teleology and the processes themselves may be causally narrated. There is, however, the requirement that the 'system' be specifiable and that it be possible objectively to ascertain necessary conditions for the persistence of that system. It is in the latter refinement that teleological analysis gains an entry.

What are the possible meanings of the statement that the function of X is 't'? First, given the requirement that functionalism be system-specific the statement would have to be extended to read: the function of item X for system Y is 't'. Translated this would become a statement that X maintains Y through 't'. As such the statement necessarily allows X a causative influence on Y. The statement allows X to account for Y through 't' in that without X a condition of system maintenance 't' would not obtain. The alternative, however, accounts 't' as the cause of X through a postulated need in Y. A social item is causally explained by referencing its consequence as necessary to the maintenance of the system of which it is a part. This is the teleology of functionalism as propounded by Kingsley Davis (see Davis, 1949; Merton, 1968; and comments by Bredemeier, 1955). The causal accounting for social items, therefore, posits certain properties of any social system which must be met for a system to persist. Some notion of system need is required because without such the functional account is equally commensurate with the caused item both existing and not existing. Conceptions of these needs or properties range from the equilibrium of Smelser to the personality integration of Parsons but their status within the whole theory is commensurate. Further, although Merton saw the danger that the substantive accounting and description of any such system property would be to confuse functionalist method with a particular configuration of society, the formal necessity of system needs for functionalism to be causally effective[2] remains even if, like Merton, one jettisons the postulates of universal functionalism, indispensability and functional unity (Merton, 1968, pp. 16 et seq.).

If we reiterate at this juncture we can gain a sense of functionalism and its problems. Functionalism was a reaction against historical schools of social theory and attempts a synchronic analysis of system properties. The function of an item is a consequence necessary to the maintenance of the system. Functionalism is structural, relating parts to wholes, and it is system-specific. Difficulties arise in identifying societies as bounded entities that can be healthy or pathological; in identifying the processes by which an item can be said to maintain a system; and in accounting for the items which perform the functions attributed to them. Although a reaction against the historical school and although wedded to atemporal correlations, functionalism never divorced itself from the problem of origins and thereby provided for its incipient teleology. As long as functionalism required a logic of causation for items by reference to system maintenance it was also in danger of reverting into tautology. For as Cohen has said 'criteria of survival of societies or cultures are difficult, if not impossible to specify' (Cohen, 1968, p. 50). A society, unlike an organism, is not bounded nor necessarily identifiable with a specific arrangement of its parts. Being denied any measure of persistence, to say that a process 'contributes to the maintenance of the system is little more than a tautology: for if the process were to change then there would by definition be a change in the system' (Cohen, 1968, p. 50). Functionalism in this guise merely states the truism that a society only persists so long as the criteria by which it is identified as a society continue to exist.

Partly in response to the lack of explanatory value of the nebulous system property of persistence, functionalism accommodated a psychology of individual motivation. Here there was to be a mechanism truly causal in an antecedent fashion for conforming behaviour. Even in this version, however, with the necessary modification to the theory of internalisation, functionalism still logically required a universal property of system integration on a normative level (Wrong, 1961).

The requirements of technical functionalism are, then, awesome. A function is a specific activity identifiable with a particular social item objectively describable and one which in specifiable ways engages a process which in further specifiable ways maintains a specified social system. Why social systems persist; how to recognise system needs; and how to account for those needs as necessarily met in one way rather than another provide the metaphysical problems of such a functionalism.

Talcott Parsons

Parsonian sociology may be seen as an attempt to refute the above characterisations of functionalism. Social order was *the* preoccupation of Parsons, but rather than specify metaphysical needs he provided a solution to the problem of order which at the same time equally solved the problem of motivation. For Parsons, man is a socialised animal. Society is built on a system of common values internalised by its members during socialisation. Through socialisation a person learns how to act in particular situations as the norms governing social life are part of his psychological make-up. So given, the person is set with a particular relation to social order. Social order is not accomplished by external constraint but internally through obligation and the units of social order are not individuals but the place of such individuals in society, as denoted by the concepts of role, norm and status. The concept of a norm is central to Parsons's sociology and he states that a norm represents a 'verbal description of the concrete course of action which is regarded as desirable' by the actor together with a 'social injunction to make certain the future actions conform to this course' (Parsons, 1937, p. 25). An actor's commitment to the norms not only solved the problem of order but, as expressed in the 'action frame of reference', united threads of Durkheim's positivism with Weber's analyses of subjectively interpreted action. Parsons criticised positivism within sociology for omitting 'all reference to an understandable normative system of rules and expectations as understood from the subjective point of view of the social actor' (Parsons, 1937, p 17). His accommodation to Weber was to include such a reference to subjectivity in the base unit of analysis. This unit Parsons called the 'unit act' and comprised an actor in a situation, the actor being in possession of values and a normative structure in common with other actors. Many such unit acts made up the orderly operation of society as a 'web of interwoven strands'. Voluntarism meant that the actor was able to appreciate what behaviour was expected from him. If he was not able so to participate in society then concerted interactions would not be possible. The action frame of reference itself signified a normative orientation to interaction, the absence of a normative schema being for Parsons equivalent to the absence of consciously controlled and directed behaviour. Parsons's social actor could appreciate his situation and act accordingly but could not choose to transcend the determinate character of that situation. As Atkinson expresses the point, '[the] actors "choice" to pursue rationally and normatively his own interests, themselves patterned by the "social system"' (D. Atkinson, 1971, p. 9). He allows that 'such analyses still retain the conception of action being subjectively meaningful to actor and scientist alike' although, as Homans might rejoin, in the application of the analyses, society 'appeared to have no actors and mighty little action' (Homans, 1964, p. 817).

As stated above, the 'action frame of reference' was given as a synthesis of converging themes in the work of Durkheim and Weber. Durkheim held the primary modes of differentiation in the structure of a society to be related to structure's functional needs. Not only were these structures and functions objectively discoverable but further, since sociology required objective facts for categorisation and analysis, Durkheim held that sociology must rid itself of pretensions to analyse internal subjective mental states. The method of comparative statistics was to hand, for if the generality of a species of behaviour varied with other established social facts then a causal correlation could be formally expressed.

Weber himself did not reject causation or objectivity in knowledge but asked that such knowledge be of understandable action sequences following an hermeneutically grasped context of motivations. Parsons saw a possible unification of the two. He believed that 'starting from the frame of reference of subjectively interpreted individual action it is open to use functional analysis to develop a generalised outline of social systems of action' (Parsons, 1947, p. 20). As such the action, however subjectively interpreted, is an emergent property of the social system itself. In order to accommodate an acting individual into such a denial of humanism, Parsons invoked Freudian psychology of the subconscious. Unit acts remained the base unit of analysis but now comprised not an acting individual in a situation but role-sets. The incumbent of the role could be motivated through socialisation and driven through subconscious needs for gratification. Interrelated sets of unit acts comprised the social totality and interdependence necessitated that a change in one area be reflected in a change elsewhere. Subjectivity is accepted as necessary to identify action-types but the essential character and existence of such actions are a system property. The subjective point of view is no longer relevant to the explanation of action, only to its analytic identity. Explanation is the province of functionalism, an analysis which looks for the conditions of persistence of social systems, these being located in a set of 'functional prerequisites'. Interdependence and differentiation remain the key elements of the theory, the primary modes of which are the functional relationships between societal prerequisites. The human being whose action is embedded in and constitutes one or other functional process leaves the scene and is allowed back only as a conveyor belt for those processes. He is indeed replaced by the concept of 'role'. Individuals occupy roles in society and behave appropriately to the requirements of role as set by its location within the normative structure of social order and as reinforced by the cultural system of value-consensus. Each role subsumes a set of obligations and expectations which must be fulfilled if the role is to play its part in the maintenance of the system. The system, seen functionally, sanctions those expectations and attributes objective motives to the actor (D. Atkinson, 1971, pp. 25-31). The action frame of reference has been replaced by functionalism.

Of what, then, is Parsonian functionalism composed? Parsons's theory is one of the objective possibilities of social order discoverable from an objective phenomenology of the unit act. For Parsons there are three possibilities when actors come together: random orientation, conflicting orientations or complementary expectations. Only the latter is compatible with the continuance of interaction. It is settled *a priori* that social order requires (needs) normatively oriented social actors occupying complementary social roles learnt through socialisation. Social systems are the emergent property of the unit act in that should the hypothetical actors have complementary expectations they will have created a collective reality partaken of by both but belonging to neither. From the unit act are taken the necessary assumptions to make 'system' a viable sociological entity. The network of social relationships which are prior to any one course of social interaction is already composed of those emergent realities generated in the hypothetical account of interactional settings. Standardised expectations, derived from a central value system, pervade action at all levels and the actor, by virtue of his socialisation and the requirement that he attend carefully to the goals and standards of the socio-cultural nexus, is assured of finding matching expectations among others with whom he interacts. That the actor can identify expectations and match his behaviour is, as has already been said, the 'voluntarism' of Parsons's theory. But individual psychology enters again into the picture. In Parsons's theory the 'system needs' are provided not by speculation regarding universal functionalism but by reference to objectively ascertainable requirements of the unit act. That these requirements are met, in other words, that there is a cement for the real world as a functioning totality, is provided by motivation and in particular from the cognitive consensus underlying each system. Parsonian functionalism as such, then, is a theory of societal equilibrium and functional interdependence. The functional prerequisites are specifiable by reference to the problem of social order and in their particular solution provide for the normative analysis of regular patterns of activity. It would, however, be inconsiderate to the reader to suggest that Parsons's own structural functionalism does not itself embody shifting orientations. As Gouldner (1971, pp. 138-282) argues, Parsons's writings can be read as an attempt to resolve at a theoretical level this cultural conflict between behaviour as system integration or as value internalisation. In working out his theoretical design for functionalism, Parsons moved through three stages in regard to social order. At first there was an emphasis on values as an 'internalised moral code' in and for itself; secondly, an emphasis on 'the importance of the gratifying outcome of individual conformity with values' and the real worldly consequences so deriving; thirdly, the usefulness or function of cultural values for system equilibrium became central and an orientation achieved to 'society as a social system comprised of interacting institutions' and the 'emphasis on voluntaristic individual commitment' is replaced by a reliance on 'the socialisation of individuals to produce the choices the system requires'. Social systems, by this third stage, were now ordained with the property of equilibrium as a derivation of their own processes, the processes themselves constituted by the 'conformity all give to the legitimate expectations of each other'. This is a Durkheimian vision of social solidarity. As Parsons said, 'my own inclination is to refer above all to Durkheim as the fountainhead of the primary fruitful trend' (cited in Gouldner, 1971, p. 163, n. 27).

This trend has resulted in what we shall call not a technical method of functionalist analysis but a doctrine of functionalist theory. The theory has now provided not only an analogy of systems with interrelated parts but has decomposed those parts into a normative structure. Other aspects of society, such as the cultural system, are subordinate to the functional prerequisites of normative order. The order provides for the ways of acting of individual members of society in the institutions of which society is composed. Patterns of action are functional and the delineation of the processes whereby the 'function' is seen as necessary to the continuance of society is an elaboration of the logical requirements of complementary expectation over random orientation or conflict, that is of the unit act.

With the proviso in mind that we shall later have to divorce the functional doctrine of Parsons from the functional method technically so called, we can look at the fate of law within the Parsonian structure.

Parsons on Law

Parsons's social system was a generalised picture of 'any' society. This general sketch of necessary societal processes could then be filled in to see how in a particular case a specified process is met. These processes Parsons termed 'pattern variables'. They represent the primary modes of differentiation within society and can be equated with the major institutionalised sub-systems. They are both necessary functions for system maintenance and the processes by which the major institutions of society fulfil their functional tasks. To understand the part played, for instance, by law in the social system, it is necessary to analyse the law's relationship to other institutions and the other pattern variables. If law be equated with the processes of 'integration' then the other processes are 'adaptation', 'goal pursuance' and 'pattern maintenance', and it is possible both to take a look at the internal workings of a chosen process or to analyse inter-process relationships. In his essay 'The Law and Social Control' (1962) Parsons gave a look at the structure and needs of the integrative process and sought to explicate how law functioned to maintain an ordered set of social relationships. His concern was not with how a particular law or even a particular legal system did so order relationships but with what is involved in *any* such ordering. More specifically, Parsons was concerned to analyse the conditions on which rests the effectiveness of a system of rules. These conditions, as necessary for the integrative process to be maintained, had to be abstract properties of any system of normative regulation and not tied to the specific content of a society's laws. Indeed, Parsons strongly advocated the neutrality of law as a generalised mechanism of social control, its non-specificity with respect to content. Law is, on this view, the real worldly counterpart to the analytic framework for society of roles, norms and statuses. In the analytic picture of society roles intersect and so normative orientations must be mutually consistent; incumbents must be motivated both to retain incumbency and act appropriately. Motivation is acquired through socialisation and standards of appropriateness sanctioned by complementary expectations. Law operates just as do these other social rules, its normative system of sanctioned expectations is the form of integration provided, an integration achieved through the form of law rather than the specific content of the laws themselves. This characterisation of law as performing an integrative function in and through normative regulation Parsons regarded as central. For on this basis one is directed to inquire into the functional requirements of the process if it is to exist and if it is to continue to exist. In other words, if law integrates then one needs to go further and inquire how the law achieves this objective. The analysis of law's effectiveness is, then, at the same time an analysis of the problems any legal system has to solve if it is to regulate social interaction.

It is important to remember here that Parsons saw only one alternative to normative regulation — chaos. Normative regulation is not just one possibility amongst other endemic possibilities for achieving social order, it *is* social order. Order comprises actors adhering to a system of rules and so the basis of the law's effectiveness can be found in an *a priori* inquiry into the necessary correlates of any rule-system. Those correlates were specified by Parsons as being internal consistency and an external domain of operation. The latter requires not only a jurisdiction so linking law to political governance via the polity's monopoly over sanctions but also the legitimacy of the system within that jurisdiction so linking law to sociality via the concept of justice and the motivation of individuals to mobilise the law on their behalf. As we shall see these inter-process relations were analysed in more detail by Bredemeier, Parsons himself stopping short at an internal analysis of law. But in this internal inquiry he assembles many and varied commonly known features of the operation of law and related those features to the necessary conditions of normative regulation. The requirement for authoritative rule interpretations embedded in the possibility of normative consistency and a sanctioning procedure to maintain such interpretations in the face of rule-infraction are each, in turn, capable of being related to specific features of legal operation. It would be too lengthy to reiterate Parsons's own particular appreciation of these features here but the point must be taken that in his analysis relating legal phenomena to pattern variables and so to the maintenance of social systems, descriptions of legal phenomena are given as resistant to alternative conceptualisations. This resistance is founded on the claimed logical structure of functional theory and herein lies the primary requirement for achieving a technical appreciation of functionalism and for eschewing the employment of functional terminology without reliance on or acceptance of the infrastructure of the method.

If we recapitulate at this point, the theory's conception of normative order is inherent in its basic analysis of social systems. Social systems, as conglomerates of unit acts, are composed of individuals performing subjectively meaningful actions. These actions have an objective context provided by the system of roles and norms and the individual is socialised into that context. The system of roles and norms, or, more obliquely, social order, is an integrated normative framework. Integration has to be provided for and is so provided for both by the essential character of norms themselves as sanctioned role expectations and by those features of normative orders which equip them to operate in specified social systems. A functional analysis of law is, then, the filling out of those tenets with empirically achieved representations of the processes in action. The analysis would describe the solutions provided by law to problems of social order and to problems of strain in the accomplishment of those solutions. Social order is explained first by the essential character of normative systems and secondly by those aspects of society and its institutions which provide for the successful operation of those systems.

Bredemeier

Bredemeier, himself not uncritical of functionalism, analysed how law interacts with the other pattern variables of a social system. Law was conceived as receiving inputs from the other pattern variables of adaptation (economy, science and technology), goal pursuance (polity) and pattern maintenance (sociality) in return for which they received the outputs of organic solidarity, interpretation and justice respectively (Bredemeier, 1962).

Bredemeier organised the relationship of law to the pattern variables: largely around the Parsonian concept of law as neutral and reactive. The law concretises role structures, duties and obligations but the efficiency of such a concretisation in the specific appearance is dependent upon the goal structure of society and the ability of society to mobilise the use of law. Further, in being mobilised the law faces problems of evidence and truth, problems which it itself, as a normative system, cannot solve. Further still, there is the problem of in what direction solutions should move social relationships, a problem whose own solution is dependent upon the law being given knowledge of the function of various species of social behaviour. All these kinds of questions and problems are external to law as a normative system. The law can operate only if provided with answers to these questions by other pattern variables. At least they have to be provided for the resultant organisation of social relationships to be functional for a particular social system. So, although the polity provides the legal system with policy goals for evaluating an anticipated role structure, it is the adaptive processes that are brought in to remove obstacles to the attainment of those goals. The integrative process provides a mechanism for their attainment by applying goals to individual cases. In so doing the law performs the act of interpretation in return for which it receives from the polity enforcement procedures. But even to apply policy to individual cases the law requires knowledge of what social relationships further rather than hinder the policy. Policy requires efficient social organisation and the law receives its knowledge of both efficient organisation and means for its attainment from the adaptive process. In return for this information on efficient organisation, the law, in concretising social relationships, returns an output of organisation or solidarity. The decision of the court on an individual case is an output of structure, the imposition of rights and obligations in the interests of efficient organisation. The pattern maintenance process provides for the possibility of legal organisation by bringing conflicts into the realm of the law, by motivating individuals to use the law for the protection of their interests and by equipping the legal personnel through professional socialisation with the means to continue their (imperfect) monopoly over the interpretation of role structures. The law in return provides pattern maintenance with the output of justice which, for functionalism, is not so much an ideal but the legal justification for meeting the demands of individualised expectations.

The above all too brief excursion into a substantive analysis is filled out in Bredemeier's own work with examples from legal practice. For present purposes, however, it is sufficient if one acknowledges the attempt to convert a static organic analysis of functional interrelationships into a dynamic process capable of both experiencing strain and accommodating to social change. Bredemeier attempts to show how on a functional view a change in one process must be reflected in either a functional or dysfunctional stress in another process. And far from being committed to a view of a necessary reassertion of equilibrium, he does go into some detail on the ways in which the balance between the pattern variables can break down. Other aspects of the legal machinery can then be appreciated for the work they do in reducing the likelihood of such strains in fact coming to pass. The functionalist theory of Parsons is composed of explicit statements concerning the equilibrium of social systems. The ends-means scheme of normative orientation in the unit act carves out the basic building blocks of sociology of norms, role-sets and so on. Explanation of order is by reference to complementary expectations and social phenomena are functional to the extent that they are necessary to maintain the normative edifice. Underlying the theory is an assumption of cognitive consensus, a common value system, and a substantive claim of equilibrium as a property of social systems. System needs are represented by functional prerequisites and the individual is locked into the system through socialisation. This functionalism commits the social theorists to a view of system needs as analogues of causal antecedents and to a view of the systems themselves as identifiable with a particular ordering of or conjunction between a normative order and a value system. Further, social processes are related to system maintenance and there has then to be postulated some variant of system needs, these being found in the logical requirements of normative structures. The inner core of functionalism is a view of society as accountable by reference to categories of norms, roles and statuses. Patterned regularities in the behaviour are the outcome of complementary expectations. The features of a pattern of action are explicable by reference to culturally acquired dispositions to act in specifiable ways and sanctioned expectations (see the careful development of this point in Wilson, 1971). Expectations are internalised to provide the fabric of a shared culture. This scheme is the Parsonian alternative to Durkheim's external constraint and it does, necessarily, limit the analysis of social items to their relationship with the postulated normative framework. Even as a method of inquiry, functionalism dictates relevant levels of questioning and relevant researchable relationships. Whatever the problems of such an approach it has the benefit of providing commensurability between varied studies. For instance, functionalism in the study of law is looking not to the legal arena. It has looked at the legal profession through both the eyes of Parsons (1962) and the more sceptical eyes of Rueschmeyer (1964). In both, the professional-client relationship is analysed by reference to the role it plays in maintaining the accredited legal ideology and, further, the role of that ideology in maintaining the whole system by reducing strain. The analyses are informative and worth attention.

In Parsonian functionalist theory, the professions were accorded the status of defenders of liberty. They were seen as a barrier between the individual and the direct effects of the exercise of political authority, one more check or balance in the constitution of liberty. The theory's liberal appreciation of the profession has to be understood on the basis of how such social groups were said to maintain a balance in the social structure or, in other words, of their structural function. The substantive analysis of the professions, in turn, is one of showing which characteristics shared by professional groups provide for the latter's ability to perform such a function. So, unlike 'trait' theories of professions which make out a check-list for professionalism (see Johnson, 1973), functionalist theory aims not merely to itemise and identify professional characteristics but theoretically to order them in line with the functions they perform. It is an attempt to state what a profession *essentially* is by reference both to the function of professions and to those features of professionalism which allow that function to be fulfilled. We have then the characteristic interrelationships between both theoretical tenets and their empirical referents. The characteristics of professions function to allow the function of professions to be maintained. The characteristics are both interrelated one to another and further interrelated to more general orderings of the wider society.

The major characteristic of professions, as attended to by functionalism, is the application of systematic and technical bodies of knowledge in the service of society's central values. Certain values of a society are so pervasive and important that specialised technical knowledge is developed for their protection. Such knowledge is not the province of 'everyman' because of the need for special and lengthy training, long periods of professional socialisation and so on. Without the ability to use the technical knowledge to evaluate services the individual consumer is at risk. The protection offered in return for the trust given to the profession, is altruistic attention in a fiduciary relationship. The standards of service are subject to collegiate control rather than control either by the state or by the market. To safeguard its expertise and to maintain the confidence of their clients are the major problems faced by professions and provide the major sources of strain.

By reference to the above propositions of functional theory, Parsons is then able to slot in empirical features of professional work. But it is not an empirical inquiry in any normal sense. It is not an empirical inquiry into, for instance, whether lawyers are self-interested or not, but one of finding features of professional organisation that can stand as the parameters of altruism. How well the theory could withstand concerted empirical attack we will better be able to state after considering the work of Rueschmeyer. For now, however, we can put forward three positive aspects of the approach. First, the theory emphasises the interdependence of professional characteristics; secondly, it may act as an heuristic comparative reference point for empirical studies; thirdly, by co-classing professions in terms of structural functions, empirical studies of lawyers, say, would have a wider and less parochial appeal than a study of the legal profession *sui generis.* In Parsons's own analysis, the legal profession is analysed as a profession first and foremost with specified functions to fulfil. The theory is asked to explain not only that function, not only the function of the normal operation of the profession, but equally, features of deviance and strain.

Rueschmeyer, in a critical analysis of the functionalist theory of professions, attempted to undercut the empirical adequacy of the Parsonian framework as applied to lawyers. Especially, he questioned the doctrines of 'central value' and 'theoretical knowledge'. In the Parsonian model both these are necessary as they underpin the profession's dependence upon internal control mechanisms and a code of ethics. Rueschmeyer argued, however, that far from being the equivalent of a value such as health, justice is open to competing interpretations and incapable of providing either a guide to, control over or standard for professional conduct. Further, while the working knowledge of lawyers involves a degree of technical refinement it is of a more pragmatic nature than medicine. It is not a science. The application of pragmatic knowledge to individual cases allows a degree of client control and evaluation of the service offered. This degree of influence is heightened by the empirical studies of lawyers' work especially their demonstration of the stratified character of the profession and the entrapment of particular strata in the service of specifiable socio-economic groups. In the face of his work situation the lawyer without an unambiguous value to fall back on is under great pressure from the particular class of society that buys his services. Equally, the international differentiations within the profession open up to doubt the reality of professional solidarity, collegiate control and a single uniform code of ethics. Rueschmeyer's analysis together with the empirical studies themselves (for instance, Carlin, 1962; Smigel, 1964) substantiates the suggestion made earlier that functionalism is fraught with difficulties in accommodating non-theoretically drawn pictures of professional organisation. On the positive side, however, the ability of Rueschmeyer to use the theory's framework in his critical analysis also substantiates the suggestion that as an heuristic model handled in an empirically attuned manner, functionalism can provide useful insights into the inner workings of lawyers as a social group.

A Reconsideration

A reconsideration of Bredemeier's study of law must stand as a last attempt to describe the formal deficiencies of functionalism before a move is made to suggest an alternative form of functional analysis. Bredemeier utilises functionalism to investigate such features of law as *stare decisis.* This is placed within the integrative task in terms of a contribution to the judicial input of interpretation. Such an analysis remains problematic, however, unless it can be related to the working conceptions of judges who operate the decision-making process. Without such a relationship not only may the analysis misconstrue the judicial task but also the analysis would be unable to adjudicate between the description offered of that task and available alternative descriptions — such as, for instance, a contention that *stare decisis* helped the courts resist claims that law should respond more adequately to changing social conditions. On the other hand, given the latter contention's change of system specificity from legal to social system, it is up to the functionalist proponent to counter-argue resistance to adaptation as itself functioning to maintain the balance between various interrelated societal structures. Their interdependence does not commit one to a view of equal significance and so, as Cohen argues on another example, 'the hypothesis, like the customer, is never wrong' (Cohen, 1968, p. 52). Such theoretical immunity will have to be removed and the removal will have to be by way of recreating 'functionalist' analyses away from the properties of social systems. Conventional functionalism cannot itself escape from the immunity of its tenets without reference to the biological analogy so much an embarrassment to present-day practitioners. Without the organic analogy there is no criteria of adjudication between competing descriptions, and with the analogy there is a notable inabililty to specify the empirical manifestations of criteria of health necessary to assess the functioning or malfunctioning of the organism's processes.

If systems analysis must give way is there an alternative? Let us take an example. Legal formality and ritual are the very type of social item meet for a functionalist analysis. As perpetrated by conventional practitioners, however, we have the problem of adjudication between competing accounts, for instance between accounts of signs of authority by reference both to confidence or to degradation, both to professionalism or to control. The alternative method is to relate legal rituals, say, to the interactional requirements of the settings in which they are found.[3] So, for instance, courtrooms provide occasions of multi-party interaction which, it can be argued, have certain similarities with other occasions of such interaction. It is possible then to investigate what function specifically-identifiable features of that interaction have in overcoming problems of multi-partyship. It can be further argued that such analyses meet the prime requirement specified earlier for functionalism, namely to investigate determinately the processes by which an item is functional for the system in which the function is said to operate. But the 'system' concerned is not a social system but a patterned activity or, in other words, situated interaction. And the processes involved are no longer to be specified simply by reference to how they are engaged in interactional structures. It must be shown that the features posited are required for the interaction to be constructed in the way that it is found to be, in other words, there is a demand that what is provided as an account of the item be shown to be criterial for members for what members do in the situation. Rather than having system needs or functional universality as tools to bridge the logical gap between consequence and existence, analysis is limited to describing the world as it is. On those occasions when analysis is able to point to interactional structures, for instance ones of formality or ritual, and demonstrate their effect on how interaction proceeds, then it is a warranted claim that without these structures the interaction would be different. Rather than maintenance of system one is on the level of the constitution of interaction. It is the here-and-now properties of functionalism that may yet be fully accomplished in the environment of interactional analyses.

Conclusion

The main argument of the chapter has been that the potential of functionalism in the sociology of law is best achieved by eschewing a motivated concern to do functionalism and to organise research by reference to the interactional structures operating in whatever aspect of the legal order attention is directed. Whether and how an interactional rather than a systems analysis will be recognised as functionalist is not particularly important. We have tried to indicate just some similarities in method.

More time was spent on identifying a technical meaning for functionalism, to distinguish mere analyses of consequence and to distinguish the doctrine from the method properly so called. It has been argued that functionalist theories of law have been theoretically unedifying though in certain aspects, and particularly by reference to the comparative use of functional models, have thrown light on particular aspects of the legal system. The major celebration of functionalism lies in its overtly sociological orientation, an orientation towards atemporal correlation, interdependence and differentiation. As a method of analysis it moves against any reification of law and conceives law as a social phenomenon. The investigation of any social phenomenon, including law, within a functionalist framework, pushes the horizons of investigation away from the particulars of the item concerned and towards its place in a larger system, however conceived. Some of the problems of conventional functionalism have been detailed in brief and presented as logically without solution for an empirically based science.

Most specifically, functionalism explains the generalised features of a generalised society rather than the actual features of actual societies, a mode of analysis which, as Homans rightly said, is of limited potential (Homans, 1964, p. 813).[4] To overcome this abstract character of the theory it is of special importance to be very specific concerning the types of questions the theory is used to answer. The utility of the functionalist method for the study of law can be greater or lesser depending on the questions the researcher wishes to address. Functionalism has, for instance, illuminated the social groupings of lawyers, whereas it has been less successful in the investigation of the origins of specific legislative enactments (see Aubert, 1966). Most specifically, functionalism is not obviously appropriate to particular studies of specific legal phenomena, for instance a proposal of legal reform, unless two conditions are met. First, the interest would have to be related to some mechanism of social integration or stability, in other words, that would have to be the intellectual interest in the phenomenon, and, secondly, the particularistics of the study would have to be generalisable into propositions concerning the character of societies or other social groups as such.

Nevertheless, functionalism in the guise of the study of the processes whereby social phenomena are related, irrespective of considerations of systems equilibrium, integration or persistence, is clearly, and I take it irrefutably, the source of the major intellectual developments of the sociology of law. As such the potential is not a change of course, nor is it necessarily the continuation of a misconceived logic. Although this chapter has given a technical description of functionalism, many studies of importance have been done under the auspices of functionalism or some other theory which, while eschewing the technical logic of functionalism properly so called, have analysed and provided insights into the relationships that constitute society. For instance, the relationship between the legal and the political system is well referenced not only by Durkheim and Weber but at a less general level in many studies of the profession and of legislation; the relationship between the legal system and the polity is referenced in studies on the impact of legislation on social change; social change studies themselves, in their concern with impact, are necessarily claiming an ability to investigate the effect of one phenomenon upon another. Even if such studies may not attain the technical sophistication of functionalism, may not partake of its logical structure and difficulties, they nevertheless may provide useful insights into the operation of law in society. The same may be said for studies ranging from the analysis of changing institutional legal forms to those concerned with the concrete experience of legal actors in, for instance, the witness box, the solicitor's office or the jury room. The potential for functionalism for such studies lies in making explicit their underlying rationale and setting limits to what we may say we knew about the origins and effects of legal phenomena. Functionalism properly understood may emphasise the body's wisdom (see Matza, 1969), but equally it accentuates the need for academic modesty in our claims on the world.

On the other hand, we must not forget that the sociology of law may, in return, be beneficial to functionalism providing a whole vista of researchable arenas central to many of the implicit claims obtaining in the theory's doctrinal statements. Especially of relevance here are the functional-conflict theorists as well as those who, though eschewing functionalist terminology, claim Renner as an intellectual guru. A reading of Renner (1949) or Chambliss on the source of legal structures and their effects on society's other sub-systems provides alternative analyses to the same phenomena encompassed in Parsons's theoretical edifice. Although it has here been suggested that such indeterminacy renders functionalism immune to empirical verification, a reliance on the method of functionalism, rather than any particular doctrine in the investigation of such phenomena as the creation of legal norms, the adjudicative process and so forth, could provide a clearer impression of how far particular doctrines are empirically supportable. In other words, functionalism may offer the sociology of law a strong empirical thrust away from general models of society. Functionalism offers freedom from myopia and in return the sociology of law offers functionalism freedom from the empirical paucity of certain of its tenets. In this chapter the requirements of empirical support have been argued as best met in studies which depart from a systems analysis and provide an, if you will, functionalism of interactional structures. Such analyses, being 'sensitive to the requirements of the immediate local setting', are functionalist in method and in meeting the requirement to specify the linkages between the existence of phenomena and the (interactional) needs of the system of which they are a part and have a high degree of descriptive adequacy. Whether functionalism will take for itself freedom from systems theory and move amongst the world of interactional structures must for now remain an issue for thought and speculation.

Notes

1. On the biological analogy see Moore (1979), and on the advent of sociology see Nisbet (1970).
2. One can note that even in the work of Bredemeier and Homans, who eschew the teleology of system needs in favour of the individual psychology of a social architect, the designed item is functional only if it can be maintained that its effect is adaptive to the continued persistence of the system of which it is a part.

3. Specific papers that may be usefully read for the purpose of reflecting on the logical strengths of a non-systems based functionalism include those of J.M. Atkinson (1976, 1978, 1979 and 1980).

4. Homans uses a legal example here stating that 'Even if a statement like: "if it is to survive, a society must possess conflict-resolving institutions", were accepted as testable...[w]hat remained unexplained was why the society had conflict-resolving institutions of a particular kind, why for instance, the jury was an ancient feature of Anglo-Saxon legal institutions' (Homans, 1964, pp. 812-13).

Bibliography

Arnold, T. *The Symbols of Government* (Harcourt, Brace and World, New Haven, Connecticut, 1935)

Atkinson, D. *Orthodox Consensus and Radical Alternative* (Heinemann Educational Books, London, 1971)

Atkinson, J.M. 'Order in Court: Some Preliminary Issues and Analysis', paper presented to the International Sociological Association Research Group on the Sociology of Law, Balatonszeplak, Hungary, September 1976

______ 'Constraints on the Organisation of Communicative Interaction in Multi-Party Settings', paper presented to the British Sociological Association Sociological Theory Group Conference, Surrey, September 1978

______ 'Notes on the Analysis of Interaction in "Formal" Settings', paper presented at the British Sociological Association — Social Science Research Council Conference on Methodology and Techniques of Sociology, Lancaster, January 1979 — Workshop 3

______ 'Understanding Formality: Notes on the Recognition and Production of "Formal" Interaction', paper produced for the Baldy Center — Centre for Socio-Legal Studies, Oxford meeting, Buffalo, 1980

Aubert, V. 'Some Social Functions of Legislation', *Acta Sociologica*, vol. 10 (1966), pp. 98-120

Badcock, C. *Lévi-Strauss: Structuralism and Sociological Theory* (Hutchinson, London, 1975)

Bauman, Z. *Hermeneutics and Social Science* (Hutchinson, London, 1978)

Baxi, U. 'Comment — Durkheim and Legal Evolution: some problems of disproof', *Law and Society Review*, vol. 8 (1974), pp. 645-51

Bredemeier, H. 'The Methodology of Functionalism', *American Sociological Review*, vol. 20 (1955), pp. 173-80

______ 'Law as an Integrative Mechanism' in W. Evan (ed.), *Law and Sociology* (Free Press, New York, 1962), pp. 73-90

Carlin, J. *Lawyers on their Own* (Rutgers University Press, New Jersey, 1962)

Carson, W.G. 'Some Sociological Aspects of Strict Liability and the Enforcement of Factory Legislation', *Modern Law Review*, vol. 33 (1970), pp. 396-412

______ 'Symbolic and Instrumental Dimensions of Early Factory Legislation' in R. Hood (ed.), *Crime, Criminology and Public Policy* (Heinemann, London, 1974a), pp. 107-38

______ 'The Sociology of Crime and the Emergence of Criminal Laws' in P. Rock and M. Macintosh (eds.), *Deviance and Social Control* (Tavistock, London, 1974b), pp. 67-90

Chambliss, W. and Seidman R. *Law, Order and Power* (Addison-Wesley, Reading, Massachusetts, 1971)

Cohen, P. *Modern Social Theory* (Heinemann Educational Books, London, 1968)

Davis, K. *Human Society* (Macmillan, New York, 1959), pp. 757-72

______ 'The Myth of Functional Analysis as a Special Method in Sociology and

Anthropology', *American Sociological Review,* vol. 24 (1959), pp. 757-72

Espinosa, E. de 'Social and Legal Order in Sociological Functionalism', *Contemporary Crisis,* vol. 4 (1980), pp. 43-76

Dore, R. 'Function and Cause', *American Sociological Review,* vol. 26 (1961), pp. 843-53

Durkheim, E. *The Division of Labour in Society* (Free Press, New York, 1933) (first published in 1893)

——— *The Rules of Sociological Method* (Free Press, New York, 1938) (first published in 1894)

——— 'Two Laws of Penal Evolution', *University of Cincinnati Law Review,* vol. 38 (1969) (first published in 1899), pp. 32-60

Gouldner, A. *The Coming Crisis of Western Sociology* (Heinemann Educational Books, London, 1971)

Grace, C. and Wilkinson, P. *Sociological Inquiry and Legal Phenomena* (Collier-Macmillan, London, 1978)

Gusfield, J. *Symbolic Crusade* (University of Illinois Press, Chicago, 1963)

Homans, G.C. 'Bringing Men Back In', *American Sociological Review,* vol. 29 (1964), pp. 808-18

Johnson, T. *Professions and Power* (Macmillan, London, 1973)

Lukes, S. *Emile Durkheim* (Penguin, Harmondsworth, 1973)

Matza, D. *Becoming Deviant* (Prentice-Hall, New Jersey, 1969)

Merton, R.K. *Social Theory and Social Structure* (Free Press, Illinois, 1968)

Moore, W.E. 'Functionalism' in T. Bottomore and R. Nisbet (eds.), *A History of Sociological Analysis* (Heinemann, London, 1979), pp. 321-61

Nisbet, R. *The Sociological Tradition* (Heinemann Educational Books, London, 1970)

Parsons, T. *The Structure of Social Action* (McGraw-Hill, New York, 1937)

——— 'Introduction' to M. Weber, *General Theory of Social and Economic Organisation* (Free Press, New York, 1947)

——— *The Social System* (Free Press, Illinois, 1951)

——— 'A Sociologist Looks at the Legal Profession', in T. Parsons, *Essays in Sociological Theory* (Free Press, New York, 1954), pp. 370-85

——— 'The Law and Social Control' in W. Evan (ed.), *Law and Sociology* (Free Press, New York, 1962), pp. 56-72

Renner, K. *The Institutions of Private Law* (Routledge and Kegan Paul, London, 1949)

Rueschmeyer, D. 'Doctors and Lawyers: a comment on the theory of the professions', *Canadian Review of Sociology and Anthropology* (1964), pp. 17-30

Schur, E. *Law in Society* (Random House, New York, 1968)

Schwarz, R. and Miller, J. 'Legal Evolution and Societal Complexity', *American Journal of Sociology,* vol. 40 (1968), pp. 159-69

Sklair, L. 'Functionalism and Deviance', paper presented to the British Sociological Association Annual Conference, 1971

Smigel, E. *The Wall Street Lawyer* (Free Press, New York, 1964)

Weber, M. *General Theory of Social and Economic Organisation,* edited by Talcott Parsons (Free Press, New York, 1947)

Wilson, T. 'Normative and Interpretive Paradigms in Sociology' in J. Douglas (ed.), *Understanding Everyday Life* (Routledge and Kegan Paul, London, 1971), pp. 57-79

Wrong, D. 'The Oversocialised Conception of Man in Modern Sociology', *American Sociological Review,* vol. 26 (1961), pp. 183-93

5 Marxism and the Analysis of Law

Alan Hunt

Introduction

This paper seeks to examine the contribution which Marxism either has made or may potentially make to our analysis and understanding of law and legal phenomena. Before directing my attention towards substantive problems it is necessary to make a few preliminary remarks which may assist in avoiding confusions and in clarifying the nature of my objectives.

The term Marxism is not unproblematic and I eschew any pretension to be the bearer of 'correct Marxism'; it is important that we remain sensitive to the significant variant forms of 'Marxism' which have a legitimate claim to draw their primary inspiration from the writings of Marx. I shall, for example, argue that some of the more recent trends in Marxist theory open up a potential for Marxist analysis of law which was not present within the orthodox 'historical materialism' which has had such a grip on Marxist thought up to the 1960s.

I want to insist that there is no Marxist theory of law that can be found in the pages of Marx and Engels which can be lifted out and applied to the analysis of law and legal phenomena. I hasten to add that this insistence does not stem from any desire to devalue the writings of Marx and Engels either in general or specifically about law. Indeed I have recently completed an edition of extracts from Marx and Engels on law (Cain and Hunt, 1979). Additionally, I take the view that Marxism does not constitute a 'general theory' that may be applied to any desired social issue or problem; in this sense Marxism is not a sociological theory in the same sense as other explicitly sociological theories which purport to have such a status, of which structural functionalism is the example that comes first to mind. Again I hasten to add that my differentiation between Marxism and other sociological theories does not lead me to the extremes of anti-sociological nihilism to be found amongst some Marxists (this anti-sociological position is best represented by Shaw, 1975).

The reason which underlies my contention that there is no 'Marxist theory of law' in the texts of Marx and Engels is that law never constituted a specific object of inquiry for either Marx or Engels. As a consequence what they actually write about law, the volume of which is surprisingly large, contains a number of very different emphases, indeed, some blatantly contradictory remarks occur. It follows then that not only is there no ready-made Marxist theory of law by bringing together the dispersed passages. A simple aggregation of the writings on law produces many fascinating suggestions, insights and problems as well as some hair-raising Victorian moralisms.[1] Some of the recent controversies between Marxists about law have stemmed from the familiar practice of differential selection; this is particularly apparent in the exchange between Paul Hirst and the authors of *The New Criminology* (Hirst, 1975; Taylor, Walton and Young, 1973, 1975).

The position that I hold implies that the development of Marxist theory of law remains very largely undeveloped. We must, of course, note the existence of certain substantive contributions; in particular the work of Evgeny Pashukanis (1978) and Karl Renner (1976) come to mind. Without entering into an analysis of this work I want merely to enter a caution against wholesale adoption of either Pashukanis or Renner. Pashukanis cannot be lifted out intact from the specific historical debates of the early 1920s within Bolshevism; and Renner must be approached with extreme caution because of the intense functionalism that underlies his apparently orthodox Marxist terminology and which thus conflicts sharply with its apparent theoretical content. Pashukanis and Renner, then, may be treated as signposts in the construction of Marxist theory of law, but it remains to be determined, through analysis and debate, whether they point in the right or even a hopeful direction.

It is, however, clear that the creation of a Marxist theory of law is an ongoing project. Such a project is related to, but distinct from, Marxist 'analysis' of law. This distinction between 'Marxist theory' and 'Marxist analysis' is pertinent in the present context because it requires us to recognise the uneven but interconnected development of these fields. The development of Marxist theory of law requires no necessary involvement with substantive analysis of legal phenomena, although such a perspective may well be a motivating condition of the theoretical project. The notion of Marxist analysis must not be taken to indicate the application of a completed or unitary theory, 'Marxism', to a given legal phenomenon; such a conception involves a simplistic positivist view of the social sciences. Rather the notion of 'Marxist analysis' designates explorations or inquiries produced 'under the sign' of Marxism; that is making use of elements of theory and concepts drawn from the Marxist tradition. Whilst it is necessary to distinguish between these two activities they do not develop autonomously. I shall argue that certain features present in Marxist theory, features which under specific intellectual and political circumstances became predominant, either impeded or distorted Marxist analysis of law. I shall go on to argue that the changed circumstances of contemporary Marxist thought are manifesting themselves in significant developments and advances in Marxist analysis of law.

It is not my intention here to discuss the historical and political transformations affecting Marxist theory.[2] Rather I shall rely on the assertion that contemporary Marxism, often labelled Western Marxism, has effected certain breaks with what again may be somewhat schematically labelled 'orthodox Marxism'. I hasten to add that this process is uneven and complex in its concrete manifestations. I shall explore the substantive content of these transformations only in so far as they affect work on the theory and analysis of law.

I wish to advance the argument that the contribution of Marxism to the study of law must be understood as operating at a number of different levels. These levels have a sequential character but are not reducible to a simple historical periodisation; we cannot therefore break this contribution down into convenient historical periods. The levels to which I wish to draw attention continue to operate alongside each other within any given period, similarly the work of a given individual or a single book or article may, on analysis, reveal the presence of more than one level. The levels of contribution of Marxism to the study of law are: the 'oppositional' or 'critical' stage, the level provided by the problematic of 'the class character of law', and what may be the highest stage, the substantive analysis of legal phenomena.

Oppositional or Critical Phase

Here the major characteristic takes the form of a reaction against dominant conceptions of law, both intellectual and popular; the reactive process sets up a series of polar oppositions to what are argued to be the characteristics of the prevailing conception of law. Let me illustrate by reference to one of the more systematic expositions of this position. William Chambliss (1976, p. 4) identifies the following amongst the major features of the dominant conceptualisation of law:

(a) the law represents the value consensus of society,
(b) the law represents those values and perspectives which are fundamental to social order,
(c) the law represents those values and perspectives which it is in the public interest to protect,
(d) the state as represented in the legal system is value-neutral,
(e) in pluralistic societies the law represents the interests of the society at large by mediating between competing-interest groups.

In marginally variant plumage this position constitutes a consensus model of law. The procedure pursued by Chambliss is to negate the tenets of one model by another in which any apparent consensus around values is a manifestation of false consciousness; rather law embodies the inequality of class-divided society, functioning to maintain and support the power and privilege of dominant economic and political interests.

It is thus within the context of a more or less explicit theoretical procedure which operates through the simple mechanism of negation or reversal that Marxism enters the scene. The role which it has to play is that of an already available theory which appears to meet some of the major characteristics of the conflict perspective; Marxism emphasises class polarity, inequality, exploitation and processes of political and ideological domination. It is significant to note that in the development of conflict perspectives Marxism is 'discovered'; authors from significantly different and even antithetical intellectual traditions adopt Marxism during the course of their active intellectual life.[3] It should be stressed that the dichotomous classification of sociological theory around a consensus-conflict axis had widespread currency in the 1960s and its application within the sociology of law was very much a by-product of these developments.

Whatever the merits of attempts to classify sociological theory around the polarity between consensus and conflict it should be stressed that Marxism should not be regarded as a conflict theory. It does not start out from phenomena of inequality or exploitation; rather its point of departure is the social relations of production. That the results of the analysis of these relations reveal, at the level of empirical analysis, results attributed to conflict theory does not legitimate the inclusion of Marxism within this label.[4]

The general significance of the harnessing of Marxism to the conflict perspective produces, as I have suggested, a reactive result. It is one which creates opportunities; it opens up a breach in the monolith of Anglo-American legal scholarship. It by no means vanquishes that enduring bastion but it creates the possibility for a radical critique of law. There is something 'new' about the radical critique of law; I want both to defend and to qualify this assertion.

The radical critique of law is 'new' in a number of important respects. First it is new in a quantitative sense, in that since the late 1960s there has been a rapidly swelling volume of literature that self-consciously adopts a radical stance. From a wide and divergent range of sources a radical literature, the varieties of which I will not explore more fully, has been produced. This phenomenon is new in a second and qualitative respect in that there is an increasingly overt concern with the development of a theoretically articulated formulation of a radical critique of law.

The radical critique at its present stage of development is essentially an orientation or even a mood or stance. The term 'radical' is used to designate a self-conscious challenge to orthodoxy which takes the form of a denial of orthodox thought. The essential challenge is to the assumption of the desirability and naturalness of law. Challenged is the assumption of the neutrality of law and of law as a necessary expression of a well-balanced and integrated society.

The radical critique tends to proceed through the negation or reversal of conventional wisdom. Law is presented as an agency of conflict, not integration, that functions to protect and preserve, not common and shared interests, but of 'dominant' interests, variously conceptualised as class or elite interests. Law is not an agency of integration but as the creator and amplifier of social inequality and disequilibrium being the bearer of class bias and privilege. The impact of the radical mode is its iconoclastic negation of conventional wisdom which is stood on its head to propose the assertion of propositions which challenge the complacent and sanctified assumptions of orthodoxy.

One consequence which is generally, but not necessarily, associated with the proponents of the radical critique is a tendency towards legal nihilism, that is towards the repudiation of law as such. The sharpest manifestation of such a position is to be found in Bankowski and Mungham's *Images of Law*. Their 'image of law' is one-dimensional; it is of law as a 'means of domination, oppression and desolation' (1976, p. 29).

The image of law encapsulated is exclusively an *instrumentalist* view of law. Law is the instrument of a ruling class which functions directly at the behest and control of dominant economic and political interests as a mechanism of oppression and domination; it is all the more successful because it is able to do so in such a way as to disseminate 'false consciousness', for example, spreading the illusion of neutrality and impartiality. Liberals and radicals connive, consciously or unconsciously, because in proclaiming the possibility of 'using law' they bind the subordinate classes more closely to capitalist values and 'exacerbate the feeling of powerlessness' (p. 29). In general the use of law 'has the effect of increasing the domination of law over people's lives' (p. 69).

It is the unarticulated and consequently unexplored theoretical assumptions that lead to the presentation of law simply as repression and false consciousness. It necessarily follows that a monolithic, one-dimensional legal order cannot be reformed or liberalised; it cannot, in general, be 'used'; any such project leads to contamination.

This phase in the Marxist theory of law does, however, mark important advances. First, it draws attention explicitly to the coercive and repressive features of law. The theoretical positions adopted within mainstream sociology of law have obliterated or obscured the recognition and acceptance of this simple proposition. I have argued more fully elsewhere (Hunt, 1976a, 1978) against the pervasive adoption of a 'law as social control' perspective. Social control is seen as a necessary consequence of social life itself and as such it is located within primary social processes and institutions, and more specifically as a product of the normative process. The consequences that flow from this position have both theoretical and ideological dimensions. In so far as social control is perceived as constraining the sanctioning it is perceived as a process that flows *naturally* from the very facts of social life itself. The constraint that is exercised through the informal mechanism of social control is seen as essentially a process of self-regulation. The unspoken corollary is the denial of the coercive or repression implying a process of control which is not a natural or spontaneous process but one which is a property of the prevailing social relations.

The second important result of the oppositional phase is to focus attention upon the law-state relationship. All too often, however, the law is *reduced* to the state and is presented as a simple instrument in the hands of the holders of state power; the state, in its turn, is similarly viewed as an instrument or mechanism wielded by the dominant socio-economic class. The tendency to a reduction of the law to the state is, in its turn, a reaction against the pervasive influence of the doctrine of the separation of powers, playing as it has a central role in nineteenth- and twentieth-century jurisprudence and also in modern sociology of law.[5] The radical response to the ideological function of the separation of powers has predominantly been simply to deny it or to label it ideological and abusing that concept in turn by presuming that ideology is to be equated with falsity. Hence we see again that while opening up an important perspective on law the reactive or oppositional character of the orientation tends to devalue or narrow the potentiality of the insight.

Marxism and the Class Character of Law

Let us now turn to consider the second phase or stage in the harnessing of Marxism to the analysis of law. This phase may be identified as one in which the paramount objective and guiding object of inquiry is provided by the problematic of 'the class character of law'. The focus is upon both the content of law and its administration. I shall argue that there are two major forms of this approach which, while apparently differing and indeed often in dispute with each other, share a basic unity of orientation.

The focus on the content of law applies Marx to the project of answering the question: what is the class content of law? This problematic has not been the exclusive concern of Marxists. For example, liberals who attach great importance to the neutrality of law as a condition of its legitimacy have posed the same question in periods when a dangerous or flagrant class partiality has manifested itself. For example, the very unradical figure of Roscoe Pound dealt explicitly in one of his earliest articles with, and I quote its title, 'Causes of Popular Dissatisfaction with the Administration of Justice' (1906). Although they have not had a monopoly it has been those operating from a Marxist perspective that have most persistently posed the question as to the class content of law.

The Marxist and leading political advocate of his period, D.N. Pritt, provides us with a classic example of this Marxist mode. In *Law, Class and Society* (1971), his perspective is essentially of a class holding state power as the makers of law and making it in accordance with their class interest.[6] This approach has been particularly evident in writings on labour law and has been taken over by non-Marxists and turned towards the more liberal problematic of the fairness of law; this is, for example, the underlying perspective of Wedderburn's influential book, *The Worker and the Law* (1971). A similar perspective underlies the more recent work of John Griffith on *The Politics of the Judiciary* (1977).

The general characteristic of this trend, with all the diversities of political position encompassed, is its essential simplicity. It posits that any element of law (and here I should stress that this applies just as much to the administration of law as it does to its substantive content) can be evaluated along some scale of partiality or bias. This position remains naive and unsophisticated because the criteria of 'class bias' are never revealed. The method of analysis is empiricist in that it is based upon undertaking an examination of a series of cases or the provisions of legislation, that is a direct examination of legal phenomena; from this are drawn conclusions of this kind, 'Look, in this series of cases workmen failed to recover damages against employers' or 'the provisions of this statute provide only limited protection to tenants', hence it is concluded that class bias is revealed. Such a position is only in a very limited sense Marxist, if so at all. It is perfectly compatible with liberal or pluralist positions.[7] Its theoretical core is the necessary assumption of a linear scale from biased to fair; or to express the same point, it necessarily rests on the assumption of the logical possibility of fair law; for the liberal 'fair law' could be achieved within the existing social system, given better laws, impartial judges, and so on, while the socialist postpones its advent until after the victory of 'the revolution'.

The alternative form of Marxist treatment of the class character of law takes as its object the function of law. Let me suggest that the pursuit of 'function' does not involve the adoption of a functionalist perspective, such a result is a possible but not a necessary consequence of such a direction of inquiry. The pursuit of the function of law embraces a wide range of different substantive positions but is marked by a shared characteristic of a greater concern to produce a theoretical analysis than was manifest in the 'class bias' trend. The central preoccupation of this type of work may be expressed very simply, it poses the question: in what way does law help capitalism? There has been a certain polarity in the type of solutions posited between what may be presented, without doing too much mischief to work which is often very sophisticated, as two trends, 'law as repression' and 'law as ideology'.

'Law as repression' has played a very important part in the socialist tradition; its literary manifestations have been part of many declarations and today finds expression in the more radical and polemical writings. It is very paramount in such American writers as Cloke (1971) and Lefcourt (1971). Also from radical America we have the product of the Union of Radical Criminologists *The Iron Fist and the Velvet Glove* (Center for Research on Criminal Justice, 1975), the imagery 'iron fist' in the 'velvet glove' reveals the fundamental theoretical and political position, the reality is the iron fist while the velvet glove of legality and legalism is a thin deception which enjoins the radical to tear it asunder and reveal the repressive reality of police and law. This same theoretical position, combined with a traditional anarchistic element, underlies Bankowski and Mungham's *Images of Law* (1976).

The other general emphasis has been on 'law as ideology'. Its roots lie in a rejection of a simple 'law equals repression' thesis while, at the same time, holding firm to a 'class law' position. This position is very explicitly at the root of Gramsci's treatment of both law and state. The major thrust has been directed towards an analysis of the forms of combination of repressive and ideological functions of law. This is most apparent in modern Marxist theory stemming from the influence of Althusser. Although Althusser has relatively little to say specifically about law his essay 'Ideology and the Ideological State Apparatuses' (1971) has had a very powerful influence on subsequent Marxist discussion of law; the most direct impact was through the writings of Nicos Poulantzas, who not only focused in some of his early essays on the Marxist theory of law (1964, 1967), but whose continuing focus on questions of the state (1973, 1978) has given his work a particular relevance for debates in the Marxist theory of law. The focus of this tradition is upon the question of 'the reproduction of the social relations of production'. Capitalism, and especially late capitalism, is not self-reproducing, but it is reproduced and perpetuated through processes which in the advanced capitalist states cannot be reduced, even propagandistically, to a process of coercion. The implications of Althusser are to focus upon the processes of complex effectivity of the non-economic levels, in particular the political and the ideological levels, in the reproduction of capitalist social relations. Law is significantly located within both ideological and political levels. The general conclusion of this tradition revolves around Poulantzas's thesis that the function of the state and of law is as the 'factor of unity', facilitating the unity of the dominant class(es) and the disunity/disorganisation of the subordinate class(es). With some terminological differences this is the position I developed through the proposition that law functions as elements of *both* ideological domination and of repressive domination (Hunt, 1976a, b).

Thus duality is present in one form or another in the majority of Marxist analyses of law. The problem which such formulations do not resolve is that, despite insisting upon the 'dialectical' character of the dichotomous elements, the position has a tendency to lapse back into 'either-orism'; that is either the moment of repression is dominant or alternatively the non-repressive is paramount. This leads back towards the conventional picture found in legal theory and sociology of law of the counter-opposition between force and consensus. The major area of exploration which is seeking to overcome the theoretical problems posed by this tendency to dualism is through the exploration of Gramsci's concept of 'hegemony'.[8]

The focus upon the function of law is also shared by another position within Marxism whose exponents have eschewed the functional perspective. The most coherent expression of this position is argued by Holloway and Picciotto. In *State and Capital* (1978) they explicitly differentiate between functional analysis, epitomised by Poulantzas, and their own position which we may label 'form analysis'. The latter derives from the West German 'state derivation' discussion whose central focus has been to 'derive' systematically — that is rigorous adherence to the logic of Marx's exposition in *Capital,* vol. I — the form of law or state from the very nature of capitalist economic relations. The specific focus of this work has been to start with Marx's opening chapter of *Capital,* concerning the nature of commodities; from this is derived the form of the legal relation, epitomised as the isolated 'legal subject' as the bearer of commodity relations. The roots of this quest lie in a reaction against those tendencies in Marxism, for example both Gramscian and Althusserian, which confer degrees of autonomy upon levels other than the economics. In its pursuit the writings of the early Soviet jurist Pashukanis have been rediscovered. There has been a certain vogue of late for Pashukanis (1978) precisely because this was his project: to derive the form of bourgeois law from the form of the commodity relation.

Yet this position retains the same fundamental orientation as the function perspective: the function of law is simply prescribed in advance by the structure of the capitalist relations of production. In other words, it is a form of essentialism in that the effectivity or function of law is inscribed, as it were, in advance in the economic relations. Law then performs necessary functions precisely because they are required and prescribed by the economic level. The denial of the autonomy of law, whether relative or absolute, does not of itself place 'form analysis' on a different theoretical terrain.

The second phase or level in the Marxist theory of law has in the main been characterised by a concern with the elaboration of general theoretical perspectives; theory produced has varied significantly from a very basic 'class theory of law' to very much more elaborated and complex theories. One of the most powerful and compelling features of Marxism has been precisely a primary thesis or class theory; I wish to suggest that this is the starting point for Marxist work, not its conclusion.[9] There is a necessary limit to the extent to which any field of Marxist analysis can be resolved or completed at the level of general theory. The discussions have raised a number of important problems, many of which relate, as I have indicated, to some of the most central and controversial problems within Marxist theory; the solution of these general problems of Marxist theory is outside the scope and ambit of Marxist theory of law and certainly of the present paper. My position then is to insist upon the importance of the development of general theory within the Marxist analysis of law. This has set it off and allowed it to stand in a healthy critical relation to non-Marxist sociology of law which has been in theoretical retreat even since Max Weber.[10]

The implication of this line of thought is that there is little possibility of the further advance of a Marxist approach to law at the general theoretical level. The possibility which is, however, opened up is to proceed to another stage.

Substantive Analysis of Legal Phenomena: The Highest Stage?

The third stage and one which has the greatest potentiality for the sociology of law is the stage at which Marxist theory and method is utilised in the substantive analysis of legal phenomena. The distinctive feature of this stage is the conscious attempt to combine the application of a developed theoretical perspective to the level of the concrete analysis. In this undertaking a significant feature is the way in which, without necessarily adopting it at the outset as a central problem, a focus has emerged on one of the more difficult theoretical problems encountered in general Marxist theory of law; a number of writings can be seen as seeking to come to grips with the relationship between the form of law, not in itself necessarily reducible to derivation from the commodity form, and the specific effects of law as interventions in social, economic and political relations. This problem has been treated within theoretical discourse in terms of mutually exclusive alternatives. Now through application in concrete analysis a convergence is being effected between the form analysis approach and the functional trends discussed above.

This stage is not merely a future prospect. There have been a number of very valuable works which, in my opinion, can be said to meet these criteria. I shall examine two such examples and attempt to draw some general conclusions concerning the potentiality of Marxism for the understanding and analysis of law. The criteria of selection upon which I have relied has been to focus upon work which is as well-known as possible in the hope that as many readers as possible have some acquaintance with the work in question and are therefore in a position to make judgements about my analysis. This is not to suggest that this is the only work that merits attention. I am somewhat reluctant to simply list works with the implied assumption that the present author has some claim to award the distinction of personal approval or of honorary mentions. As a compromise I will first make some brief comments on a number of pieces of work which also deserve fuller discussion. First, let me mention an essay in close proximity to Thompson's book which I will have more to say about (1975); Douglas Hay's essay 'Property, Authority and the Criminal Law' (1975) arose from the same project at Warwick University, focusing on the social order of eighteenth-century England. He engages with the problem of understanding the increasingly important role of criminal law of property offences of legitimising the existing forms of property relations during a century when statutes provided a substantive law of unbridled severity and yet in which the number of executions did not rise as might have been anticipated. From this brief indication of its subject-matter it is evidence that Hay engages directly with the problem we have already encountered, namely, the interpenetration of ideological and repressive functions of law.

It is not without its significance that historical studies form such a substantial proportion of my references. Another one which deserves fuller discussion is that provided by John Foster's discussion (1974) of the class struggle in Oldham in the early nineteenth-century; of particular importance is his discussion, under the heading of 'Labour and state power', of the struggles for control over the developing policing system, which took place at both local and national level.

My third suggestion for a work deserving of fuller attention is Balbus's study (1973) of the legal response to Black urban militancy in the USA. His findings are that despite expectations the legal response is least repressive in the wake of the major conflagrations that received the greatest public attention; whereas the participants in the smaller riots received the full repressive rigour of the law. The power of his analysis is perhaps somewhat blunted by the single-minded way in which he pursues this general finding; it tends to leave him insensitive to other issues within the politics of law enforcement.

The two works I will discuss, despite the apparent dissimilarity of their subject-matter, constitute closely related endeavours. E.P. Thompson's *Whigs and Hunters* (1975) is a study of the statute of 1723, commonly known as 'the Black Act'.[11] On the other hand, *Policing the Crisis,* by Stuart Hall and his colleagues from the Centre of Contemporary Studies at Birmingham (1978), focuses upon the much more recent phenomena of 'mugging'; in this study the period under examination is 250 years after the Black Act, the central event from which the work emanates is 'the Handsworth mugging' for which sixteen-year-old Paul Storey was sentenced to 20 years' detention.

The common core of these two studies is that they both start out from a very specific, almost microscopic, social phenomenon. Now for studies that are explicitly Marxist this raises certain problems. Marx engaged in little direct discussion of methodological questions, but his major intervention was the Introduction to the *Grundrisse* (1973), particularly 'The Method of Political Economy' (pp. 100-8). A literal reading of this text would suggest that Marxist studies should not start out from the phenomenal forms in which reality first presents itself. It is on a rather formalistic presentation of those passages that Paul Hirst, in his polemic with radical deviancy theorists, insisted that, 'Crime and deviance are no more a scientific field for Marxism than education, the family or sport' (1975, p. 204). He poses as the alternative: 'The objects of Marxist theory are specified by its own concepts, the mode of production, the class struggle, the state, ideology; etc.' (1975. p. 204). This very restrictive insistence on the retention of Marxist virginity, whilst registering some very timely reservations against tendencies operating under the label of Marxism in the field of deviancy, cast a pall of doubt over those seeking to come to grips with problems of law, crime and deviance from a Marxist perspective. By casting aside the prohibition these two works have not only made important substantive contributions but have cleared the ground theoretically for much more work. It is not without significance that both works are explicitly historical; this is more obviously so in Thompson's case and this may be seen as drawing upon one of the few areas in which Marxist scholarship has been consistently strong over a number of decades. But *Policing the Crisis* is also historical in a way which presents the authors with the very real methodological difficulty of treating a contemporary social phenomenon historically. Yet much of the sensitivity which the book achieves stems from the care with which the historical location of the events is carefully constructed.

The 'historical' character of these works requires further comment. It has become a commonplace to insist that a central feature of Marxist analysis is the methodological requirement of historical specificity. Yet Marxism has no monopoly over historical method. What these studies do indicate is the capacity, through adherence to the injunction of historical specificity, to penetrate beyond the phenomenon under examination and to thereby explore the wider dimension within which that object is located. Hence the study of the Black Act derives its power precisely because it is a study of the manner in which the social order of the new bourgeois society was constituted. Similarly the study of the 'mugging' phenomenon takes on meaning within the crisis of social order during the period of a different type of transformation.

The process of inquiry therefore starts with the phenomenon itself and proceeds to the explication of the social relations within which the phenomenon is located. Thus, for example, it becomes possible to pierce the ideological rhetoric of the Act itself through the discovery that the defendants who were its victims did not 'fit' with these expectations. Rather specific forms of alliance and communality of interest between yeoman farmers and the cottagers of the deer forests were revealed. Similarly, mugging is set in the interplay between the transformations of race relations and the social construction of a wider social crisis within which these relations themselves were derived from those very transformations. Again, we are led to the framework of socio-political relations within which those processes take meaning as both indicators and bearers of specific forms of crisis within those relations.

It is in the course of this movement from the phenomenon to the constitution of social order that both works come to engage with presenting a theoretical level necessary to the full elaboration of their findings. We find certain differences between the two texts. E.P. Thompson writes a conclusion containing his reflections on 'the rule of law'; the theoretical tone of this discussion is, I want to suggest, more naive than its content. Thompson presents himself as doing battle with 'a sophisticated, but (ultimately) highly schematic Marxism' (1975, p. 259) which, though not named, can be nobody other than Althusser.

Yet the reality is that it is not with Althusser but 'an older Marxist tradition' with which he is actually struggling. This theoretical confusion means that he is not able to advance very far upon the exploration of the theoretical implications of his analysis. What is most important is the decisive and powerful manner in which he insists upon the necessity of a specific analysis of the effects and implications of the rule of law which cannot be reduced to mere ideology. Yet theoretically Thompson speaks in the name of a position which insists upon the 'relative autonomy' of the instances of the non-economic levels; there is no awareness that there may be any problems or difficulties associated with the adoption of this theoretical stance. Now is not the time to explore this issue which is playing a role of growing importance in contemporary debates within Marxism, it is sufficient to note the absence of any awareness of possible deficiencies or weaknesses in his powerful prose.[12]

On the other hand, Hall and his colleagues are fully alert to the latest developments, debates and intricacies in Marxist debates. However, so much are they aware of the specific theoretical issues that it intrudes into and divides up their text; this reaction may be somewhat subjective but I had the feeling that the two theoretical chapters had been written quite separately from those dealing with the materials more immediately relating to mugging. This problem of separation cannot be levelled as a simple criticism of the text or its authors; the question of the relationship between theoretical discourse and empirical materials presents itself as a bigger problem for Marxists since they do not adopt the simple positivist solution of treating theory as a resource, to be applied and tested through the data. Further, it needs to be borne in mind that Marxists have the authority of Marx for distinguishing between the order of inquiry and the order of exposition. So some practical separation, as expressed in the organisation of chapters, is inevitable. Taking these considerations into account still leaves problems about the relationship between theory and empirical materials. At its most successful the text powerfully established the 'realness' or materiality of ideology and thereby leaves out an important theoretical strand.

The text is less successful with its treatment of 'crisis'. The early chapters establish the 'panic' that surrounded 'mugging' in 1972. The difficulty emerges in the way that this is linked to the socio-political crisis of post-1968 British society. 'Crisis' sometimes proclaims itself unambiguously but more often it does not present itself in such unmistakable terms. Hall and his colleagues are aware of the problematic relationship between the Left and 'crisis'; the Left has tended to present every stage of the transformation of modern capitalism as being a 'crisis' and more often than not has labelled it the 'final crisis'.[13] It is important to ensure that the existence of crisis conditions is carefully established and not assumed. It must be recognised that there are difficulties inherent in treating the contemporary period historically. Yet *Policing the Crisis* opens itself up to objection precisely because the contemporary 'crisis' of civil society in Britain is established by the method of partial selection; by the selection of descriptive elements whose accumulation is taken to be proof of both the fact and the form of 'the crisis'. It is not my purpose here to pursue the problem of the identification of social crisis but rather to establish that it has inescapable implications for our more immediate concern, namely the analysis of law. *Policing the Crisis* moves from 'the crisis' to an analysis of law, especially with regard to the mobilisation of law as a means of effecting strategic political goals, in particular the attempts to use law to discipline labour. The problem I want to point to is that this analysis is prejudged and predetermined by its 'crisis' designation. Hence the conclusion of a trend to authoritarianism or towards a law-and-order society is pregiven by the initial location of the analysis. Now it must be insisted that Hall and his colleagues avoid the simple conspiracy theory of law discussed previously.[14] The weakness of the treatment of crisis has its effect in the uni-dimensional analysis of the course and direction of the legislation of the 1970s.

The object of these criticisms is to suggest that a significant element of the analysis is directed at understanding the nature and direction of legislative action over a limited period of time. It is precisely this attempt to come to grips with concrete reality[15] that is the most positive feature of the project which resulted in *Policing the Crisis*; and the book itself marked a reaction against a certain theoreticist trend within contemporary Marxist analysis. I have expressed reservations about elements of this analysis: first, not to detract from its significance and, second, to suggest that they stem from certain theoretical presuppositions which themselves require re-examination.

The importance and potentiality of Marxism for the analysis of law lies then not in any pre-ordained superiority or in any guarantee of success over all other theoretical positions. Its strength, which is its ongoing potential, is in the dynamic of the interaction of its theoretical development and growth with its harnessing to the analysis of law and its effectivity in historically specific circumstances.

Notes

1. See Engels on the causes of female crime and prostitution in 'The Condition of the Working Class in England' in *Marx-Engels Collected Works,* vol. 4 (Lawrence and Wishart, London, 1975).

2. For such a discussion see amongst the rapidly growing literature, L. Colletti (1972a); L. Althusser (1969); P. Anderson (1976); R. Miliband (1977); A. Cutler, B. Hindess, P. Hirst and A. Hussain (1977, 1978).

3. In the general field of radical sociological theory Alvin Gouldner is an important example of this process of discovering Marxism; in the field of sociology of law and criminology we may observe the same process in the work of William Chambliss and of Richard Quinney. Additionally it should be noted that this is predominantly an American phenomenon resulting from the repression of Marxism in the post-war period of the Cold War and McCarthyism.

4. For full discussion of the status of Marxism as social theory see, for contrasting positions, A. Swingewood (1975) and G. Therborn (1976).

5. Note in particular the role played by the 'separation of powers' in P. Selznick (1969), Talcott Parsons (1962) and R. Pound (1906, p. 279).

6. In fairness to Pritt it is important to stress that in the Introduction to the second volume he explicitly renounces a simple instrumentalist position and insists that the working class through its struggles can and do influence the content of law.

7. See, for example, by its persistent and very effective application in the influential works by B. Abel-Smith and R. Stevens (1966) and by Wolfgang Friedmann (1959).

8. See in particular A. Gramsci (1971), especially pp. 5-14, 55-60, and 228-39. The most impressive work seeking to develop the heuristic potential of 'hegemony' has been in S. Hall *et al.* (1978).

9. See the fuller argument developed by S. Hall (1977) concerning the relation between 'simple' and 'complex' levels of analysis in Marx's writings.

10. I argue this position less schematically in A. Hunt (1978) chs. 5 and 6.

11. 9 Geo I, c.22; the 'black' referred to are the 'Walthams Blacks' who were reputed to black their faces and maraud in the deer forests of south-east England.

12. See in particular the debate initiated by Hindess and Hirst; for a résumé of their position with regard to relative autonomy see P. Hirst (1977, pp. 125-54).

13. See, for an interesting discussion of the role of 'crisis' in Marxist politics, G. Hodgson (1975) and L. Colletti (1972b).

14. See above pp. 96-7.

15. It was Lenin who defined Marxism itself as 'a concrete analysis of a concrete situation'; 'Kommunismus', *Collected Works,* vol. 31 (Lawrence and Wishart, London, 1966), p. 166.

Bibliography

Abel-Smith, B. and Stevens, R. *Lawyers and the Courts* (Heinemann, London, 1966)
Althusser, L. *For Marx* (Allen Lane, Harmondsworth, 1969)
——— *Lenin and Philosophy* (New Left Books, London, 1971), pp. 123-80
Anderson, P. *Considerations on Western Marxism* (New Left Books, London, 1976)
Balbus, I.D. *The Dialectics of Legal Repression* (Russell Sage, New York, 1973)
Bankowski, Z. and Mungham, G. *Images of Law* (Routledge and Kegan Paul, London, 1976)
Cain, M. and Hunt, A. (eds.), *Marx and Engels on Law* (Academic Press, London, 1979)
Center for Research on Criminal Justice, *The Iron Fist and the Velvet Glove* (Center for Research on Criminal Justice, Berkeley, 1975)

Chambliss, W. 'Functional and Conflict Theories of Crime' in W. Chambliss and M. Mankoff (eds.), *Whose Law, What Order? A Conflict Approach to Criminology* (John Wiley, New York, 1976), pp. 1-28
Cloke, K. 'The Economic Basis of Law and State' in R. Lefcourt, *People: Essays to Demystify Law, Order and the Court* (Random House, New York, 1971), pp. 65-80
Colletti, L. *From Rousseau to Lenin* (New Left Books, London, 1972a)
——— 'Bernstein and the Marxism of the Second International' in L. Colletti, *From Rousseau to Lenin* (New Left Books, London, 1972b), pp. 45-108
Cutler, A., Hindess, B., Hirst, P., and Hussain, A. *Marx's 'Capital' and Capitalism Today* (Routledge and Kegan Paul, London, 1977 and 1978) vols. I and II
Foster, J. *Class Struggle and the Industrial Revolution* (Weidenfeld and Nicholson, London, 1974)
Friedmann, W. *Law in a Changing Society* (Stevens, London, 1959)
Gramsci, A. *Selections from the Prison Notebooks* (Lawrence and Wishart, London, 1971)
Griffith, J.A.G. *The Politics of the Judiciary* (Fontana, Glasgow, 1977)
Hall, S. 'Marx's Theory of Class' in A. Hunt (ed.), *Class and Class Structure* (Lawrence and Wishart, London, 1977), pp. 15-60
Hall, S., Critcher, C., Jefferson, T., Clarke J. and Roberts, B. *Policing the Crisis* (Macmillan, London, 1978)
Hay, D. 'Property, Authority and the Criminal Law' in D. Hay *et al., Albion's Fatal Tree: Crime and Society in Eighteenth Century England* (Allen Lane, Harmondsworth, 1975), pp. 17-63
Hirst, P. 'Marx and Engels on Law, Crime and Morality' in I. Taylor, P. Walton and J. Young, *Critical Criminology* (Routledge and Kegan Paul, London, 1975), pp. 203-30
——— 'Economic Classes and Politics' in A. Hunt (ed.) *Class and Class Structure* (Lawrence and Wishart, London, 1977), pp.124-54
Hodgson, G. *Trotsky and Fatalistic Marxism* (Spokesman, London, 1975)
Holloway, J. and Picciotto, S. *State and Capital* (Edward Arnold, London, 1978)
Hunt, A. 'Perspectives in the Sociology of Law' in P. Carlen (ed.) *Sociology of Law* (Sociological Review Monograph No. 23, University of Keele, 1976a), pp. 22-44
——— 'Law, State and Class Struggle', *Marxism Today*, vol. 20 (1976b), pp. 178-87
——— *The Sociological Movement in Law* (Macmillan, London, 1978)
Lefcourt, R. (ed.) *Law Against the People: Essays to Demystify Law, Order and the Courts* (Random House, New York, 1971)
Marx, K. *Grundrisse* (Penguin, Harmondsworth, 1973)
Miliband, R. *Marxism and Politics* (Oxford University Press, Oxford, 1977)
Parsons, T. 'Law and Social Control' in W. Evan (ed.) *Law and Sociology* (Free Press, Glencoe, 1962), pp. 56-72
Pashukanis, E.B. *Law and Marxism* (Ink Links, London, 1978)
Poulantzas, N. 'L'examen Marxiste de l'Etat et du droit actuel', *Les Temps Moderne* (Aug/Sept. 1964)
——— 'A propos de la théorie Marxiste du Droit', *Archives de Philosophie de Droit*, vol. 12 (1967)
——— *Political Power and Social Classes* (New Left Books, London, 1973)
——— *State, Power and Socialism* (New Left Books, London, 1978)
Pound, R. 'Causes of Popular Dissatisfaction with the Administration of Justice', *American Law Review*, vol. 40 (1906), pp. 729-49
Pritt, D.N. *Law, Class and Society* 4 vols., (Lawrence and Wishart, London, 1971)
Renner K. *The Institutions of Private Law and their Social Functions* (Routledge and Kegan Paul, London, 1976)
Selznick, P. *Law, Society and Industrial Justice* (Russell Sage, New, York, 1969)
Shaw, M. *Marxism and Social Science* (Pluto Press, London, 1975)
Swingewood, A. *Marx and Modern Social Theory* (Macmillan, London, 1975)

Taylor I., Walton P., and Young J. *The New Criminology* (Routledge and Kegan Paul, London, 1973)

______ *Critical Criminology* (Routledge and Kegan Paul, London, 1975)

Therborn, G. *Science, Class and Society* (New Left Books, London, 1976)

Thompson, E.P. *Whigs and Hunters: The Origins of the Black Act* (Allen Lane, Harmondsworth, 1975)

Wedderburn, K.W. *The Worker and the Law* 2nd edn (Penguin, Harmondsworth, 1971)

6 The Contribution of the Critical Theory of the Frankfurt School to the Sociology of Law

Hubert Rottleuthner

In writing on the contribution of the critical theory of the Frankfurt School to the sociology of law, it may be well for me to begin with several qualifying remarks. First, I know of no systematic contributions to the sociology of law by the most prominent figures of the Institute for Social Research, namely Max Horkheimer, Theodor W. Adorno and Jürgen Habermas; and I would regard it as less than helpful simply to look through their writings on the chance I might discover some modest contribution or other. Similarly, I will not venture to speculate on what Adorno might have said, had he been asked for his views on socio-legal questions.

Secondly, I fear that I may well have a prejudice against the writings of the Frankfurt School. To be sure, I studied philosophy and sociology (and some law) in Frankfurt, I attended Adorno's lectures, and I wrote my thesis under the supervision of Habermas. In the early 1970s, however, I began reading analytical philosophy and I learned more about empirical research methods than would seem appropriate to a disciple of the Frankfurt School. I fell prey to what Habermas would have denounced as 'scientism' had he been aware of my position. I am, then, writing today as an apostate, and the effort to report on my former confessions and their relation to my professional work raises familiar problems. Still, I hope to have enough hermeneutical sense to provide a useful sketch on aspects of critical theory.

I will suggest, in particular, that the Frankfurt School does have contributions to make to the sociology of law. But I should add here a further qualification. My remarks obviously do not permit a comprehensive account of critical theory, nor of the history of the Frankfurt School and its theoretical development. I will limit my efforts to a short outline of some crucial aspects of critical theory.[1] Considering the variety of topics that have been the concern of members of the Frankfurt School — from Chinese history to pop music — and considering the anti-systematic, almost aphoristic, trait in Adorno's writings in particular, it would, I think, be a bit absurd to search for remarks relevant to the sociology of law. One can attempt to reconstruct the legal theory hidden in the work of Marx but it would be simply foolish to try the same with Horkheimer's or Adorno's work.

One final qualification is that I am not going to discuss the work of either Franz Neumann or that of Otto Kirchheimer (see, for example, Burin and Shell, 1969; Gurland, Kirchheimer and Neumann, 1943; Kirchheimer, 1939; Neumann, 1944, 1957; Rusche and Kirchheimer, 1939) both members of the Institut für Sozialforschung (Social Research), as it came to be called during its period of exile in the United States. For a few years both were affiliated with the Institute. During this period, as in earlier years, they wrote on such topics as the law in fascist Germany, on correlations between social structure and punishment, and on the development of the Weimar Republic. Their illuminating articles were grist for the mills of critical lawyers, in particular for the critical law students of the 1960s, and they are still to be valued as important theoretical statements on the relations of law, politics and society. But I shall not discuss the work of these two authors, since I do not regard them as representative members of the Frankfurt School.[2] Allow me to explain what I mean by 'representative members' by referring to the writing of the two classic figures of the Frankfurt School, Horkheimer and Adorno.

The Critical Theory of Horkheimer and Adorno

The critical theory of Horkheimer and Adorno has three characteristics. In the subsequent discussion, these will serve to clarify the differences between the original version of the critical theory and its further development through Habermas. Later I shall attempt to link these characteristics with corresponding themes in the sociology of law to which critical theory does contribute.

First, critical theory, as developed by Horkheimer, is a normative field within social philosophy (Horkheimer, 1972, contains a fundamental exposition of critical theory). It is guided by a practical interest, namely the fundamental change of society. Not only does the critical social scientist describe, explain and predict events and processes as extrinsic to him, but he is himself a political member of the society in which he acts. He has to unify these two activities in the work of the critical theorist.

It has frequently been observed that we do not find in Horkheimer and Adorno any attempt to clarify their concept of a better society. They have even refused to give programmatic advice for changing society and to specify the goals they were aiming at. This unwillingness was sometimes linked to the Jewish taboo against calling God by his right name (for example, Horkheimer, 1967, pp. 311-12).

Critical theory uses many of the classical dichotomies to interpret what it assumes to be a distorted world. We find a separation between subject and object, general and singular, name and thing, civilisation and nature, reason and nature, perception and object, and so on. The world is described in a highly persuasive language, a language full of complaint and mourning. Occasionally one finds an expression of hope and reconciliation (Horkheimer and Adorno, 1947, p. 223), but this hope is never left unchallenged. As Jay puts it, writing about Horkheimer: 'Philosophy as he understood it always expresses an unavoidable note of sadness, but without succumbing to resignation' (1973, p. 47). Aside from the positive concepts of abandonment, or, given its sexual overtones, perhaps surrender *(Hingabe)* (Adorno, 1964, p. 72), and of reconciliation or salvation, we find but one central critical tool, namely the confrontation of the existing social reality with the norms and ideals that are claimed to be realised (for example, Horkheimer and Adorno, 1947, p. 292). In short, we have here the concept of 'immanent critique' developed by Hegel and Marx.

A second distinctive feature of the Frankfurt School is the philosophy of history set forth in the 'dialectic of the Enlightenment': the suppression of external nature is always accompanied by a repression of the inner human nature itself. The growing technical domination of nature is mirrored in a similar notion of man himself as an object of increasing domination. Mankind has surmounted the old myths; the disenchantment of the world has led to a separation between man and nature. This alienation from the calculable and reified world, however, is but a dialectical corollary to human self-alienation and both self- and other-renunciation. Reason *(Vernunft)* ceases to mean the reconciliation of contradictions, and is reduced to an instrument of calculation and adaptation. Science itself has fallen victim to a new myth: the scientistic or positivistic myth of fact, of that which is the case. The instrumental manipulation of nature by man is paralleled by a manipulation of man to man, a new barbarism among men.

As a third characteristic we can see the attempt to develop a comprehensive theory of present society. Horkheimer and Adorno used categories reminiscent of Marx, but neither dealt systematically with Marx's political economy. Both are convinced that in the present capitalist societies the principle of exchange penetrates all human relationships. Everything becomes an exchangeable good, including the products of the so-called 'culture industry'. Along with this extension of the capitalist market mechanisms to the sphere of culture and to the whole 'superstructure' of society, Horkheimer and Adorno both observed the growing power of public administration, an overwhelming tendency toward a totally 'administrated world' *(verwaltete Welt).* Both aspects, the dominance of the exchange principle and increasing administrative power, result in an absolute supremacy of the society over the individual. There is an irreversible trend towards the disappearance of the autonomous individual.

Horkheimer and Adorno did not deal systematically with socio-legal themes, nor can we find in either of them any systematic remarks on the ideological function of law. In but a single paragraph of his *Negative Dialektik* does Adorno define law as the 'prototype of irrational rationality' *(Urphänomen irrationaler Rationalität)* (1966, p. 302).

> The law enthrones a principle of equality that is of a merely formal nature and hence becomes the hiding place of substantive inequality, owing to the fact that essential differences are struck down. Thus, this concept of equality turns into a surviving myth in a world where the undoing of myths is only apparent.[3]

If law could serve in this way as a paradigm of the dialectic of the enlightenment, it is surprising that Adorno gave so little attention to legal phenomena. Perhaps his unwillingness was due to his horror of definition, conceptual systems and formalism — qualities he ascribed to the scholarly disciplines dealing with law (1966, p. 302). There is only a brief article, namely 'Sexual Taboos and the Law Today', which is concerned with legislative and judicial problems in the light of psychoanalysis (Adorno, 1963). The proposals that he makes for further criminological research in this field have not lost any of their interest.

Thinking of critical theory today, one is particularly interested in the work of Jürgen Habermas, to whom I now turn. While there is evidence that Habermas is increasingly concerned with socio-legal questions, I would argue that he is at the same time moving further away from the original Frankfurt School.

Habermas

I have identified three distinctive features of critical theory, namely, its normative implications, its philosophy of history and its comprehensive theory of the present capitalist society. Taking this classification as a blueprint for the presentation of Habermas's approach. I shall exclude the following two topics. First, unlike Horkheimer and Adorno, Habermas wrote extensively on problems within the theory of science, especially on the logic of the social sciences (Habermas, 1967, 1968a). His dispute with Hans Albert, the satrap of critical rationalism in Germany, was one of the highlights of the so-called *Positivismusstreit* (Adorno, 1969). I will not go into details; space does not allow for a discussion of Habermas's interpretations and misunderstandings of analytical philosophy and critical rationalism. What is more, Habermas has revised his opinions on analytical philosophy to a considerable degree.

Secondly, Habermas attempts to reconstruct a fundamental social theory in the form of a communication theory based on universal pragmatics. But this very ambitious theory has not yet been sufficiently elaborated, nor have its single elements been worked out consistently. One still finds a variety of different attempts to classify types of action, pragmatic universals, forms of communication, communication-media and so on (1976a, p. 132; 1976b, c). Therefore I shall not deal with this still rather sketchy theory. Instead, I will look at the work of Habermas in the light of the three features of critical theory I mentioned earlier.

Normative Theory of Communicative Ethics

In contrast to Horkheimer and Adorno, Habermas makes his normative assumptions explicit and attempts to prove them systematically. He no longer relies on the method of immanent critique. Since bourgeois consciousness has grown cynical as traditional ideals have come to be discarded, it no longer makes sense to confront reality with the hollow shells of Christian or Liberal values (1973b, pp. 53-4; 1976a, pp. 10-11, 52). Habermas is convinced that we cannot any longer deduce our material value assumptions from higher principles; on the other hand, we cannot reduce rational ethics to an empirical analysis of behaviour or to a linguistic analysis of evaluative utterances or sentences either. Today the only way of coping reasonably with practical problems is to specify the formal procedures of a moral discourse. Unlike his predecessors, Habermas develops a normative theory of communicative ethics — 'without', he says, 'being afraid of false positiveness' (1976a, pp. 66-7).

Habermas develops his concepts on the basis of a theory of action. The first step is a distinction between types of action, namely non-social action (technical, instrumental) and social action (strategic or communicative). We do not find a final classification of types of action, but, rather, a variety of attempts (1968a, 1976a, pp. 32-5, 132, 170, 261; Habermas and Luhmann, 1971, pp. 114-15). He goes on to assert that by performing a speech act during communicative action (or consensual action) we raise four *'validity claims'* (1973a; 1976a, pp. 11, 339), namely those of the intelligibility (or comprehensibility) of the utterance; of the truth of its propositional contents; of the adequacy or correctness, legitimacy or rightness; and of the veracity or credibility of the speaker. These validity claims are usually taken for granted. But they can be 'problematised' once the communication has been disturbed, for example, when the truth of a proposition or the legitimacy of a value judgement or a norm formulation has been called into question. In such a case the participants have to negotiate their validity claims in order to carry a consensual interaction. The participants then no longer perform a communicative action but engage in theoretical or practical *discourse* in which the relevant claim to validity is examined.

Habermas takes the following features to be characteristic of all 'discourse' (1973a, pp. 148-9, 152; 1976a, pp. 85-8, 132, 170, 343; Habermas and Luhmann, 1971, pp. 115-22; 1973, pp. 214, 238-52). They do not compel their participants to act; co-operative search for truth is the only permissible motive. They do not provide processes whereby information can be acquired. (They are purged of action and experience). The validity claims are made 'problematic' *(virtualisiert)*. In principle those affected are participants in the discourse. The participants express and interpret their needs.

The outcome of discourses consists of a consensus among participants who either recognise or reject a validity claim. But we have to distinguish between a merely accepted consensus and a rational one. For only a rational consensus provides us with a criterion for a correct assessment of validity claims. Habermas asserts that a reasonable consensus is one that has been achieved in an *'ideal speech situation'*.

(For this concept and the features mentioned subsequently, see 1970b, pp. 371-72; 1973a, p. 152; 1973b, pp. 296-8; 1976a, pp. 343-45; Habermas and Luhmann, 1971, pp. 122, 136-41; 1973, pp. 252-60.) He argues that the design of an ideal speech situation is necessarily implied in the structure of potential speech; this idea is necessarily presupposed whenever we give reasons in communication, just as the validity claims are implied in normal communicative interaction. Engaging in discourse *means* that we presuppose the fulfilment of the conditions of an ideal speech situation.

Undistorted or unconstrained discourse is marked by three features: there is no compulsion other than the compulsion of argumentation; no form of domination exists; every participant has an equal opportunity to choose and perform the possible speech acts; and every participant can freely change the linguistic levels (putting forward propositions, norm formulations, intentional/self-representative expressions, and so on).

Up to this point I have simply described the opinions of Habermas rather than criticised them. But let me now make some critical remarks. What is the logical status of the four validity claims implied in every speech act that aims at mutual understanding? And what is the status of the presupposed and anticipated ideal speech situation? Does Habermas assert *empirically* that everyone who wants to achieve a rational agreement *in fact* presupposes that the conditions of an undistorted communication will be fulfilled? Or does he *recommend* those participants to assume that the ideal speech situation exists, in order thereby to achieve a consensus? Or is it only *by definition* that a 'rational' consensus is one that is obtained under ideal conditions? Habermas's reference to a 'normative foundation inherent in the very structure of social action', or to 'formal conditions of discourse', or to 'basic rules of rational speech' (1976a, p. 194; Habermas and Luhmann, 1973, pp. 258-9) or to 'the basic structure of verbal behaviour' (1976a, p. 339) is not very illuminating.

I doubt whether an ideal such as the lack of domination and compulsion, the ideal of equal opportunities and symmetry, can be found in the 'structure of possible speech' without committing the naturalistic fallacy. Perhaps Habermas is here returning, albeit tacitly, to a field he was concerned with before he developed this theory of communicative ethics. Habermas first introduced the notion of an undisturbed communication when he was considering problems of psychoanalysis and the concept of ego-identity (1973b, pp. 195-231, 264-301). Discussing the latter, he combined classical German philosophy with the empirical results of social psychology. He worked out a special type of systematically distorted communication, one that psychoanalysis is concerned with. In everyday communication we find misunderstandings that cannot be eliminated in the usual way since the participants are not able to perceive and interpret their own motives. To resolve such distortions takes special therapeutic skill, theoretical background assumptions, and normative patterns of 'normal' interaction and 'balanced' ego-identity. I suppose that Habermas projected those normative patterns into the 'basic structure of possible speech'.

Theory of Social Evolution

Habermas's attempt to bring philosophical reflection closer to the empirical sciences marks another difference between himself and Horkheimer and Adorno. To be sure, this was also the goal of the founders of the Institute for Social Research, a goal which, however, they never attained to any significant degree. Here they failed, in particular, in their highly speculative writings on the philosophy of history and in their writings about the present society. (I shall return to this point below.) Instead of a pessimistic or negative philosophy of history, we find in Habermas a theory of social evolution, one built upon the results of anthropological, ethnological and historical research (1973a, pp. 19-41; 1973b, pp. 389-98; 1976a, pp. 9-48, 129-267). Habermas is unique in choosing, as a frame of reference for his evolutionary theory, fundamental concepts from the cognitive psychology of child development (Piaget, Kohlberg). He distinguishes the *logic of development* from the *dynamics of development*. The former may be understood as the sequence of possible structures that can be rationally reconstructed (forming the logical scope of possible development), and the latter, as the description and explanation of actual learning processes, the analysis of the conditions on which the evolutionary process depends (1973a, p. 27; 1976a, pp. 154, 248).

Socio-evolutionary learning processes are stimulated by system-problems that cannot be resolved by means of the 'steering capacities' available (that is the potential for influence within sectors of the socio-environmental system). A crisis emerges whenever a social system cannot manage a problem by means of its own 'organisation principle' *(Organisationsprinzip)*. One precondition of evolutionary learning is that the available capacities of cognitive knowledge are being applied and are being institutionalised as an expression of the currently accepted 'rationality structure' *(Rationalitätsstruktur)*. The institutionalisation of such a rationality structure is accompanied by the inauguration of a new organisation principle. Such a principle forms the institutional kernel that determines the specific mode of social integration. Seen from a historical perspective we can distinguish the following modes of social integration (1973a, pp. 31-40; 1976a, p. 169), namely, familial and relationship patterns (in archaic cultures); political class domination (in traditional societies); and the economic system with an unrestricted market mechanism and formal legal relations (liberal capitalist societies). (The definitions of historical periods in Habermas are also inconsistent — 1973a, pp. 30-41; 1976a, pp. 26-9, 97-101, 135, 172-3.) Each mode of social integration sets conditions for a new societal level or standard of learning. As a consequence the economic forces of production may then be developed further, limited only by the level of techno-organisational knowledge and skill.

Habermas (1976a, pp. 31, 35) holds that normative structures of society have their own history — their own processes of rationalisation — and are not simple reflections of the economic infrastructure; and that the development of such normative structures, as they establish a new mode of social integration during each stage of this development, is the real pacemaker of social evolution. He interprets the course of history as a cumulative progress with various dimensions (1973a, pp. 16, 22; 1973b, pp. 202-5, 390-2; 1976a, pp. 156, 194). These are the development of the economic forces of production, which is accompanied by an increase in empirical knowledge; the expansion of 'steering capacities' (here meaning 'political influence'); and the change of normative structures and general interpretations of the world *(Weltbilder).* Habermas gives careful consideration to the development of normative structures. He discerns a historical development in a number of patterns of universal justification or legitimation (1976a, pp. 277-81). These are mythological, cosmological, religious and ontological patterns, and also, formal-procedural types of legitimation beginning with Rousseau's *Contrat social.* A new and higher level would be reached if mankind were to achieve the institutionalisation of discourses, or so he asserts. (For the problem of institutionalisation of discourses, see 1971a, pp. 31-3; 1973b, pp. 378-88; and Habermas and Luhmann, 1976a, p. 340; 1973, p. 265.)

This rather optimistic view is an extension of the findings of Piaget and Kohlberg concerning the homologous development in the moral judgement of the child (1973b, pp. 207-19, 396-8; 1976a, pp. 13-30, 135, 171-3). By analogy to this ontogenetic development Habermas reconstructs the history of morals as a process of increasing universalisation and internalisation of normative demands. Moreover, he extends the six steps of moral consciousness in Kohlberg, steps that end with a post-conventional level characterised by conscience orientation towards universal ethical principles, by introducing a seventh step; and it is not surprising that this last step is the realm of universal linguistic ethics or an ethics of discourse (1976a, p. 83).

Habermas claims to put forward a self-reflective theory of social evolution. Hence we can interpret his attempt to establish an ethics of discourse as a perhaps overly ambitious effort to provide a new and higher organisation principle in history. Discourses constitute a system-wide learning mechanism *(systemrelevanter Lernmechanismus)* (1971a, p. 31); they form a level of learning that can cope more effectively with problems that are at present unresolved.

Theory of Late Capitalist Societies and of Crisis

The holistic approach of Horkheimer and especially Adorno was oriented more towards an ideology-critique than towards a politico-economic theory. The two classical figures were concerned with phenomena of the 'superstructure', with the culture industry and mass culture, with bourgeois consciousness, and in particular with the all-embracing and penetrating fetishism of commodities *(Warenfetischismus).* Habermas, however, borrows categories and employs results from political economy and from recent theories of government (1973a; 1976a, pp. 271-328). He refines them in his theory of late capitalist societies, a theory that consists primarily of an analysis of the relations among the three major social systems: the economic system, the political-administrative system, and the socio-cultural system.

We also find in his work a theory of crisis; it consists of a classification and description of various types of crises related to the three sub-systems (1973a, pp. 66-128): within the economic system, specifically an economic crisis (over-investment and realisation crises); within the political system, specifically a crisis of rationality (a lack of political steering capacities) and a legitimation crisis (a lack of mass loyalty); and within the socio-cultural system, specifically a motivation crisis (alienation, retreat or protest).

The main purpose of Habermas's crisis theory is to answer the question of whether advanced (or late) capitalism is able to overcome its crisis tendencies regularly and consistently, and, in particular, whether it could overcome its economic crises — those seen by Marx to herald the inevitable demise of the capitalist system. Habermas puts forward the thesis that economic crises appear to have lost their revolutionary impact. Economically induced crises have been successfully turned into or transformed into crises of the political-administrative system. State administration is now challenged by a paradoxical situation. On the one hand, economic constraints demand state intervention, but on the other, the administration has to allow the basic mechanisms of a capitalist economy to remain unchanged, for example, freedom of investment. Habermas leaves unanswered the question as to whether the other types of crises will bring about a revolutionary change in the capitalist system.

Habermas's New Version of Critical Theory

Before I turn to Habermas's contribution to the sociology of law and to what in his writings we can apply to our socio-legal studies, let me summarise the differences between the orthodoxy of the Frankfurt School, as represented by Horkeimer and Adorno, and the approach of Habermas.

Normative implications

As I mentioned earlier, the differences between Horkheimer and Adorno, and Habermas on the normative implications of their approaches lie in the fact that Habermas articulates his normative assumptions explicitly and attempts to prove them systematically. While Adorno, in *Minima Moralia* wrote his 'Doctrine of a Good life' *('Lehre vom richtigen Leben')* full of distress (knowing full well that you cannot lead a good life in this disrupted world), Habermas develops a universal linguistic ethics. But Habermas claims that by this discoursive ethics he is carrying on a basic pattern of dialects, one emphasised by Hegel and by Adorno, namely the dialectic of the general and the individual. According to Habermas, this dialectical scheme is derived from the model of everyday communication and can be made plausible by referring to the structure of normal interaction (1971b, p. 192). As soon as individuals talk to each other they claim to be perfectly unique subjects, but paradoxically their individuality can only be comprehended in general terms and categories. Similarly Habermas detects the dominance of society over the individual only within the power relations characteristic of systematically distorted communication *(Gewaltverhältnisse systematisch verzerrter Kommunikation)* (1971b, p. 193).

Habermas viewed the imminent downfall of the individual, but he renews the concept of ego-identity and other humanist values. He argues that Adorno, in his critique of the 'totally socialised society' *(total vergesellschaftete Gesellschaft)* had to presuppose the ideal of the autonomous individual (1976a, p. 65). Whereas Adorno mourns the alienation of man, Habermas argues optimistically for a discourse undisturbed by any form of domination. A third dissimilarity mentioned earlier is that Habermas no longer believes in the feasibility of immanent critique.

Philosophy of History

Comparing the 'Dialectic of the Enlightenment' with Habermas's theory of social evolution, one finds a striking difference in the amount of empirical content in the latter and, still more striking, the elimination of any dialectical pattern in the interpretation of historical development in Habermas. He reconstructs history as a process of refinement for the human species *(Bildungsprozess der Menschengattung)* (1973b, p. 233). The only dialectical moment Habermas posits (here referring explicitly to the 'Dialectic of the Enlightenment') is that there is no linear progression but rather, that at every new level of learning new challenges are produced. As you acquire more efficient problem-solving capacities, new problems come to mind (1976a, pp. 181, 257, 285) — a trivial pattern that can also be found in, for example, Popper (in Adorno, 1969, p. 103)

Theory of the Present Society

Habermas stresses the distinction between a critique of the ideology (a concern to which Adorno applied his energies admirably) and a theory of late capitalist societies (Habermas, 1971a, p. 198). What Adorno regarded as the fundamental mechanism of capitalist societies (namely the principle of equivalent exchange) is for Habermas only the basic ideology of the bourgeoisie (1976a, pp. 308, 327). According to Habermas this ideological pattern is collapsing: market exchange no longer is the pre-eminent mechanism or structure of social relations. No longer is social integration brought about by the economic market; instead, that has become the task of the political system (1973a, pp. 59, 76, 83, 117). Increasingly, exchange relations are replaced by administrative action. As a result the basis of fetishism of commodities *(Warenfetischismus),* so emphatically criticised by Adorno, has vanished (1973a, p. 97).

In contrast to Adorno's approach, Habermas, well-informed about political economy and theories of state, develops a theory of late capitalism that explains the crisis tendencies and steering capacities of the political system. To sum up: Habermas sticks to the great themes of critical theory, but one finds marked differences from the critical theory of the old Frankfurt School in his writings. This schism makes it difficult to carry over the label 'critical theory' to the writings of Habermas.

Habermas's Contribution to the Sociology of Law

Thus far I have argued that Habermas is moving further and further away from the original Frankfurt School, but that he shows at the same time an increasing concern with socio-legal questions. I want now to turn to this remarkable trend.

In the earlier writings of Habermas, legal questions played a considerable role. There he was rather concerned (for example, in 1962; 1971a) with the history of bourgeois legal thought such as natural law and, in 'Zum Begriff der politischen Beteiligung' (1958, reprinted in 1973b, pp. 9-60), with legal doctrine in the field of public law. In his later writings on methodology and the theory of science (1967, 1968a), however, he mentions neither law nor legal doctrine. Amazingly, for Habermas, hermeneutical sciences are oriented towards a practical type of 'knowledge-constitutive interest' *(erkenntnisleitendes Interesse),* that is an interest 'in the preservation and expansion of the intersubjectivity of possible action-orienting mutual understanding' (1972, p. 310). But this is just what we can regard as a goal of the legal sciences: to interpret norms in order to preserve intersubjective communication or, in the case of a conflict, to maintain social integration. But, rather than dealing with legal doctrine and judicial action, Habermas traces a practical knowledge-constitutive interest in the field of historical sciences (a field in which there has typically been more interest in the continuity of tradition than in the preservation of actual inter-subjectivity). None the less, by applying our scheme we can uncover the following contributions of Habermas.

Communicative Ethics

The model of undistorted communication or an ideal speech situation is at the core of Habermas's communicative ethics. This model can be applied in an analysis of courtroom interaction — and has, indeed, been so applied, not by Habermas himself, but by some of his followers (for example, Rottleuthner, 1971). Obviously the language of the courtroom does not fulfil the standards of an ideal speech situation. (Habermas would not even call it a discourse but rather a type of strategic activity.) But one can use the concept of undistorted communication as a critical pattern, one that brings about an awareness of the actual distortions and asymmetries in court proceedings. Yet the idealised model of undistorted communication is purged of empirical content to such a degree that one can hardly identify actual inequalities and distortions. It is therefore not surprising that Habermas's concept of discourse has recently been interpreted as suggesting a normative theory of argument in the field of legal theory (Alexy, 1978, pp. 134-77). On the other hand, an empirical analysis of courtroom behaviour lends itself much more readily to categories and principles of conflict theory — a perspective which, surprisingly enough, is all but ignored in the writings of Habermas notwithstanding the fact that he is, after all, concerned with problems of conflict and consensus.

In his recent work Habermas mentions that intersubjectivity, as a function of law and morality, is preserved as conflicts arise (1976a, pp. 13, 20, 74, 135, 171-2). But he regards conflict resolution through the application of legal or moral rules as a continuation of communicative action by other means. In this sense, he speaks of 'consensual' conflict resolution. This notion, I believe, does not fit his idealised concept of 'consensus' (mentioned above). Whenever participants in a social conflict appeal to legal rules or at least to legal institutions, it is most unlikely that conflict will be resolved by consensus. Even an agreement in court may not comply with the requirements of a real consensus. And in a criminal procedure the accused certainly does not 'consent' to his being jailed.

Habermas also blurs an essential distinction between law and morality. In contrast to morality, law consists not only of rules of social action but also of (secondary) rules that guide the application of (primary) rules. Furthermore, law consists of constitutive rules that structure institutions, and these institutions, in turn, apply and enforce the primary and secondary rules. But in another context Habermas realises that the institutionalisation of the judge's role (the role of a third party who is empowered to hand down binding decisions) marks a crucial point in the evolution of society. For Habermas it even marks the beginning of the state (1976a, pp. 177-9, 272). Yet Habermas is not concerned with questions of legal institutions; instead, he treats moral and legal issues alike, namely on the level of the actor's orientation (compare Schelsky, 1978, pp. 12-16).

Social Evolution

Here I turn to the evolutionary aspect in Habermas. In his theory of social evolution normative structures gain a prominent place. In particular Habermas lends great weight to structures of action (the differentiation between action, role, norm and principle; the various types of action; and the increasing compartmentalisation of certain types of action within specific social sub-systems, for example, strategic action in economic relations); to structures of general interpretations in so far as they are constitutive of the law and morals, for example, in the form of doctrines of legitimation; and to structures of moral and legal conflict resolution. As to the latter Habermas states an increasing tendency towards rationalisation of the law in a number of dimensions (1976a, pp. 264-5). These are universalisation: the field of economic-strategic activities is controlled according to *general* statutes; legalism: law and morals, legality and morality are divided; conventionalism: the law is treated as a conventional medium which can intentionally be changed, criticised, but which also demands justification; and formalism: private subjects gain a field of autonomous economic activities unhampered by state regulations. Now Habermas maintains that he has found a parallel between this pattern of modern law and, at the ontogenetic level, a state of moral consciousness. What is characteristic of modern law is also characteristic of the post-conventional stage of moral consciousness (à la Kohlberg).

One can raise some doubts about this thesis. I am uncertain about the empirical adequacy of Habermas's description of the development of law and, in particular, his remarks on modern law. It was none other than Max Weber (1967, pp. 345-6) who pointed to a tendency of derationalisation in the law. The indicators of this derationalisation have become more apparent since then, namely an increasing use of indefinite statutes, an enormous number of more 'specific' legal measures not fitting the standards of 'general' rules, the restriction of dispositive rules by standards of social responsibility and reasonable demands, the judicial application of moral standards, and the interpretation of judicial reasoning not guided by logical procedures but by psychological attitudes and motives. It is just these tendencies that Habermas's colleague Klaus Eder (1978) has identified in an article recently published in *Soziale Welt*.

It is amusing to see that Eder also treats these features as indicators of a 'post-conventional' state. So one has to choose which of the two, Habermas or Eder, has operationalised and applied the notion of 'post-conventionalism' properly (Eder changes explicitly the meaning of 'post-conventionalism' as originally introduced by Kohlberg). Thus at the level of concept formation it does not seem to be easy to translate notions from the psychology of child development to such complex phenomena as the development of law, let alone to the establishment of an evolutionary rank ordering among legal and moral systems!

This leads to a central problem in Habermas's approach — the parallel between ontogenetic and social development. He regards the analogy as justified particularly in the field of law, for the structures of law consciousness are homologous in the individual just as they are in the human species. On the one hand, they are incorporated in the legal (and moral?) institutions, and on the other, they are expressed in the legal/moral judgements and behaviour of human individuals (1973a, p. 107, referring to 1967, pp. 290-305; 1976a, p. 13). This double nature of law has been discussed a good deal. Legal rules serve from the point of view of the actor to facilitate mutual orientation towards the actions and expectations of the other. One can also look upon the law as an institutionalised order which is relatively independent of an individual's actions, motives and attitudes.

But it is just this problem of institutionalisation with which Habermas cannot cope, for he constructs legal categories from the perspective of the actor. He excludes from his analysis the objective function of legal norms and institutions and deals only with the patterns of justification in the mind of the individual acting within social institutions. A working group of the Starnberg Max-Planck-Institut (Eder *et al.*, 1978) is now concerned with the analysis of historical change in the legitimation-patterns as seen in legal texts. Habermas does not analyse the system functions of the law. He explicitly remarks that the rationality of the law consists not of its efficient contributions on a systems level but only of the patterns of rationality, mentioned above, that refer to a certain type of action (1973a, pp. 121-3; 1976a, pp. 260-7). But how would Habermas interpret, say, the law-and-economy approach?

I might summarise the questions Habermas leaves — as far as the issues of legal institutions and system functions are concerned — to our future efforts. What does 'institutionalisation of the law' mean? Which are the system functions of the law that cannot be conceptualised from the point of view of the individual actor? Are there really 'objective' system functions to which the law contributes?

Theory of State and Crisis

It is not surprising that Habermas makes no further reference to legal phenomena in his theory of state and crisis. He could have mentioned the law in connection with the crisis of legitimation (for example, is the concept of the rule of law still feasible for the legitimation of the present capitalist state?), but law is systematically excluded from the analysis of state intervention in economic systems. Such intervention is usually accomplished by legal means — but that is not Habermas's concern.

Having examined Habermas critically, it should be clear that sociology of law ought to consider more seriously the problems of a theory of state, emphasising the study of politico-legal steering mechanisms in socio-economic processes. Furthermore, legal sociologists should give more weight to an empirical analysis of legislative processes, that is the actual formation of state law. This field of research has been left too long to speculation and to indiscriminate 'derivations' from basic conditions of capitalist societies.

I might add other topics in the study of Habermas that suggest further areas for joint work by social scientists and academic lawyers. I doubt — and presumably academic lawyers do too — whether the instrument of immanent critique has actually become obsolete. Habermas himself said that law requires justification, precisely because it is changeable. And it is one of the tasks of lawyers to justify and/or criticise legal measures by invoking existing norms and principles. But the lawyers' strategies of justification and/or critique suffer from a paucity of empirical reference. Academic lawyers do not describe social events or conditions in such a way that one can determine whether these events represent an application of the norms and principles, abstract as they may be. I presume that this mode of dealing with norms, values and principles creates the impression of being vague, arbitrary and, hence, obsolete. Empirical 'operationalisation' of ideals and values, the denotation of their factual referents, should be made the object of co-operative efforts by both academic lawyers and social scientists. For it is the task of empirical sociologists to develop indicators for such complex social states of affairs. Since values or value-predicates have a descriptive element or meaning and do not merely function as emotive expressions, a promising field of co-operative work is opened up.

A similar field of investigation can be seen in the evolution of law.

Under the heading of 'legal culture' legal sociologists have for some time been dealing with the problem of formulating indicators appropriate to a comparison of different legal systems. Generally these studies are limited to existing legal and societal systems. But their scope should be broadened to include indicators that allow for a reconstruction of the ontogenetic development of law. This might well be a future task for legal historians, sociologists of law and for cultural anthropologists too.

Notes

1. I shall not deal with Walter Benjamin's work, concerned as it is with aesthetics; furthermore, I shall not deal with the writings of Herbert Marcuse and his theoretical development (but see, as a contribution relevant to legal theory, Marcuse, 1934). I am grateful to Stanley L. Paulson for valuable help in refining my English.
2. On their relationship to the Institute of Social Research see Jay (1973, pp. 143-50).
3. A loose translation of the sentence: 'In ihm wird das formale Aquivalenzprinzip zur Norm, Versteck der Ungleichheit des Gleichen, in dem die Differenzen untergehen; nachlebender Mythos inmitten einer nur zum Schein entmythologisierten Menschheit.' A similar interpretation can be found in Negt (1975, pp. 61-2).

Bibliography

Adorno, T.W. 'Sexualtabus und Recht heute' in *Eingriffe* (Suhrkamp, Frankfurt am Main, 1963) pp. 99-124

——— *Minima Moralia,* 2nd edn (Suhrkamp, Frankfurt am Main, 1964; 1st edn 1951)

——— *Negative Dialektik* (Suhrkamp, Frankfurt am Main, 1966)

——— *Der Positivismusstreit in der deutschen Soziologie* (Luchterhand, Neuwied-Berlin, 1969); English translation — *The Positivist Dispute in German Sociology* (Heinemann, London, 1976)

Alexy, R. *Theorie der juristischen Argumentation* (Suhrkamp, Frankfurt am Main, 1978)

Burin, F.S. and Shell, K.L. *Politics, Law and Social Change: Selected Essays of Otto Kirchheimer* (Columbia University Press, New York, 1969)

Eder, K. 'Zur Rationalisierungsproblematik des modernen Rechts', *Soziale Welt* (1978) pp. 247-56

Eder, K., Frankenberg, G. Rödel, U. and Tugendhat, E. 'Projektvorschlag: Die Entwicklung von Gerechtigkeitsvorstellungen und Begründungsverfahren im modernen Recht als soziologisches Problem, Starnberg', an unpublished paper (1978)

Gurland, A.R.L., Kirchheimer, O. and Neumann, F. *The Fate of Small Business in Nazi Germany* (Library of Congress, Washington, D.C., 1943)

Habermas, J. *Strukturwandel der Offentlichkeit* (Luchterhand, Neuwied-Berlin, 1962; 4th edn, 1974)

——— *Zur Logik der Sozialwissenschaften* (Beiheft 5 der Philosophischen Rundschau, 1967) (new edn, Suhrkamp, Frankfurt am Main, 1970) pp. 71-310

——— *Erkenntnis und Interesse* (Suhrkamp, Frankfurt am Main, 1968a; new edn, 1973) (English translation — *Knowledge and Human Interests,* Heinemann, London, 1972)

______ *Technik und Wissenschaft als 'Ideologie'* (Suhrkamp, Frankfurt am Main, 1968b)
______ 'On Systematically Distorted Communication', *Inquiry*, vol. 13 (1970a), pp. 205-18
______ 'Towards a Theory of Communicative Competence', *Inquiry*, vol. 13 (1970b), pp. 360-75
______ *Theorie und Praxis*, 4th edn (Suhrkamp, Frankfurt am Main, 1971a) (English translation — *Theory and Practice*, Heinemann, London 1974)
______ *Philosophisch-politische Profile* (Suhrkamp, Frankfurt am Main, 1971b)
______ *Knowledge and Human Interest* (Heinemann, London, 1972)
______ *Legitimationsprobleme im Spätkapitalismus* (Suhrkamp, Frankfurt am Main, 1973a) (English translation — *Legitimation in Crisis* Beacon Press, Boston, 1975)
______ *Kultur und Kritik* (Suhrkamp, Frankfurt am Main, 1973b)
Habermas, J. and Luhmann, N. *Theorie der Gesellschaft oder Sozialtechnologie – Was leistet die Systemforschung?* (Suhrkamp, Frankfurt am Main, 1971)
______ 'Wahrheitstheorien' in H. Fahrenbach (ed.), *Wirklichkeit und Reflexion* Walter Schulz zum 60. Geburtstag (Neske, Pfullingen, 1973), pp. 211-65
______ 'Sprachspeil, Intention und Bedeutung. Zu Motiven bei Sellars und Wittgenstein' in R. Wiggershaus (ed.), *Sprachanalyse und Soziologie* (Suhrkamp, Frankfurt am Main, 1975), pp. 319-40
______ *Zur Rekonstruktion des historischen Materialismus* (Suhrkamp, Frankfurt am Main, 1976a)
______ 'Was heisst Universalpragmatik?' in K.O. Apel (ed.), *Sprachpragmatik und Philosophie* (Suhrkamp, Frankfurt am Main, 1976b), pp. 174.272
______ 'Universalpragmatische Hinweise auf das System der Ich-Abgrenzungen' in J. Habermas, *Seminar: Kommunikation, Interaktion, Identität* (Suhrkamp, Frankfurt am Main, 1976c)
Horkheimer, M. *Zur Kritik der instrumentellen Vernunft* (Fischer, Frankfurt am Main, 1967)
______ *Critical Theory* (The Seabury Press, New York, 1972)
Horkheimer, M. and Adorno, T.W. *Dialektik der Aufklärung* (Querido, Amsterdam, 1947)
Jay, M. *The Dialectical Imagination. A History of the Frankfurt School and the Institute of Social Research 1923-1950* (Heinemann, London, 1973)
Kirchheimer, O. 'Criminal Law in National Socialist Germany', *Studies in Philosophy and Social Sciences VIII*, vol. 3 (1939)
Marcuse, H. 'Der Kampf gegen den Liberalismus in der totalitären Staatsauffassung' reprinted in H. Marcuse, *Kultur und Gesellschaft I* (Suhrkamp, Frankfurt am Main, 1934), pp. 17-55
Negt, O. 'Zehn Thesen zur marxistischen Rechtstheorie' in H. Rottleuthner (ed.), *Probleme der marxistischen Rechtstheorie* (Suhrkamp, Frankfurt am Main, 1975), pp. 10-71
Neumann, F. *Behemoth: The Structure and Practice of National Socialism, 1933-1944*, rev. edn (Oxford University Press, New York, 1944)
______ *The Democratical and the Authoritarian State: Essays in Political and Legal Theory* (Free Press, New York, 1957)
Rottleuthner, H. *Zur Soziologie richterlichen Handelns II* (1971), reprinted in *Rechtswissenschaft als Sozialwissenschaft* (Fischer, Frankfurt am Main, 1973)
Rechtswissenschaft als Sozialwissenschaft (Fischer, Frankfurt am Main, 1973)
Press, New York, 1939)
Schelsky, H. 'Die Soziologen und das Recht', *Rechtstheorie*, vol. 9 (1978), pp. 1-21
Weber, M. *Rechtssoziologie*, 2nd edn (Luchterhand, Neuwied-Berlin, 1967)

7 The Principle of Exchange as a Basis for the Study of Law

Anthony Heath

The starting point of exchange theory is that most, although not all, social interaction can be conceptualised as the exchange of goods and services analogous, although not identical, to those which take place within the more usual economic context. Peter M. Blau, one of the founders of exchange theory, observed that

> Social exchange can be observed everywhere once we are sensitized by this conception to it, not only in market relations but also in friendship and even in love . . . as well as in many social relations between these extremes in intimacy. Neighbours exchange favors; children, toys; colleagues, assistance; acquaintances, courtesies; politicians, concessions; discussants, ideas; housewives, recipes. The pervasiveness of social exchange makes it tempting to consider all social conduct in terms of exchange, but this would deprive the concept of its distinctive meaning. People do things for fear of other men or for fear of God or for fear of their conscience, and nothing is gained by trying to force such action into a conceptual framework of exchange. (Blau, 1964, pp. 88-9)

The central idea here is that a great many interactions in daily life are, as Blau puts it, 'contingent on rewarding reactions from others' and 'cease when these expected reactions are not forthcoming' (Blau, 1964, p. 6). Excluded from this conception of social exchange is behaviour which is not motivated by the return but by a sense of duty or by some other internalised value. The actions of the man who believes in the rightness of his cause and is not affected by the praise or blame of others cannot be included in the category of exchange. Nor can behaviour which is lacking in motive. The man who really is 'drunk and incapable' and the housewife who has a neurotic compulsion to go shoplifting cannot sensibly be said to be engaging in social exchange, whatever the views of the police or magistrate may be. Social exchange may be pervasive but on this definition it is not all-inclusive.

This aspect of exchange theory comes under what might be called the 'debunking' function of sociology. The sociologist shows that things are not really quite what they seem and that apparently high-minded behaviour has its low-minded side. Thus, in theory, we help our friends voluntarily without thought of return; academics share knowledge out of a disinterested pursuit of truth; politicians advance policies because they are in the national interest; but, in reality, sordid considerations of self-interest are likely to be present too. After a while we are not quite so willing to help the friend who never gets round to reciprocating; we stop sending Christmas cards to people who always forget us. More often than we might like to think, our actions are contingent upon others' reactions.

Various examples of this can be found in the area of law. Thus the police, for example, in theory decide to prosecute on the basis of the strength of their case against the accused and of the evidence that he did, in fact, commit the alleged offence. But, in practice, they will be influenced by other considerations, in particular the willingness of the alleged offender to co-operate. The extreme case is the one where all charges are dropped in return for evidence which will lead to the conviction of other offenders, but this merely represents a dramatic instance of a much more common phenomenon. For example, if the alleged offender is willing to co-operate by pleading guilty, he may be charged with a lesser rather than a more serious offence. Co-operation is thus exchanged for leniency.

There are two conditions which make this kind of transaction possible. First, the police have discretion — they have some latitude in how they enforce the law. Second, the alleged offender has something which the police want — he can present them with a quick and easy conviction which saves time and trouble, or he can admit to a number of other offences which can then be 'cleared up', improving the record of detected crime. In short, each party has something which the other wants, and by exchanging they are both made 'better off' than they would have been without the transaction.

A crucial point is that exchanges of this kind should not be regarded as examples of malpractice and individual failings but rather as structural features of the legal system. It is the fact that the decision to prosecute is vested in the police rather than an independent prosecutor and that promotion or a good reputation are linked to one's success in clearing up offences that makes the exchange viable.

Another example is Parsons's famous comparison of professional and business motivations. He began by contrasting the egoism of the businessman with the apparent altruism of the professional man such as the doctor or lawyer. 'The business man has been thought of as egoistically pursuing his own self-interest regardless of the interests of others, while the professional man was altruistically serving the interests of others regardless of his own.' (Parsons, 1954, p. 36) On this view professional men stood above considerations of financial gain, devoting their lives instead to the 'service' of their fellow men, but against this Parsons argued that the motivation of both groups was essentially the same; it was the pursuit of success, of which a large component was the attainment of high standing in one's occupational group. In business, he wrote,

> this will involve official position in the firm, income, and that rather intangible but none the less important thing 'reputation', as well as perhaps particular 'honors' such as election to clubs and the like. In medicine it will similarly involve size and character of practice, income, hospital and possibly medical school appointment, honors, and again reputation. The essential goals in the two cases would appear to be substantially the same, objective achievement and recognition: the difference lies in the different paths to the similar goals, which are in turn determined by the differences in the respective occupational situations. (Parsons, 1954, p. 44)

In the professions, therefore, the institutional arrangements make it in the self-interest of the actors to engage in apparently altruistic behaviour. The professional who fails to attend to the interests of his clients will lose the respect and esteem of his colleagues and his behaviour will be moulded by these informal sanctions. There is thus a system of 'indirect' exchanges, service to clients' needs being exchanged for reputation among colleagues.

The main point which the exchange theorist would wish to draw from Parsons's example is that intangibles like reputation may be as valuable to men as the monetary incentives which the more familiar economic exchange typically involves. And one of the main aims of exchange theory is to broaden the range of 'valuables' which we recognise to be exchanged. As Homans has suggested, 'from apples and dollars, physical goods and money, [economics] needs to be extrapolated so as to apply, for instance, to the exchange of intangible services for social esteem in a market that is far from perfect' (Homans,

1961, p. 12). True, these intangibles may not always be quite so valuable as monetary benefits. The growth of malpractice suits brought against medical practitioners in the USA suggests that Parsons's analysis may be a rather over-idealised one, itself in need of debunking, but the general point is none the less a valid one: institutional arrangements can, in principle, establish a system of indirect exchanges which make it in the self-interest of some men to spend their time helping others.

The first step in exchange theory, then, is to identify what is actually being exchanged and by whom. Different writers move in different directions. On the one hand, a more sociological tradition examines the morality of social exchange — the norms and expectations which govern the exchange of gifts or favours — and the social implications of this distinctive morality. On the other hand, a more economic tradition applies the techniques of economic analysis and, in particular, the 'rational model of man' to this broader category of social exchange. Let us consider these in turn. (The following two sections are based on Heath, 1976.)

Morality of Social Exchange

Economic exchange in our society is governed by a complex system of legal rules, and social exchange too is regulated by an analogous, although less explicit, code of rules. Blau suggested two rules which he saw as fundamental to social, as opposed to economic, exchange. The first is the obligation to make a return. This is the famous norm of reciprocity. The man who accepts a favour thereby incurs a moral debt which thus, in a sense, gives the donor a hold over him. The second is the rule that the nature of the return cannot be bargained about but must be left to the discretion of the one who makes it. This is what often gives social exchange its deceptive appearance of voluntary generosity. Blau summarises his position as follows:

> Social exchange differs in important ways from strictly economic exchange. The basic and most crucial distinction is that social exchange entails *unspecified* obligations. The prototype of an economic transaction rests on a formal contract that stipulates the exact quantities to be exchanged . . . Social exchange, in contrast, involves the principle that one person does another a favor, and while there is a general expectation of some future return, its exact

nature is definitely *not* stipulated in advance. (Blau, 1964, p. 93, italics in the original)

This distinctive feature of social exchange, Blau goes on to argue, means that it must be based on trust; the giver can never be sure that he will receive an appropriate return. But if reciprocation does occur the trust between the participants is strengthened and this trust may form the basis for further and perhaps more significant transactions. Social exchange, then, unlike purely economic exchange, gradually transforms the relations between the partners and establishes bonds of fellowship between them.

To determine how far these considerations affect transactions between police and offenders would be an interesting ethnographic exercise. Does overt bargaining occur, and is it regarded as improper by the participants or the public? To the lay mind corruption might well be thought to begin when explicit bargains are put to the defendant in place of more general 'understandings' which he is at liberty to disregard. Again, does the acceptance of favours from informants in the underworld place the police officer under a diffuse moral obligation which might, in principle, compromise his independence? True, information received may be paid for in cash, but the sociological analysis of these transactions suggests that they cannot be regarded as purely economic exchanges which have no further implications for the relations between the participants.

A hypothesis which the sociologist might wish to advance, therefore, is that the nature of the policeman's task, and the incentives which the official criteria for promotion place before him, make it in his self-interest to engage in social exchange with potential or actual offenders and their associates and thus generate a new social relationship with them which makes him vulnerable to corruption. On this view it would be naive to expect to have a police force which could be both incorruptible and efficient in the detection of crime. Vulnerability to corruption may be an inevitable price of efficiency.

Economic Analysis of Exchange

Once so much social interaction is conceptualised as an exchange of goods and services, it is tempting to apply the techniques of analysis which have served the economist so well in the analysis of economic transactions. The corner-stone of these techniques is the theory of rational choice. Broadly speaking, it begins by assuming that men have given goals, wants or 'utility functions' (they come down to much the same thing). It then assumes that these goals cannot all be equally realised — men live in a world of scarcity and must select between alternative courses of action — and that men will therefore choose the course which has the highest 'pay-off'. To do so is to choose rationally. In Robbins's much-quoted words, economics is a 'science which studies human behaviour as a relationship between ends and scarce means which have alternative uses' (Robbins, 1932, p. 15), and it is therefore a science which is appropriate wherever scarcity and choice apply and not uniquely to transactions in conventional economic markets.

The economic analysis of rational choice next makes a basic distinction between risky and riskless choices. Where there is no risk each course of action open to the individual has a single known outcome or consequence, whereas in the case of risky choices a number of possible outcomes may follow from any given course of action. In situations of risk the economist assumes that numerical probabilities can be assigned to the likelihoods of each of the various outcomes occurring — if they cannot he defines the situation as one of uncertainty and holds that alternative models of rationality (derived from game theory) must be employed. These will not be discussed here.

In the cases of riskless and risky choices, however, the economist puts forward two simple principles of rationality. In the former case he merely assumes that the individual will rank all the options open to him in order of preference and will then select the one that comes at the top of his list. This is usually called the principle of 'utility maximisation': to choose the most preferred option is to choose the one that yields most utility. In the latter case the principle is somewhat more complicated. It states that the individual should weight the utility of each possible outcome by the probability of its occurrence and should then choose the course of action whose combined outcomes have the highest weighted utility. This is called the principle of *expected* utility maximisation. The basic idea is still the same: compare the pay-offs of alternative courses of action and choose the one which yields the highest pay-off. In computing these pay-offs, however, the individual has to take into account all the possible consequences of a given act, their utilities, and their probabilities of occurrence. (For some problems with these computations see Heath, 1974.)

So far in this section nothing has been said about exchange itself. Indeed, the theory of rational choice can be applied as well to interactions with the non-human environment where we can hardly talk of exchange — for example, the decision whether to take an umbrella or not — as it can be to social exchange. But the basic economic analysis of exchange follows easily enough. All it says is that the transaction will take place only if *both* partners believe it to yield the highest pay-off of all the options currently open to them. The exchange, therefore, enables both participants to be better off than they would have been without it. We should note, of course, that this does not necessarily mean that they will be better off than they were *before*. The alleged offender may be better off pleading guilty to a lesser charge than guilty to a more serious one — it may be the best option currently open — but the exchange certainly will not make him better off than he was before being apprehended. The distinction may be viewed as one between a voluntary and a coerced exchange (see Heath, 1976, p. 19). The Black youth stopped 'on sus' by the Special Patrol Group faces a coerced transaction; whatever he does now he is likely to be worse off than if he had been able to continue on his way unmolested. And such coerced exchanges are likely to have diametrically opposed consequences and social implications from those described by Blau in the case of the voluntary exchange of favours.

I shall not attempt here to describe the many further steps which have been taken in the 'pure theory' of the sociology or economics of exchange. Instead, I shall take three examples in the area of law and law enforcement. First, I shall look at the rational choice analysis of crime such as has been put forward by economists such as Becker (1976) and Ehrlich (1973). Second, I shall consider the social exchanges involved in plea bargaining as described by Baldwin and McConville (1977), and third, I shall take the economic analysis of law presented by Posner (1973).

Rational Choice Theory of Crime

Gary Becker has suggested that 'a useful theory of criminal behavior can dispense with special theories of anomie, psychological inadequacies, or inheritance of special traits and simply extend the economist's usual analysis of choice' (Becker, 1976, p. 40). In deciding whether or not to commit an offence a potential offender can be thought of as comparing the pay-offs from criminal and non-criminal activities. Crime is a risky activity and so the principle of expected utility maximisation is appropriate. The pay-off from criminal activity will clearly include the likely gains from successful crime, but against this must be set the severity of the punishment, if caught and convicted, weighted by the probability of such arrest and conviction. The net pay-off from crime must then be compared with the alternative uses to which the time spent on crime could have been put, such as engaging in legitimate paid employment (if any is available), watching television (if he has one), or aimlessly wandering the streets (if homeless and unemployed).

There are a number of immediate inferences which can be drawn from this analysis. Crime will tend to be more common among those for whom the 'opportunity cost' as economists call it (that is the utility of the alternative uses to which the time could have been spent) is low. In other words, we would expect higher crime rates among those with poor job opportunities, poor leisure outlets, unpleasant home conditions, and the like. Furthermore, we would expect that the higher the probability that the commission of a given type of offence will be followed by arrest and conviction, the less likely the individual is to commit such an offence. Similarly, the greater the likely punishment is, the greater will be the deterrent effect. And of course there is some evidence that this is the case. The most common offences are those for which the penalties and the probabilities of conviction are low.

While it is perhaps easiest to appreciate this analysis in the context of crime motivated by pecuniary considerations, there is no need to restrict it in this way. It is at least a good hypothesis that crimes against the person, just as much as crimes against property, will be deterred by high rates of conviction or harsh penalties. There is also good evidence that sexual offences are related to the alternative opportunities for legitimate sexual activity. Svalastoga, in his study of rape in Denmark, found that rape was primarily committed by single men; was related to the sex ratio among unmarried persons; was lower in the capital city where the alternative of commercial prostitution was more readily available; was most common among unskilled or rural workers of whom, Svalastoga concluded, 'it is hard to escape the conclusion that the violence of this group is a tool used by a category of people who have less chance than most people to learn more refined ways of social persuasion or to acquire the means whereby favours are bought and not taken by force' (Svalastoga, 1968, p. 286).

Prima facie, then, there is considerable plausibility in the rational-choice approach to crime. There are, however, some difficulties with it. There are grounds for believing that crime rates are more responsive to changes in the probability of detection than in the severity of punishment. This at first seems inconsistent with the basic principle of expected utility maximisation. To rescue the approach the economists have introduced the concept of 'risk preference'. Consider two alternative offences which yield identical expected utility to a particular offender, but in one of which this is obtained by a mild punishment weighted by a high probability of conviction and in the other of which the same result is obtained by a harsh punishment weighted by a lower probability of conviction. The 'risk preferer' is defined as the man who will choose to commit the second offence, the 'risk avoider' as the man who will choose the first offence, and the individual who is 'risk neutral' is the one who is indifferent between the two alternative crimes. It can be seen that, if offenders and potential offenders are risk preferers, increasing the likelihood of detection and conviction will have a greater deterrent effect, and conversely if they are risk avoiders. By definition, only if they are risk neutral will the predictions of the basic principle of expected utility maximisation hold. Unfortunately there is no independent empirical evidence that offenders actually are risk preferers.

An alternative answer to the problem is to take account of what is called the 'rate of time discount'. Other things being equal, the utility of a distant event is less than that of an identical present event — we tend to discount future gains or losses, and the more distant the future benefit or cost is the less weight it has in our present calculations. Increasing the length of prison sentences, therefore, will have relatively little effect since the additional time spent in prison is going to be even further in the future and thus even more heavily discounted. It is often claimed that the social groups from whom most convicted offenders are drawn have a relatively high rate of time discount — in the language of sociologists they prefer present to deferred gratification — and thus lengthening potential sentences is likely to be particularly inappropriate for this group. We might add that this analysis yields two further testable inferences: the deterrent effect of increasing prison sentences will be less than that of increasing fines but will be greater for white-collar than for blue-collar offenders.

Negotiated Justice as Exchange

'Negotiated justice' has become the general term for the kind of transaction where the defendant is persuaded by counsel, sometimes even when he protests his innocence, to plead guilty in return for a lesser sentence. It is a practice which Baldwin and McConville have convincingly shown to be rather widespread, but one which they find objectionable. They argue that 'the established practice of allowing some reduction in sentence in return for a plea of guilty has allowed a situation to arise (and in one sense may be seen to have created it) in which unfair pressures have been placed upon defendants to plead guilty' (Baldwin and McConville, 1977, p. 7).

To explain the occurrence of the practice Baldwin and McConville turn to look at the costs and benefits which each side obtains. Although they do not actually use the language of rational choice, theirs is none the less a layman's attempt to use an economic model of exchange. In the case of the defendants they argue that 'the greater the disparities, or, more accurately, the anticipated disparities, between sentences following a guilty and a not guilty plea, the greater the risk that innocent defendants will plead guilty' (p. 107). In other words, defendants are faced by a situation of risk if they plead not guilty and while they transform the possibility of conviction into a certainty by changing their plea, they may be more than compensated by the fact that this increase in probability is now weighting a smaller sentence.

But it is not enough to show what is the pay-off for the defendant. If the transaction is to occur it must also be the best alternative course of action open to counsel as well. If he had, for example, a financial stake in longer trials, we might instead expect him to put pressure on the defendant to plead not guilty. Baldwin and McConville argue as follows:

> It is also arguable that counsel's primary interests inevitably lie with the court system and not with the defendant . . . There is often great pressure upon counsel to deliver what the system wants, and one of the over-riding requirements is, as we see it, administrative efficiency, which is greatly assisted by — indeed in large part dependent upon — a steady flow of guilty pleas. The discount system is itself one manifestation of this concern. It may well benefit counsel, who may be briefed for the prosecution on the next case, to work within the administrative goals of the system, to ensure a steady flow of cases. (Baldwin and McConville, 1977, p. 111)

Both sides thus benefit from the negotiation, although it is hard to see on this account why it is in any way unfair. It is only if there is some risk of conviction if he pleads not guilty that the defendant, on the pure rational choice model, could possibly find the expected utility of a guilty plea to be greater than that of the not-guilty plea. If he is sure of his innocence there is no good reason, short of maladministration of justice, for changing his plea.

One response to this, of course, is that there may always be some possibility of an 'error' in the administration of justice if the defendant pleads guilty. However sure he is of his innocence he is never going to be completely certain of an acquittal. There is always an element of risk which thus gives the discount argument some force. However, there is another reason, apart from error, for agreeing with Baldwin and McConville's misapprehensions. Suppose that the defendant really is guilty but that the evidence against him is unclear. There is thus an unambiguous situation of risk. Now the principle of expected utility maximisation tells the defendant to compare the two alternative courses of action, multiply the probability by the utility in each case, and choose the one with the greater pay-off (or, in this case, the smaller negative pay-off). Now this weighting of utility by probability is all very well as a rather general account of what people tend to do in this kind of situation (which is all that the economist usually needs), but it clearly will not do as a literal description of the defendant's thought processes. Indeed, strictly speaking it will be an illegitimate and impossible task for him unless he has an interval scale of utility and a ratio scale of probability (for further details of this see Heath, 1974). But, in practice, the defendant will never have more than *ordinal* scales; he will know that the probability of conviction is increased if he pleads guilty, but not by how much it is increased, and he will know that the size of the sentence will be reduced, but again not by how much. He has to balance the increase against the decrease, but there is no way in which he can make them commensurable and, given that he only has ordinal rankings of the probabilities and sentences, application of the principle of expected utility maximisation becomes logically unsound. He is faced with what might be called an *impossible* decision.

It is my hypothesis that, when faced with balanced or impossible decisions of this kind, people resort to a variety of supplementary rules or procedures for coping with the situation. Thus they may search for further information or for precedents, postpone the decision (probably the most common tactic) or delegate it to others. But in the present example there is no further information to be collected and postponement is not a viable option. The tendency will therefore be to delegate the decision to someone 'who should know better' (although, in fact, the decision is just as much an impossible one for anyone else). There is evidence that this happens in transactions between professionals and clients, and Baldwin and McConville also happen to show that it is precisely what some of the defendants they interviewed did. They allowed their barristers to make the decision for them. As one defendant reported, 'I agreed to plead guilty but it wasn't my decision; I had no choice about it' (Baldwin and McConville, 1977, p. 50).

The theory of 'impossible decisions' explains why so many defendants allowed themselves to be persuaded by their barristers to change their plea. They had no rational grounds for making the decision themselves, and it is this which made them vulnerable to the suggestions of counsel and introduced an element of impropriety. But why should counsel be blamed? The decision is equally impossible for him. Baldwin and McConville cannot actually show that their advice was wrong and not in the defendant's best interests.

The answer, of course, is that there are incentives on counsel to attend to other considerations than his client's. But Baldwin and McConville's account of the pay-offs facing counsel are excessively vague. There is no explicit account of how the pressure is put on him to work with the administrative goals of the system. Does he have better promotion chances if he ensures a steady flow of cases? Does he earn more money? Does he secure better working relations from court officials? Practical pay-offs of this kind are surely needed rather than a nebulous 'shared interest'.

In fact Baldwin and McConville do suggest a more practical interest which counsel has, namely lack of familiarity with the case.

> The demands of the court and of their practice in general are such that few barristers can be sure, even if the brief is delivered in good time, that they will be available to conduct a particular defence. Counsel may, therefore, be understandably reluctant to spend an undue amount of time on a case ... The result is, as many solicitors have told us, that some barristers are often not sufficiently familiar with the brief properly to advise the defendant ... Another difficulty is that the barrister who ultimately undertakes the defence is quite often not the person initially selected. In such cases, the brief is commonly returned so late that it is almost impossible for a barrister to give the case adequate consideration. Because of lack of preparation, it is possible that some barristers may be reluctant to undertake the defence of a case in court. (Baldwin and McConville, 1977, pp. 110-11)

Lack of familiarity exposes the barrister to the possible ridicule of his fellows if he puts up an inept performance in court. His reputation may suffer, and this gives him a good practical reason for urging guilty pleas on his client.

For Baldwin and McConville the discount principle is the main villain of the piece and the institution which they wish to reform. But if my analysis is sound, the problem is not quite so simple. On the one hand, abolition of the discount principle would not eliminate the difficulty faced by defendants if there were other sources of uncertainty, for example, if the police were still allowed to vary the charge according to the defendant's willingness to co-operate. And on the other hand, the more objectionable features of the system could be removed if there were no incentive on barristers to influence the defendant's plea. It is, moreover, something of a scandal in its own right if counsel are regularly ill-prepared, and surely this should be the target of reform. Baldwin and McConville do not always remember that there have to be two sides to any negotiation and that reform can therefore be directed at either side. One possibility here would be to allow solicitors to do more of the defence than they customarily do at present. They are more likely to be familiar with the case, and Baldwin and McConville's own evidence shows that it is the barristers rather than the solicitors who put pressure on the defendants to change their pleas. There is at least as good a case for reforming the arrangements for defence as for principles of sentencing.

Economic Analysis of Law

Perhaps the most famous example of the application of an economic approach to the study of law is Posner's *Economic Analysis of Law* (1973). It is, however, a very different kind of exercise from the two which we have looked at so far and raises distinctly different issues. To be sure, Posner, like exchange theorists such as Blau and Homans, attempts to apply economic analysis to examples of social behaviour outside the usual scope of the market, but there the similarity stops.

The famous example of the engine sparks will make Posner's approach clear. He argues as follows:

> If a railroad is to enjoy the exclusive use of its right of way it must be permitted to emit engine sparks without legal limitation. The value of its property will be impaired otherwise. But if it is permitted to emit engine sparks, the value of adjacent farmland will be impaired

> because of the fire hazard created by the sparks. Is the emission of sparks an incident of the railroad's property right or an invasion of the farmer's? And does anything turn on the answer?

Posner's answer is to suggest a general economic principle for deciding in cases of conflicting land or other property use which party shall have the right to exclude the other. The right, he says, should be assigned to the party whose use is more valuable. Thus

> Suppose that the right to emit sparks, by enabling the railroad to dispense with costly spark-arresting equipment, would increase the value of its property by $100 but reduce the value of the farmer's property by $50 because it would prevent him from growing crops close to the tracks. If the farmer has a legal right to be free from engine sparks, the railroad presumably will offer to pay and the farmer will accept compensation for the surrender of his right. Since the right to prevent spark emissions is worth only $50 to the farmer but imposes costs on the railroad of $100, a sale of the farmer's right at any price between $50 and $100 will make both parties better off. If instead of the farmer's having a right to be free from sparks the railroad has a legal right to emit sparks, no transaction will occur. The farmer will not pay more than $50 for the railroad's right and the railroad will not accept less than $100. Thus, whichever way the legal right is assigned, the result, in terms of resource use, is the same: the railroad emits sparks and the farmer moves his crop.

It can be seen that Posner is using the same general principle of exchange that we described earlier: an exchange will take place only if both parties expect to be made better off by it than they would in its absence. In this case both parties would be better off if the railroad buys the right to emit sparks from the farmer at some price between $50 and $100. Now why should the law intervene here? Why should not our two participants go ahead and make the exchange if they wish? The answer lies in transaction costs. The process of exchanging property rights is itself costly, and if, in the present case, it costs more than $50, it will not be worthwhile for the railroad to undertake the transaction. The right is worth only $100 to him, and if the total cost, that is the price plus transaction cost, comes to more than this, there is no point in going ahead. But this, argues Posner, will lead to a maldistribution of resources. The right to emit sparks is more valuable to the railroad. If the farmer retains it, and no exchange takes place because of the transaction costs, we are clearly in a suboptimum position. Posner's point is that voluntary exchange will, in the absence of external impediments, lead to the optimum allocation of resources and the law should therefore be used to enable the participants to get as close as possible to the same end-state that voluntary exchange would achieve. Thus he asserts:

> The right should be assigned to the party whose use is more valuable — the party, stated otherwise, for whom discontinuance of the interference would be most costly. By assigning rights in accordance with this principle the law can anticipate and thus obviate the necessity for a market transaction.

Posner is thus making the extremely important point that the law is not needed if the voluntary actions of self-interested individuals will get to the desired result in any event: what it can do is enable men to get to a desirable result that they could not otherwise reach. The classic example here is the prisoners' dilemma. I imagine that this is familiar to most people and I will not therefore describe it at length. The main point is that, in the absence of any social rules, the rational self-interested behaviour of the two prisoners will lead to what is, for them, the joint worse outcome, namely substantial periods of imprisonment for both of them. Only if there is a rule prohibiting confessions can they reach their joint optimum. One point of social rules (although by no means the only one) may be to enable people to reach optima that they could not otherwise attain.

But let us return to Posner. His primary focus is not the explanatory task of explaining why the law is what it is (although he does in passing raise this), but the normative task of suggesting what the law *should* be like. He is engaged in an application of what is known as welfare economics, whereas exchange theorists have always tended to apply what is usually called positive economics. He is not making predictions that can be empirically refuted but ethical conclusions whose acceptance must depend on the persuasiveness of the premisses.

This in itself is no bad thing. If welfare economics is a legitimate activity, and I believe that it is, then it would seem at least as reasonable to extend its application to the legal field as it is to extend any other aspect of the economic approach. If exchange theorists have neglected welfare economics, then so much the worse for them. The crucial point, however, is that in evaluating an ethical theory of this kind a different set of criteria must be used. What we must do is scrutinise the premisses upon which the ethical edifice is built to see if they square with our own moral intuitions. Now the crucial premiss upon which Posner's edifice is built is that value is to be measured by the consumer's willingness to pay. Thus he states that 'efficiency is a technical term: it means exploiting economic resources in such a way that human satisfaction as measured by aggregate consumer willingness to pay for goods and services is maximized. Value too is defined by willingness to pay.' Now we must allow Posner his own moral intuitions, but they may not be widespread. Leff (1974) brings out the point neatly:

> Let us say that a starving man approaches a loaf of bread held by an armed baker. Another potential buyer is there. The baker institutes an auction; he wants cash only (having too great doubts about the starveling's health to be interested in granting credit). The poor man gropes in his pockets and comes up with a dollar. The other bidder immediately takes out $1.01 and makes off with the bread. Now under Posner's definitional system we must say that the 'value' of the bread was no more than a dollar to the poor man because he was 'unwilling' to pay more than that. An observer not bound within that particular definitional structure might find it somehow more illuminating to characterise the poor man's failure as being the result of being unable to pay more than a dollar. But one cannot, consistent with Posner's system, say any such thing.

Fortunately, there is nothing in exchange theory which requires us to equate value with willingness to pay. True, most exchange theorists would agree that what a man is prepared to do is often the best guide to what his values are, but a man may be prepared to do more things than simply hand over money. After all, if the baker had been unarmed, the starveling might have been prepared to mug him in order to obtain the bread, and it would not be all that far-fetched to suggest that his willingness to engage in a more extreme form of action indicates that the bread had greater value for him.

On this revised account we might suggest that the most efficient allocation of resources is that where those who are prepared to go to the most extreme lengths to get things should be allowed to keep them. After all, if the unarmed baker hands over the bread to the starving man they are presumably engaging in a transaction which makes both of them better off than they would be in any of the alternatives at that moment open to them. The baker prefers to hand over the bread rather than be mugged, and the starving man prefers to get his hands on the bread and so take his chance on being caught and convicted for theft. True, this does not come within Blau's definition of exchange, for he specifically excluded actions taken for fear of another man, but is the exclusion sensible? Blau (1964) writes:

> An individual may give another money because the other stands in front of him with a gun in a holdup. While this could be conceptualised as an exchange of his money for his life, it seems preferable to exclude the result of physical coercion from the range of social conduct encompassed by the term 'exchange'.

But I am not convinced that it is preferable. The same principles of rational choice presumably apply to these 'coerced transactions' as much as they do to voluntary ones. By concentrating on voluntary transactions rather than coerced ones, it seems to me that both Blau and Posner are tending to lend support to the view that 'all is for the best in this best of all possible worlds'. If people can be made better off, they would presumably enter into voluntary exchanges in order to do so. All that needs to be done to achieve this idyllic state of affairs is to remove all impediments to voluntary exchange. But this, of course, is to ignore the ethical problem that some people, even when impediments to voluntary exchange are removed, may be desperate for things that they cannot reach by voluntary exchange.

Where, then, does this leave us? One strategy is to return to classical utilitarianism where the criterion for judging social arrangements such as laws is aggregate utility. Thus if the bread increases the starving man's happiness more than the rich man's, the bread should go to him. Quite aside from philosophical objections to utilitarianism, however, the social scientist is likely to object to the impossibility of making inter-personal comparisons of utility. It is this that led the economists to positions like Posner's which do not make interpersonal comparisons of utility. For Posner the crucial idea is that situation A is preferable to situation B if those who gain in the switch from B to A could adequately compensate those who lose in the switch and still be better off. We need intra-personal comparisons for this but no more.

This deals splendidly with the case of the engine sparks, and it is not a principle which we should reject. It is not, however, a *sufficient* principle for dealing with ethical issues, as the case of our starving man shows. Alas, I am in no position to suggest what a sufficient principle would be. Indeed, I suspect that it is dangerous to suppose that there might be one. Rather, the programme which I would wish to sketch out for exchange theory would be to separate the ethical from the empirical issues. Thus we have the empirical task of establishing what the costs and benefits of different legal arrangements are for those subject to them. What I have in mind here is a cost-benefit analysis of law in which costs and benefits are not defined economically but in terms of the participants' own subjective experience of them as costs and benefits. Thus the stigma of poverty would have to be included just as much as the financial costs of poverty.

This programme will clearly be somewhat different from, and additional to, the explanatory task that I had assigned exchange theory earlier. We are not trying to explain why the law is the way it is but rather to describe what the pay-offs of different legal arrangements are for those affected. But, in keeping with the general orientation of exchange theory, the pay-offs must be extended to include intangibles, such as social honour and reputation, as well as material ones. The enterprise is not unlike the functionalist one of discovering the unintended consequences of different social institutions, but whereas the functionalist is concerned with the consequences for that nebulous entity, society, the exchange theory is concerned with its consequences for the different individuals and groups involved. Having completed this empirical task (and these five words hide an enormously complex and difficult task), we can proceed to the ethical evaluation of the different sets of consequences. I do not believe that there are any elegant principles like Posner's that can do the whole job for us. If the exchange theorist has anything to offer at this point it is again the empirical investigation of what ethical principles members of society themselves believe to be appropriate. Social justice in exchange has been extensively studied by writers such as Homans and Blau, but no one pretends that it is any substitute for ethical argument.

Bibliography

Baldwin, J. and McConville, M. *Negotiated Justice: Pressures to Plead Guilty* (Martin Robertson, London, 1977)

Becker, G.S. 'Crime and Punishment: an Economic Approach' in G.S. Becker, *The Economic Approach to Human Behavior* (University of Chicago Press, Chicago, 1976), pp. 39-85

Blau, P.M. *Exchange and Power in Social Life* (Wiley, New York, 1964)

Ehrlich, I. 'Participation in Illegitimate Activities: a Theoretical and Empirical Investigation', *Journal of Political Economy*, vol. 81 (1973), pp. 521-65

Heath, A.F. 'The Rational Model of Man', *European Journal of Sociology*, vol. 15 (1974), pp. 184-205

______ *Rational Choice and Social Exchange* (Cambridge University Press, Cambridge, 1976)

Homans, G.C. *Social Behaviour: Its Elementary Forms* (Routledge and Kegan Paul, London, 1961)

Leff, A.A. 'Economic Analysis of Law: Some Realism about Nominalism', *Virginia Law Review,* vol. 60 (1974), pp. 451-82

Parsons, T. 'The Professions and Social Structure' in T. Parsons, *Essays In Sociological Theory* rev. edn (Free Press, New York, 1954), pp. 34-49

Posner, R.A. *Economic Analysis of Law* (Little Brown, Boston, 1973; see now 2nd edn, 1977)

Robbins, L. *An Essay on the Nature and Significance of Economic Science* (Macmillan, London, 1932)

Svalastoga, K. 'Rape and Social Structure' in M. Truzzi (ed.), *Sociology and Everyday Life* (Prentice-Hall, Englewood Cliffs, 1968), pp. 279-89

8 Law as a Social Phenomenon

David N. Schiff

The interplay between legal theory and sociological theory can be researched for many different reasons, but an exploration of sociological theory by a legal theorist needs some explanation. My concern is not with sociological theory as such, it is with the development of a working model by which law may be understood as a social phenomenon. It might be that there are some connecting links between legal and sociological theory which have been ignored, been evaded, remained disguised, or for some reason or other been misconceived. I hold the view about 'misconceptions'; the view that law is normative, that law is an ought, and that the methodology of much traditional sociology is inappropriate for the study of such a normative, institutional phenomenon. However, I also hold the view that certain approaches within sociology are particularly apposite for the study of law as a social phenomenon. What is apposite is the theme of this article.

Social Behaviour and Law

Can law be studied in terms of behaviour? What relevance has the relationship between the behaviour the law prescribes and actual behaviour for the social study of law? Is it possible to draw any conclusions about law from facts which demonstrate that certain behaviour conforms to it, while other behaviour deviates? Does it matter that one may be able to show that a good number of people have changed their behaviour in accordance with a change in the law? Many questions of this nature have been answered in the positive by those wishing to study law as a social phenomenon. For example, Timasheff writes 'in general, legal norms actually determine human behaviour in society' (Timasheff, 1937, p. 226). Underlying a significant proportion of legislation is the assumption that there is some link between the behavioural patterns embodied in the law, and the actual behaviour of individuals. Surely it is trite to question that assumption. If tomorrow a statute were passed which required that one should drive on the right, and we all did so, or at least the vast majority, can it be questioned that the law affected behaviour, and even more, that the law was effective in so doing? However, two uncertainties about the relationship between law and behaviour remain. How does law affect behaviour and how can that effect be measured? For it is rarely the case that the behaviour required by a new law is as clear-cut, as obvious, as that in my example. Take the Race Relations Acts 1965, 1968 and 1976: the non-discriminatory behaviour required is difficult to perceive, the relationship between overt and covert discrimination, between that discrimination which remains lawful and the unlawful, between racial and non-racial discrimination, all cloud the actual behaviour referred to in the Acts. We need to know how law affects behaviour and how that effect can be measured in order to be able to explain what law does. But can we do either of these things?

How does Law Affect Behaviour?

The standard argument is that law is a means of social control and contributes to the creation or maintenance of social order. That argument rests on the ability of law to control behaviour and to create uniformity in behaviour. It has often been suggested that one of the characteristics of law which distinguish it from other normative control mechanisms is the sanction, and that law functions to create order by application of the sanction for those who deviate and by dread of the sanction for those who obey. Of course, it may be that people obey for other reasons than fear, and it is not sufficient to measure the control function of law by the number of people who obey through fear, indeed fear in any positive sense may only be part of the reasons of a few people's obedience. This argument raises a whole set of questions about the relationship between legal and social norms about which there is a considerable literature. Some jurists have inclined to the view that the indirect effect of fear of sanction is significant. For example, Karl Olivecrona writes

> this does not, however, imply that we live under an ever-present sense of fear of the legal force. The psychological situation is normally of another kind. The human mind has a marvellous adaptability. It is intolerable to live under the stress of constant fear.

> Consciously or unconsciously we try to avoid it by adjusting ourselves to the prevailing conditions. (Olivecrona, 1939, p. 147)

If law's violence and its ability to control is the physical sanction, and the application of the sanction is a fact in the world of time and space, is the sanction the key to the relation between law and behaviour? If people obey because of use of or fear of the sanction, why do those who carry out the sanction obey? If they do so because of another sanction, why do those who impose that sanction obey? An infinite regression is involved. There is also a pervasive socially relevant argument. The facts of obedience and disobedience and their related sanctions or fear of sanctions are only relevant once it is shown that the legal rule and its sanction or provision for enforcement is known or appreciated, simply because people might or might not have acted in that way despite the legal rule. It may be that the sanction is crucial, but can it be proved to be so? Only if its (the sanction's) impact can be measured.

Can Law's Impact be Measured?

A logical problem is involved in the desire to measure legal impact. Law is an ought, it is a set of normative ideas which exist in the heads of those who make, apply or feel obligated to them. Behaviour or regularity is a matter of fact, but in logical terms you cannot derive that behaviour (that fact) from a law (that norm), since the fact and the norm are mutually non-logically derivative.[1] Equally, in logical terms, the fact that a sanction will be applied is not derivative from the legal norm that it ought to be applied. If it cannot logically be deduced that someone acted in a particular way because of a particular law, can it be shown as an effect (the action) of a cause (the law)? The answer to be given here is no: that social research cannot demonstrate a causal relationship between the application of past or future sanctions, the premiss of a legal norm, and the effect of compliance and non-compliance. The argument on which this conclusion is based is that since no logical deduction can be based on a directive statement (such as law) whereby logical deduction must be premised on descriptive statements, and since cause and effect analysis assumes the state of logic just as, in Merleau-Ponty's terms, all scientific discourse presupposes the 'pre-objective' world (see Kullman and Taylor, 1969, pp. 116-37), cause and effect research equally requires to be premised by descriptive statements. This argument forms part of a wider set of arguments which amount to a phenomenological critique of 'objective meaning' (Schutz, 1972, pp. 31-8, 241-9), and of cause and effect methodology within social scientific inquiry (Natanson, 1970, ch. 3; Schutz, 1974, ch. 4; Zaner, 1970, ch. 1). It presents the need to underpin the analysis of law's effects by asking foundational questions about the 'intentionality' of law, its inter-subjective meaning (see Gurwitsch, 1973, pp. 102-19; Natanson, 1973, ch. 5).

There are standard ways in which the dilemma presented by such a critique, between the 'is' of action and the objective world and the 'ought' of consciousness and directives such as law, can be circumvented. In philosophical terms 'if' clauses may be used, in sociological terms 'operational definitions' may be formulated. Neither of these is, however, able to resolve the problem. For example, I agree with David Silverman's argument that 'attempts to construct operational definitions of different forms of the family (for example, nuclear, extended) and then to establish social structural causes and effects of such forms are logically misguided' (Silverman, 1972, p. 5). In this sense an equation between social control and social order may be formulated, but to include legal control in such an equation is a reformulation inconsistent with logical analysis. Hence law's impact cannot be measured in a logico-meaningful way, and neither can it be shown that law causes behaviour either in conformity to or deviant from it. So, in these terms, one cannot analyse social behaviour as law governed. Clearly it is nonsense to talk of law compelling obedience, as there is no natural consequence of obedience to law following the making of a law. However, there is something necessary and obvious in the idea that some correspondence between law and behaviour exists. It is to an alternative explanation of this correspondence that I now turn.

Law and Reality

Jurisprudence has been bedevilled by the notion of dualism in law. This dualism finds expression in contrasts such as that between the ideal and the real in law, validity and efficacy of law, norm and fact as law. It is the relation between these contrasts as part of concepts of law that puzzles those who have recognised them. Whereas a jurist such as Kelsen denies law's reality or factitivity:

> A sociological concept of law is just as impossible as a mathematical concept of a biological phenomenon or an ethical concept of the physical phenomenon of the freely falling body. Hence every attempt to create sociology of law must result in simply speaking, in

> a general way, of social phenomena. (Kelsen, 1915, cited in Timasheff, 1939, p. 22)

others have reacted by inclining to a dualistic view of the nature of law:

> The fact that one recognizes the normative character of law, conceiving of law as a system of binding norms, does not in itself afford any solution to the problem of the relation of law to reality. For even if law must be conceived as an ideal content of mind, this of course, does not prevent the law being characterized at the same time by its positivity. Its foundations are factual decisions, modes of action, feelings of obligation, in short psycho-physical realities. The problem arises precisely because law — as Kelsen has expressed it — appears both as 'Sollen' and as 'Sein', in spite of the fact that these two categories logically exclude one another. (Castberg, 1957, p. 36)

A dualistic view of the nature of law has significant implications for the social study of law. For it implies that law is not simply a fact, and that legal impact cannot be measured simply in factual terms. An examination of the nature of law is, then, a prerequisite to the understanding of law as a social phenomenon and thereby a prerequisite to an examination of what law does. As such a conceptual question rather than an empirical one is the basis of such study. In traditional terms the requirement is for recognition of 'the distinctively legal' as an idea. As Selznick has argued 'whatever the merits of the sociological school in having called attention to the need for a realistic jurisprudence, the failure to offer a theory of the distinctively legal has been its cardinal weakness' (Selznick, 1968, p. 50). However, so that law as a social phenomenon can be understood within its social context as 'the construction of social reality inclusive of legal reality' (Schiff, 1976, p. 294), what needs to be attained is a methodological approach to the study of social phenomena which, without misconstruing legal phenomena, allows for their interrelated study. Such a methodological approach must be suited to the study of law as normative, as conceptual, as an ought, as an ideal, as ideas in people's minds.

The Nature of Action

'In "action" is included all human behaviour when and in so far as the acting individual attaches a subjective meaning to it' (Weber, 1947, p. 88). Can Weber's notion of *Verstehen* be applied to law? In what sense do we as individuals attach subjective meanings to legal phenomena?

When we talk of acting 'lawfully' or 'unlawfully' what do we mean? The normative ideas embodied in the rules of law may represent to us a number of different things, depending on the way we conceive of law, our knowledge of law or laws, our opinions, our dispositions, in effect, our attitudes. Attitude here is not meant to include purpose, but other elements that make up our consciousness about law, our way of looking at it. The dispositional states that we represent to the external world by acting or behaving in certain ways that are normative in the sense that they include our values and ideas of what we ought or ought not to do, our sentiments, our meanings. The normative is characteristic both of law itself, and the dispositional states of mind we have about it.

Winch has argued that many of the theoretical issues raised in the social sciences belong to philosophy rather than science. As such they can only be settled by *a priori* reasoning rather than empiricism. For example, he says:

> the central problem of sociology, that of giving an account of the nature of social phenomena in general, itself belongs to philosophy. In fact, not to put too fine a point on it, this part of sociology is really misbegotten epistemology. I say 'misbegotten' because its problems have been largely misconstrued, and therefore mishandled as a species of scientific problem. (Winch, 1958, p. 43)

Winch takes the example of what constitutes social behaviour, and argues that this question, rather than requiring an empirical investigation, demands an 'elucidation' of the concept of social behaviour. This elucidation he gives by reference to 'rules': 'the analysis of meaningful behaviour must allot a central role to the notion of a rule; that behaviour which is meaningful (therefore all specifically human behaviour) is *ipso facto* rule-governed' (Winch, 1958, pp. 51-2). By formulating this analysis, whether right or wrong, Winch devalues the concept of explanation in the social sciences, and replaces it by that of 'understanding'. For example, social behaviour can be understood, made meaningful, by means of rule notions (see generally, Borger and Cioffi, 1970). Action is, in this sense, merely a symbolic representation of subjective understanding. The relationship between behaviour (that is action) and the rule is that of giving meaning and developing understanding.

The Idea of Rule

In recent jurisprudential literature, law has been classified as rules (Hart, 1961). This classification has the benefit of flexibility, in that law can be looked at as different types of rules — duty-imposing, power-conferring, rules about capacity, and so on (Cohen, 1962) — rather than as a one-dimensional command with a sanction attached (Austin, 1832, Lecture I). There is a movement away from consideration of law in terms of power and its mechanism of enforcement, to attitude and response to legal norms. Similar analyses relating law and attitude, finding 'the doctrine of human conviction as a basis for legal rules' (Van Houtte and Vinke, 1973, p. 13) have many origins. The best developed analyses are theories relating ethical and legal values. The attitudes or convictions of individuals have been considered to be the necessary preconditions for 'binding' legal rules in a number of theories.[2] Many modern studies are developed in order to 'realise the extent to which changes in tempo and in values in the social groups involved, have fundamentally changed the social milieu of our law' (Van Houtte and Vinke, 1973, p. 16). Such a movement is centred on the idea of rule. Hart's 'Concept of Law' is rule-based and includes the notion of the internal attitude of the members (or, at least the officials) of the community subject to the law. For, as he argues, someone not involved with the internal workings of a society will be unable to apprehend the attitude of its members to the legal demands made of them, since his only means of doing so will be through their overt behaviour. This assessment leads him to the study of attitude and its relation to law in action:

> What is important is that the insistence on importance or seriousness of social pressure behind the rules is the primary factor determining whether the rules are thought of as giving to obligations. (Hart, 1961, p. 84)

Equally, the idea of rule is present in much modern sociological literature. Of course, rule to a jurist and rule to a sociologist are quite different: 'Where the lawyer or the legal scholar talks about rights and expectations he does so with normative intentions . . . The sociologist, on the other hand, uses the same terms to describe, reveal and explain' (Aubert, 1969, p. 9). Winch, as has already been noted, addresses himself to the idea of rule as a means of understanding behaviour. Ethnomethodological sociology, in its pragmatic desire to understand action in its situational context and particularly the study of language and reasoning as basic social phenomena, has included the study of the common-sense rules that make determination of meaning possible (see Wieder, 1971, pp. 107, 221). Symbolic interactionism, particularly in Goffman's writings, concentrates on implied rules of behaviour which integrate the situation (see Goffman, 1963). Phenomenological sociologists, relying heavily on the writings of Schutz (for example, 1963, pp. 231, 302), and concentrating on revealing 'the actual meanings used by members and to show how they are constructed' (Phillipson, 1972, p. 119) in their everyday use, are reliant on a study of 'the basic rules that allow meaningful action to proceed' (Phillipson, 1972, p. 149; see generally, Collett, 1977; Douglas, 1973). This brief summary is meant to do no more than state the obvious; as jurists and as sociologists we have at least a shared concern with rules.

Normative and Interpretive Rules[3]

The idea of shared rules has been explored in sociological theory by many. The main emphasis in much traditional sociology has been to explain deviance from rules rather than utilise notions of rules as a means of understanding conforming behaviour. Equally sociological interest in legal rules has centred on attempted explanations of deviance, hence the developed criminological literature. However, recent developments in criminology have considered conformity to legal rules, the rules themselves, the statistics and so on as problematic (symbolic interactionists for example; see Rubington and Weinberg, 1968). This reorientation is mirrored in other fields of sociological interest (for example, Young, 1971). It has become apparent that the nature of order, regularity and conforming behaviour, cannot be explained simply by demonstrating the existence of formal or informal rules or norms. In an interactional sense, understanding conformity depends on *orientation* to the rules as implied, perceived or used. This, in turn, depends on knowledge of, understanding of and recognition of the rules, disposition and attitude to them. The relationship between the normative and interpretive characteristics of rules becomes of significance. For, whereas legal rules are normative in the sense they say what one ought, that is what one may, can or should do, they are also interpretive. Understanding the interpretive characteristic of legal rules requires that research centres on such questions as why do people obey law, how is legal significance given to their actions by individuals and the related questions of knowledge, understanding and recognition of legal rules. That law is normative but is nevertheless a constituent part of social reality can be understood since legal rules do not simply explain behaviour but may give meaning to individuals for their behaviour. Orientation to legal rules, whereby people interpret their actions in relation to and derive meaning from legal rules, is one of the means by which, in their interactions, the nature of law as a social phenomenon is constructed by members of a given society.

Legal Rules as Social Phenomena

It has been the case that lawyers studying the social relations of law have concentrated on what might broadly be called efficacy studies. This may be described as sociological jurisprudence namely, 'the purposive evaluation of legal rules' (Schiff, 1976, p. 295). That sociologists should concern themselves with this rather limited enterprise is, I would argue, not justifiable. A much more fruitful area of study, derived from my previous arguments in this article is: to what extent are legal rules, individually and collectively and of the various kinds, part of the shared common-sense knowledge, part of the everyday reasoning through which social life in our society proceeds? Taking Thomas's statement that 'if men define situations as real, they are real in their consequences' (Thomas, 1928, p. 584) for the study of law as a social phenomenon envisaged, it is law as individual members perceive it, know it and understand it, that requires to be evaluated, not those internally complex definitions of law of lawyers, judges, jurists and others concerned with the practical administration of the law. Once we have gained knowledge about people's knowledge and perception of law and individual laws (see, for example, Podgórecki, 1973, p. 65), we can go on to examine to what extent legal rules are used and manipulated by individuals, in other words, to what extent they are part of social life at the microcosmic level at which social order is constructed. Do members of our society orientate themselves towards their perceptions of legal rules, or are legal rules peripheral to the underlying fabric of order and conformity in our society? What is the relevance of statements such as 'that's alright, it's legal' or 'that's illegal' or 'it's not really a crime' for attempted understanding of social settings and their organisation? How important is law at this level of social reality? To be able to give answers to some of these questions would enable a whole plethora of more traditional jurisprudential questions to be considered in a more satisfactory way, for example, what are the limits of law, how important is law to the maintenance of social order, can a society be envisaged without law? It is, I would argue, a task for sociologists, particularly those who, as phenomenological, ethnomethodological (see Psathas, 1977, pp. 73-98) or interactional sociologists, are interested in studying society and social phenomena on a microcosmic level, to research into and produce data on the type of questions listed above.

Limits of Legal Sociology

The sociological study of specific legal phenomena, particularly legal situations such as the courtroom, the solicitor's office or the jury room, offers useful examples of processes of interaction, 'organizational socialization' (see Bittner, 1965; Manning, 1971), typification, symbolisation and social construction. In fact, the courtroom is an extreme example of social construction. It is the case in which total observance to law is theoretically expressed, and yet the situation is such that the law often remains in question, and its determination has to be effected during the course of a hearing. The ordered meaning ultimately decided upon is constructed in the course of debate between the conflicting parties and their representatives, with the help of suggestions from the judge. However, social life offers numerous examples outside the official province of lawyers, in which orientation to legal rules is made in the course of everyday reasoning, and a common-sense knowledge, a reality about law, constructed. Just as Berger and Luckman (1966, p. 27) have argued that 'it is precisely this "knowledge" that constitutes the fabric of meanings without which no society could exist', so it is here argued that it is precisely this 'everyday knowledge of law' that constitutes the fabric of meanings without which no idea of law as a social phenomenon could exist.

A paradigm is offered for the study of legal rules as social phenomena in the lawyer's study of the interpretive work of the judge. Judicial activity at the highest levels centres round the interpretation of legal sources (statutes, decided cases, and so on). It is therefore not surprising that, at least in some circles, judicial behaviour and reasoning, the characters and opinions of judges have received detailed study: particularly from the jurisprudential school known as the American Realists (Schubert, 1963; Schubert and Danelski; 1969; see generally, Harvard Symposium, 1966). It is the *judicial disposition* which gives meaning to rules of law, it involves orientation to the rules, interpretation of them, determination of legal meaning and attribution of legal consequences. The significance of law as a social phenomenon lies in an equivalent mental activity of members of a given society in the course of everyday life. It is by no means only in legal situations that one finds the judicial disposition, that is orientation to legal rules, interpretation and attribution by one individual to another of legal significance for that other's actions, or, maybe more important, of legal meaning for one's own actions. This mental activity *is* law in action, it goes on every day in many situations, it is socially pervasive and significant.

Methodological Problems

The nature of analyses in the sociology of law which attempt to relate law and social behaviour (see particularly, Timasheff, 1937, 1938, 1939, 1944, 1957), social control (see, for example, Pound, 1942; Ross, 1901), social progress[4] or social change (see, particularly Sumner, 1907; also, Dror, 1959; Rose, 1956), is that they imply consistency between sets of social facts and the law. As already argued in the section on social behaviour and law, there are methodological and logical problems with such attempts. Such problems arise because law is normative. Law as a theoretical idea is a norm, it says what ought to, not what necessarily does or will, happen or has happened. The social facts to which law is related are considered to be descriptive facts, amenable to cause and effect analyses, facts, as Homans (1967) argues, having the value of testability. The relationship between law and such social facts represents a methodological imbalance. This methodological imbalance is of the same order as that which has been formulated to criticise positivistic explanations in the social sciences. For example, two of Silverman's seven propositions of an 'Action Frame of Reference' are that 'sociology is concerned with understanding action rather than with observing behaviour' and 'positivistic explanations which assert that action is determined by external and constraining social or non-social forces, are inadmissible' (Silverman, 1970, pp. 126-7). The attempts to construct a logic by which a relationship between the social forces (for example, social progress or social change) and the law can be formulated do not satisfy the needs of a coherent methodological base. However, understanding action through subjective meanings of individuals orientating to legal rules, disposition towards and consciousness of legal rules are consistent with this 'action approach' and also methodologically coherent. The attitude (including those notions of subjective meaning, disposition and consciousness) of individuals in relation to legal rules can be characterised as normative. It includes the notions of what the individual believes he ought or ought not to do as a matter of law, his manipulations and utilisation of legal rules in order to set his standards and values.

Relation of Law and Values

The ancestry of the theory of the relation of law and values is long, the pedigree of those who have contributed is outstanding. Until, however, the modern school of jurisprudential thought, known as the Scandinavian Realist,[5] developed their ideas, the influence of law on values, rather than values on law, was little considered. There has been scant regard for the question as to how, if at all, values embodied in the law have become embedded in the social fabric and the processes of socialisation and objectivation.[6] Such questions are significant to the approach to law as a social phenomenon outlined in this chapter. There is evidence to suggest that the passing of time and a network of communication (Aubert, 1966, p. 99) are the important elements in the process of acceptance of legal rules. More detailed analysis of how this occurs, if it does, or at least when it occurs on the level of everyday experience needs to be made available. Whereas it may be the case that sociological interest in law has for some time been neglectful, with maybe good reason, in that its inquiry into the rules which *do* govern social relations rather than institutional norms such as law was seen to be paramount, there has now re-opened an area of interest for some sociologists which they could well consider.

Law and Social Order

The assumption that law creates or helps maintain social order is one that may be belied by analysis of legal rules as social phenomena envisaged in this chapter. The increasing use of law as a legitimate means of interference in previously private areas of social relations may, on a micro-level, have the effect of undermining the expectations and inherent order associated with these situations. The ability to reorientate to what is perceived as changes in legal standards is taken for granted by most of those involved in the process of legislation. The gross distinctions in many areas of law between law in the books and law in action, the apparent inability of the law to solve or even improve some of the many areas of social disadvantage which it has attempted to deal with, the ineffectiveness of legal mechanisms in fields such as industrial relations and commerce, can all be explained in numerous ways. It may be argued that the content of the law requires change or its form some amendment, for example, greater powers to administrative bodies, or the imposition of duties on such bodies rather than merely discretionary powers, or the greater use of penal sanctions, or whatever. Of course, some of these arguments will always be relevant and right in terms of the manifest purposes of certain legislation, but behind them lies an assumption about the potential of law, which assumption can only be adequately assessed by analysis of the everyday effect of legal rules on the consciousnesses of those to whom they are meant to apply. That law and order are interrelated particularly in the light of an apparently high rate of legal change is a hypothesis which needs to be tested at the level of individual orientation to the expressed legal rules.

Conclusion

It has been suggested in this chapter that some of the developments in sociological theory (for example, phenomenological) and some of the research strategies of complementary developments (for example, ethnomethodological) are particularly apposite for a more fruitful interchange between law and sociology, and potentially mark out a significant movement towards a sociology of law. If that is the case it may be worth ending on an optimistic note. Whereas it has been argued that lawyers, namely Roman jurists, were among those first to study in a systematic form the nature and types of social relations (Sorokin, 1928, p. 498), and whereas law was a major concern of some of the founding fathers of sociology (Weber, 1954; and Durkheim, 1933), it is maybe modern sociologists who have the greatest opportunity of developing the relationship between the two disciplines in a substantial way. To the extent that sociologists can highlight for lawyers the impact of law in everyday life and the nature of law as a social phenomenon, they will enable jurists to answer their more traditional questions in a more satisfying way.[7]

Notes

1. There is a vast literature on this, but probably the most accessible source is A. Ross, *Directives and Norms* (Routledge and Kegan Paul, London, 1968), especially chs. 3 and 6.
2. See W. Friedmann, *Legal Theory* (Stevens and Sons, London, 1967) pp. 29 and 85, on Krabbe's 'the sense of justice', Del Vecchio's 'sentimento guiridico' and Petrazhitsky's 'intuitive law'.
3. See T.P. Wilson, 'Normative and Interpretive Paradigms in Sociology' in J.D. Douglas, (1971, p. 57); A.V. Cicourel, *Cognitive Sociology (Language and Meaning in Social Interaction)* (Penguin, London, 1973), ch. 1 'Interpretive procedures and normative rules in the negotiation of status and role', pp. 11-41.

4. Such an analysis can be found in the extreme positivism of Auguste Comte. Rather than refer the reader to Comte's voluminous works on the subject, I suggest that the best surveys of his writing on the subject are in H. Cairns, *Law and the Social Sciences* (Kegan Paul, London, 1935) and G.D. Gurvitch, *L'Idée du Droit Social* (Vrin, Paris, 1931). Also see Herbert Spencer's evolutionary approach: H. Spencer, *The Principles of Sociology* (Williams and Northgate, London, 1897-1906), vol. 2, pt. 5, ch. 14, 'Laws'.

5. The acknowledged founder of this approach is Axel Hagerström. See his *Inquiries into the Nature of Law and Morals,* translated by C.D. Broad, (Almqvist and Wiksell, Stockholm, 1953). The other main contributors known to English readers are V. Lundstedt, K. Olivecrona and A. Ross: V. Lundstedt, *Legal Thinking Revised* (Almqvist and Wiksell, Stockholm, 1956); K. Olivecrona, *Law as Fact,* 2nd edn (Stevens and Sons, London, 1971); A. Ross, *On Law and Justice* (Stevens and Sons, London, 1958); A. Ross *Directives and Norms* (1968). For a useful short account, see H.L.A. Hart, 'Scandinavian Realism', *Cambridge Law Journal,* vol. 18 (1959), p. 233.

6. Much of the analysis in P.L. Berger and T. Luckman (1966), could be applied to law in this context. Also, see J.L. Tapp, 'The Psychological Limits of Legality' in J.R. Pennock and J.W. Chapman (eds.), *The Limits of Law* (Lieber-Atherton, New York, 1974), pp. 46-75.

7. There is a debate concerning the primacy of jurisprudence over sociology of law or sociology of law over jurisprudence. This debate covers the subject-matter to be studied, the method by which knowledge about the subject matter is to be gained, and the means by which it is to be evaluated. The argument is, on the one hand, that sociology of law determines what law is and jurisprudence then develops its inquiries on the basis of a subject-matter received from the sociology of law; the main support for this argument being that 'effectiveness' is a prerequisite to the existence of a legal order, and effectiveness is a fact which can only be established by social scientific and not philosophic methods. The contrary argument puts the view that jurisprudence establishes what law is, and that sociology of law should develop its inquiries on its received object of study. The main support for this argument lies in the normative nature of legal phenomena, that the nature of law cannot be discovered by use of social scientific methods. My conclusion to this article suggests a complementary view of sociological and juristic interest in law.

Bibliography

Aubert, V. 'Some Social Functions of Legislation', *Acta Sociologica,* vol. 10 (1966), pp. 99-120

______ (ed.), *Sociology of Law,* (Penguin, London, 1969)

Austin, J.L. *The Province of Jurisprudence Determined* (Weidenfeld and Nicolson, London, 1832), Lecture I.

Berger, P.L. and Luckman, T. *The Social Construction of Reality* (Penguin, London, 1966)

Bittner, E. 'The Concept of Organization', *Social Research,* vol. 32 (1965), pp. 239-55

Borger, R. and F. Cioffi, (eds.) *Explanation in the Behavioural Sciences,* (Cambridge University Press, Cambridge, 1970)

Castberg, F. *Problems of Legal Philosophy,* 2nd English edn (Oslo University Press, London, 1957)

Cohen, L.J. 'The Review of Hart's Concept of Law' *Mind,* vol. 71 (1962), pp. 395-412

Collett, R. (ed.) *Social Rules and Social Behaviour* (Basil Blackwell, Oxford, 1977)

Douglas, J.D. (ed.) *Understanding Everyday Life (Towards the Reconstruction of Social Knowlege)* (Routledge and Kegan Paul, London, 1971)

Douglas, M. (ed.) *Rules and Meanings (The Anthropology of Everyday Knowledge)*

(Penguin, London, 1973)
Dror, Y. 'Law and Social Change', *Tulane Law Review*, vol. 35 (1959), pp. 787-802
Durkheim, E. *The Division of Labour in Society*, translated by G. Simpson (Glencoe, New York, 1933)
Filmer, P., Phillipson, M., Silverman, D. and Walsh, D. *New Directions in Sociological Theory* (Collier-Macmillan, London, 1972)
Goffman, E. *Behaviour in Public Places: Notes on the Social Organization of Gatherings* (Free Press, New York, 1963)
Gurwitsch, A. 'On the Intentionality of Consciousness' in R.M. Zaner and D. Ihde (eds.), *Phenomenology and Existentialism* (Putnam, New York, 1973), pp. 102-19
Hart, H.L.A. *The Concept of Law* (Oxford University Press, Oxford, 1961)
Harvard Symposium, 'A Symposium: Social Science Approaches to the Judicial Process', *Harvard Law Review*, vol. 79 (June 1966), pp. 1551-1628
Homans, G.C. *The Nature of Social Science* (Harcourt, New York, 1967)
Ihde, D. and Zaner, R. (eds.) *Interdisciplinary Phenomenology* (Martinus Nijhoff, The Hague, 1977)
Kullman, M. and Taylor, C. 'The Pre-Objective World' in M. Natanson (ed.), *Essays in Phenomenology* (Martinus Nijhoff, The Hague, 1969), pp. 116-36
Manning, P.K. 'Talking and Becoming: A View of Organizational Socialization' in J.D. Douglas (ed.) *Understanding Everyday Life* (Routledge and Kegan Paul, London, 1971), pp. 239-56
Natanson, M. (ed.) *Essays in Phenomenology*, (Martinus Nijhoff, The Hague, 1969)
______ *The Journeying Self (A Study in Philosophy and Social Role)* (Addison-Wesley, Reading, Massachussetts, 1970)
______ *Edmund Husserl (Philosopher of Infinite Tasks)* (Northwestern University Press, Evanston, 1973)
Olivecrona, K. *Law as Fact* (Oxford University Press, Oxford, 1939)
Phillipson, M. 'Phenomenology Philosophy and Sociology' in P. Filmer *et al.*, *New Directions in Sociological Theory* (Collier-Macmillan, London, 1972), pp. 119-63
Podgórecki, A. 'Public Opinion on Law' in Podgorecki *et al.* (1973), pp. 65-100
Podgórecki, A. *et al. Knowledge and Opinion about Law* (Martin Robertson, London, 1973)
Pound, R. *Social Control through Law* (Yale University Press, New Haven, 1942)
Psathas, G. 'Ethnomethodology as a Phenomenological Approach in the Social Sciences' in D. Ihde and R. Zaner (eds.) *Interdisciplinary Phenomenology* (Martinus Nijhoff, The Hague, 1977), pp. 73-98
Rose, A.M. 'The Use of Law to Induce Social Change', *Transactions of the Third World Congress of Sociology*, vol. VI (1956), pp. 52-63
Ross, E.A. *Social Control: A Survey of the Foundation of Order* (Macmillan, New York, 1901)
Rubington, E. and Weinberg, M.S. (eds.) *Deviance: The Interactionist Perspective* (Collier-Macmillan, London, 1968)
Schiff, D.N. 'Socio-Legal Theory: Social Structure and Law', *The Modern Law Review*, vol. 39 (May 1976), pp. 287-310
Schubert, G.A. *Judicial Decision-Making* (Free Press of Glencoe, New York, 1963)
Schubert, G.A. and Danelski, D.J. *Comparative Judicial Behaviour* (Oxford University Press, New York, 1969)
Schutz, A. 'Concept and Theory Formation in the Social Sciences' and 'Common-sense and Scientific Interpretation of Human Action' in M. Natanson (ed.) *Philosophy of the Social Sciences* (Random House, New York, 1963), pp. 231-49
______ *The Phenomenology of the Social World* (Heinemann, London, 1972)
______ *The Structures of the Life World* (Heinemann, London, 1974)
Selznick, P. 'The Sociology of Law', *International Encyclopaedia of The Social Sciences*, vol. 9 (1968), pp. 50-9
Silverman, D. *The Theory of Organisations* (Heinemann, London, 1970)

______ 'Introductory Comments' in P. Filmer *et al. New Directions in Sociological Theory* (Collier-Macmillan, London, 1972), pp. 1-12

Sorokin, P.A. *Contemporary Sociological Theories* (Harper, New York, 1928)

Sumner, W.G. *Folkways* (Ginn, Boston, 1907)

Thomas, W.I. *The Child in America* (Knopf, New York, 1928)

Timasheff, N.S. 'What is "Sociology of Law"?', *American Journal of Sociology*, vol. 43 (September 1937), pp. 225-35

______ 'The Sociological Place of Law', *American Journal of Sociology*, vol. 44 (September 1938), pp. 206-21

______ *An Introduction to the Sociology of Law* (Greenwood Press, Westport, Connecticut, 1939)

______ 'The Social Reality of Ideal Patterns', *Journal of Legal and Political Sociology*, vol. 2 (1944), pp. 66-83

______ 'Growth and Scope of the Sociology of Law' in H. Becker and W. Boskoff (eds.) *Modern Sociological Theory in Continuity and Change* (The Dryden Press, New York, 1957), pp. 424-49

Van Houtte, J. and Vinke, P. 'Attitudes governing the acceptance of legislation among various social groups' in Podgorecki *et al. Knowledge and Opinion about Law* (Martin Robertson, London, 1973), pp. 13-42

Weber, M. *The Theory of Social and Economic Organization*, translated by A.M. Henderson and T. Parsons (The Free Press, New York, 1947)

______ *Max Weber on Law in Economy and Society* (Harvard University Press, Cambridge, Massachussetts, 1954)

Wieder, D.L. 'On Meaning by Rule' in J.D. Douglas (ed.) *Understanding Everyday Life* (Routledge and Kegan Paul, London, 1971), pp. 107-35

Winch, P. *The Idea of a Social Science and its Relation to Philosophy* (Routledge and Kegan Paul, London, 1958)

Young, M.F.D. (ed.) *Knowledge and Control: New Directions for the Sociology of Education* (Collier-Macmillan, London, 1971)

Zaner, R.M. *The Way of Phenomenology (Criticism as a Philosophical Discipline)* (Bobbs-Merrill, Indianapolis, 1970)

Zaner, R.M. and Ihde, D. (eds.) *Phenomenology and Existentialism*, (Putnam, New York, 1973)

Zimmerman, D.H. 'The Practicalities of Rule Use' in J.D. Douglas (ed.) *Understanding Everyday Life* (Routledge and Kegan Paul, London, 1971), pp. 221-38

9 The Symbolic Dimension of Law and Social Control

Arthur Brittan

It is impossible to define symbolic interactionism with any degree of precision. One thing we must be clear about is that we are not talking about a formal theoretical scheme. Many people call themselves symbolic interactionists, but this does not mean that they necessarily agree about its aims, methods and rationales.

For some practitioners the focus of interest is in the actual forms of interaction. They are concerned with problems of interaction style, the way in which social forms influence the content of the communication process. They are represented by Hugh Dalziel Duncan, Kenneth Burke and perhaps Goffman. Although not generally acknowledged, one of the sources of this emphasis on interaction style is Simmel's discussion of social forms and the nature of sociality (Simmel, 1950).

For others, the central problem of symbolic interactionism is the relationship between the self and the social matrix from which it is presumed the self derives. Here, the emphasis is on the way in which there is an interplay between the self as process, and society as process. Both the self and society are constituted of the same kind of stuff, namely symbols, particularly linguistic symbols. In other words, I can only know who I am because others have indicated to me that I am a certain kind of social object. In return, I accept or reject these indications. By so doing, I contribute to the ongoing process of symbolic interaction thereby constituting both myself and others as moments or aspects of the ongoing social process. The self and society are therefore indivisible — they are not opposing forces. It is precisely this tendency to downgrade the contradiction between self and society which fuels some of the adverse criticism levelled against symbolic interactionism. It is seen as being far too concerned with presenting a picture of individual and social life which is devoid of any tension and conflict. It operates with an over-optimistic image of human nature, and an overwhelming indifference to the realities of power and inequality. (This is something I shall come back to later in this chapter.) More than any other practitioner it is George Herbert Mead who provides the central arguments and commitments of this central dimension of symbolic interactionism. He is also responsible for some of the ambiguities and difficulties which have plagued advocates of his theory of the social origin of the self. What has emerged from these difficulties is a basic contradiction between those practitioners who have seen Mead as a cultural and symbolic determinist, and those who have argued that he was far more committed to voluntarism than is generally realised. Whatever the pros and cons of this debate there can be no doubt that Mead can be read in a multiplicity of ways. The critical thing is that, for Mead, reflexivity is at the core of all mental and social phenomena, that is the individual's ability to talk to him/herself (Mead, 1967).

A third emphasis among researchers and theorists in the interactionist camp concentrates on the situation and the 'definition of the situation'. They insist that interaction should always be seen as performances in situations. I am referring to the dramaturgical model of Goffman and others. The dramaturgical model contextualises human behaviour in terms of analogies drawn from the stage. Of course, it does not go so far as to claim that all behaviour is dramatic, or that the entire fabric of social life can be defined as one vast stage on which human conduct is validated. Nevertheless, for most practitioners, behaviour is construed as being under the control of audiences who evaluate, applaud, approve and disapprove of this or that performance. In other words, social control is exercised by the public and audiences who have certain expectations about the appropriateness or inappropriateness of particular performances. The perfomer must know how to act in a situation, he must be able to read the cues and codes embedded in that situation, he must be able to dramatise the situation reflexively.

In its extreme form, this model reifies self-consciousness to an extraordinary degree. It assumes that human beings are actors who always 'know' they are 'on-stage', and who consciously plan a performance in order to meet the requirements of a role. Obviously such an extreme self-consciousness is untenable. However, Goffman, for example, has argued that the dramaturgical model has been misunderstood and distorted by its interpreters. The misunderstanding is responsible for the way in which it has been elevated to the status of 'pop sociology' especially in the United States.

Underpinning these various emphases and strategies are a number of broad philosophical themes which seem to coexist in an uneasy alliance.

Philosophical Themes

American Pragmatism

There is no disputing the fact that symbolic interactionism is fundamentally an American product. Its central propositions derive from pragmatism. Mead (1967) is described as a pragmatist, having strong links with both William James (1949) and Thomas Dewey (1929). This is reflected in the cardinal importance that he places on the 'act' as a process — a process linking selves to others. Crudely, men construct themselves by some kind of trial-and-error process, that is they construct themselves as self-conscious entities by acting in the world with others. The ethos of pragmatism is conducive to an optimistic interpretation of social reality. Social problems can be overcome by conscious application of knowledge to areas of tension and conflict. Ideologically, it mirrors the belief of American liberalism that all social problems can be solved by the application of education and scientific tools to the policies of local and central government.

A dominant assumption of this pragmatic liberalism is that human beings construct their own identities. Identities can be negotiated. The individual negotiates with his or her parents, peers, teachers, employers, policemen, friends and so on. In a sense, this notion of identity negotiation is premised on the belief that all men in American society are free to pursue their own interests provided there are no impediments to hamper such a process. It is precisely the task of social science, so it is argued, to find ways and means to circumscribe and overcome these difficulties.

A corollary to this assumption is the belief that the optimum set of conditions for identity negotiation is a legal framework which allows the individual to construct himself or herself without the coercive apparatus of agencies of social control. Of course, in the real world these optimum conditions do not obtain, so it is the task of the social scientist and legislator to understand the way in which social problems distort and stultify human relationships. The aim of the ideal symbolic interactionist-interventionist strategy is to provide a framework in which individual autonomy replaces social control and legal absolutism. In practice, this has led to the development of a multiplicity of methodological case studies in which social problems and deviance are defined in terms of audience criteria. It is the audience which categorises and evaluates individual behaviour, and it is the audience which, in the final analysis, confirms or rejects particular kinds of identity claims. Hence, in its applied form, liberal pragmatism or symbolic interactionism is directly concerned with the problem of deviance and the societal construction of negative identities. Labelling theory comes to be seen as the test of the viability of the perspective.

Phenomenology

Whether they acknowledge it or not, most symbolic interactionists adopt a phenomenological stance. Although W.I. Thomas's hackneyed phrase 'If men define situations as real, they are real in their consequences' (Thomas, 1932) derives from a pragmatic view of the world, it is in keeping with the phenomenological insistence that the world is given meaning by lived experience. In addition, it can be claimed, although not necessarily demonstrated, that contemporary symbolic interactionism has ties with *verstehende* sociology, especially Weber.

In recent years, the phenomenological strand in symbolic interactionism has been challenged by the growth of social phenomenology and ethnomethodology. The antecedents of this growth are in Europe rather than the United States. Social phenomenology derives from an amalgam of interpretive sociology and Husserl's (1931) phenomenology as mediated through Schutz (1972), while ethnomethodology has strong affinities with linguistic philosophy. To a certain extent the emergence of the new 'creative sociologies', as Monica Morris (1977) calls them, has meant that symbolic interactionism no longer has the monopoly of the loyal opposition in American sociology. (In the European context it never has had this privileged status.)

On the whole, symbolic interactionists have not been concerned with the kinds of procedures and strategies which interest ethnomethodologists. Most symbolic interactionists are, in principle, ready to concede that social structure has some meaning independent of our interpretation of it, as long as it is continuously negotiated and renegotiated, whereas ethnomethodologists argue that the concept of structure is problematic — it cannot be taken for granted. Indeed, ethnomethodologists argue that symbolic interactionism is rooted in a traditional common-sensical image of the social world which does not allow it to transcend the obviousness of its conceptual tools. Be that as it may, the point is, for symbolic interactionists, social structure is defined in terms of 'negotiated order'. It may be a fiction but it is a fiction that has direct consequences for those whose everyday lives are apparently 'real' because they accept society's 'fictive' nature as the 'real' world.

Symbolism and Literary Criticism

Although pragmatism and phenomenology have had important influences on symbolic interactionism, perhaps equally important, although not necessarily obvious, is the debt owed to philosophers such as Ernst Cassirer and Susan Langer as well as philosophically oriented literary critics like Kenneth Burke (1969). One result of this influence has been to push some practitioners into a stance in which all cultural conduct is reduced to language and the negotiation of meaning. In this respect terms such as motive, feeling, emotion, attitude and cognition disappear to be replaced by the notion of 'situated action'. Because human beings live in a symbolically mediated world, then it is assumed that there is nothing beyond the symbol except other symbols. Instead of motives we now talk of accounts, meanings and reasons.

In other words, the stability and reality of the world depend on the meaning that human actors give to it — symbols are the means we use to drive back chaos and absurdity. Thus, in some versions of interactionism, we are presented with absurdity as the ultimate rationale for human action. Language and symbolisation prop up society. There is no essential meaning to be found in the world and society — they are all constructions. Such a posture lends itself to an extreme relativism in which all symbolic systems have equal value, and all moral and belief systems are relegated to the historical dustbin. Moreover, institutions and legal practices are seen as mere appendages to culture. Structure is an illusion — an epiphenomenon.

This is undoubtedly a very far-fetched claim. But is is a claim that informs a great deal of the work of practitioners who work in the so-called newer creative sociologies. Its implications for a theory of social control are, to say the least, highly controversial.

However contradictory these philosophical themes appear to be, they have one profound consequence for symbolic interactionism, they push it into an anti-behavioural and anti-reductionist posture. Symbolic interactionists situate sociology and social psychology outside a natural science framework. In particular they reject the scientism of systems theory and functionalism.

As described by Herbert Blumer, interactionism consists of three basic premisses:

> *First,* human beings act towards things on the basis of the meaning that things have for them. *Secondly,* these meanings are a product of social interaction in human society. *Thirdly,* these meanings are modified and handled through an interpretative process that is used by each individual in dealing with the signs he encounters. (Quoted in Meltzer, Petras and Reynolds, 1977.)

The historical roots of these premisses are found not only in Mead, but also in Cooley (1964) and Dewey (1929).

Blumer sees symbolic interactionism as a set of interpretive procedures which allow us to make sense of our own interpretations of other people's interpretations. In doing sociology, one is doing no more than 'human actors' or 'members' do as participants in social relationships. Participants are continuously engaged in acts of interpretation mediated through symbolic discourse. Accordingly, it is argued, language is the medium and mechanism whereby participants become aware of the interaction process, that is they become capable of a dual dialogue between their own selves as participants, and the reflexive selves of other participants. This dialogue is central to the socialisation process. Consequently, from this point of view, socialisation is more than a process to induce social conformity (although it is true to say that a determinist reading of Mead might push us into assenting to such a proposition). If socialisation is a reflexive dialogue between participants, then it follows that the individual is both submerged in and apart from society. Reflexivity ensures that the concept 'individual' is both a social and atomistic phenomenon. By this I mean that while Mind, Self and Society are aspects of the communicative process, that is of the interplay of reflexive selves, they simultaneously are aspects of the way in which each individual defines himself or herself as a unique phenomenon. Individual uniqueness has its origins in social nexus which permits each individual to symbolise himself or herself as unique. At least this assumption is believed to hold true for those societies in which the concept, individual, has some kind of meaning. Obviously, it fits in nicely with the ideology of individualism which saturates pragmatic liberalism.

We have then a picture of symbolic interactionism which appears to be highly contradictory. On the one hand, there is the view which sees it as yet another form of cultural determinism in which the symbol is promoted to an almost mystical efficacy. Human beings are socialised in such a manner that they seem to be nothing more than symbolic cyphers. Culture plays its little games with participants so that the whole notion of individuality is seen as being merely a collective delusion. On the other hand, there is the perspective which suggests that participants are not passive spectators and victims of an overarching symbolic universe, but on the contrary, *are* co-partners with others in the construction of their own identities. So we have, as I have suggested in another context, two contrasting images of symbolic interactionism.

> The first has strong affinities with *linguistic relativism,* the second with what could be called *symbolic romanticism.* Linguistic relativism asserts the reality of symbolic forms in the shaping of self and society — language becomes 'the' paramount reality. Symbolic romanticism stresses the indeterminacy of self-other negotiations; language becomes a means for the negotiation and renegotiation of identity. In the first case critics have pointed to the submergence of structure in culture, a tendency in which there seems to be no room for the action of economic and political forces, and in which the internalisation of norms and values ensures the cohesion of society. Language is poured into man — the self being nothing more than a repository of symbols. In the second case, criticism is directed against the haphazard way in which language becomes a set of labels to categorise internal states. Individuals name themselves, devise social strategies and construct identities at will. Such a perspective, it is argued, fits in nicely with bourgeois romantic individualism. (Brittan, 1977, p. 6)

The sociological and cultural absolutism explicit in linguistic relativism has obvious affinities to the domain assumptions of mainstream sociology especially functionalism in that it tends to treat individuals as if they are on the receiving end of determinate social forces which are introjected into the individual's psychic system. From this point of view, power and reward-cost contingencies are implicit in the cultural system; it is assumed that all participants are passive in the face of such overwhelming odds. However, such a stark and blatant determinism is, in my view, due to an unfortunate interpretation of Mead's discussion of the 'generalised other'. The 'generalised other' is treated in this interpretation as though it is equivalent to society itself. Accordingly, it is impossible to distinguish between the notion of individual identity and the society in which this identity is nourished.

A further consequence of this position is that deviance is treated as if it were simply a function of inadequate socialisation. The deviant is seen as a person who has not been exposed to the appropriate socialisation techniques, and who therefore has not internalised the values and norms of society. In short, linguistic relativism posits a world in which conduct is shaped by role demands so that any departure from these demands is seen as deviant.

Symbolic romanticism is obsessed with the problem of identity negotiation. Although it accepts that there are limits set by the framework of social obligations, it seems to argue for a scenario in which identity is continuously made and remade in countless social encounters. Who and what we are will depend on the situation, on the way in which each situation is defined and interpreted. Hence, identity is multifaceted — there is no uniform core to the self. Nevertheless, behind the masks presented for confirmation in this or that context, it is assumed that the individual knows who he is, and that he can somehow project an identity consonant with particular situations. Implicit in this assumption is the belief that identity is ultimately something that one constructs and makes for oneself.

However, such a far-reaching voluntarism is severely limited by the realities of everyday life. In a sense, it is an ideal type found only in interactionist monographs. Very few interactionists are so naive as to claim that this is the way the world is, but they *do* claim that the self is always up for negotiation. For example, take the problem of stigma, legal or otherwise. The stigmatised person is usually seen as a victim of some kind of labelling process by others. *Others* identify him as a certain kind of social object who deserves a specific kind of consideration of a negative or positive nature. By being labelled a thief, it is argued, an individual is forced into a situation in which he has no choice but to accept the consequences of the deviant label. Law-enforcement officers reinforce this self-image by their actions in apprehending the thief. The whole game of activities related to solicitors, magistrates, sentencing, prison, experiences with other prisoners, relationships with family and friends and so on — all this imposes on the thief as a direct attack on his perception of himself. He has no other choice but to define himself as a thief. Now this scenario is a bit too neat. It suggests that there is a one-to-one correspondence between social definitions and self-definitions. As one commentator puts it,

> One sometimes gets the impression from reading this literature that people go about minding their own business and then 'wham' bad

> society comes along and slaps them with a stigmatised label. Forced into the role of a deviant, the individual has but little choice but to be deviant. (Akers, 1968, pp. 455-65)

Now the symbolic romanticist agrees that the stigma 'thief' is rooted in societal reaction to the 'thief's' behaviour or perceived attributes, but he disagrees with the claim that the thief must of necessity accept the societal definition and incorporate it into his self-image. Certainly, they admit, the dice are loaded against the thief, but for a thief to define himself as a stigmatised object there must be an element of negotiation. The thief construes himself as a thief precisely because he is a party to the negotiations. He does not have to accept the labelling agency's stigma. Indeed, the role thief may come to be positively evaluated in the same way as the role of a judge is presumed to be positively evaluated in so-called normal or straight society.

But, and this is an important 'but', there is no suggestion that the thief makes himself in a frenzy of self-creation. In the final analysis even symbolic romanticism must and does accept the basic postulate of the societal reaction view of deviance (as expressed in the work of Becker (1963), Goffman (1961), Lemert (1972) and others), namely that deviance is a function of social control and not the other way round. Lemert puts it this way:

> This is a large turn away from the old sociology that tended to rest heavily on the idea that deviance leads to social control. I have come to believe that the reverse idea (i.e. social control leads to deviance) is equally tenable and the potentially richer premise for studying deviance in modern society. (Lemert, 1972)

The point is that labelling implies a group of people who are in a position of power, authority, or who have access to resources which enable them to apply the labels to those persons whose behaviour they find threatening, or whose conduct they find morally reprehensible. In Western societies, it is argued, deviance will inevitably be defined in terms of class criteria so that crimes against property and so on, are far more easily identified than white-collar crime such as fraud and embezzlement. Moreover, various elites, bureaucrats, law-enforcement officers, social workers and other so-called helping professions tend to define deviant acts in terms of cognitive categories which are external to the acts themselves. From this point of view, deviance is a social construction intimately tied to the distribution of power and scarce resources. Social controllers manufacture deviance in the same way, it is claimed, that psychiatry manufactures mental illness. The helping professions are part and parcel of this process because they accept at face value the assumption that deviants can be identified. Accordingly, so the argument goes, there is a vicious circle from the official definers to the target individual. Once his behaviour is stigmatised it becomes legitimate to treat him as a person who deserves such treatment.

A powerful objection to labelling theory is that it tends to focus on the victim or the stigmatised person. Although it stresses the class differentials of the definers and the stigmatised, it nevertheless places a disproportionate amount of emphasis on the weakness and powerlessness of those groups of people who are at the margins of society, or who are weakened by their lack of access to the decision-making process. Hence, there are literally hundreds of participant observer studies of deviance of working-class crime, but a relative paucity of studies of the powerful. There is no way in which it could be said that poverty is simply an identity, a function of labelling, yet in some reports we are invited to believe that poverty generates identities which are defined as being rewarding and valuable.

However, despite these objections, it would seem to me that the investigation of negative identity does have some important implications for our understanding of the way in which various groups of individuals behave under situations of stress and deprivation. In this respect, symbolic interactionists do not make broad and spectacular claims for their case studies. In general its typical approach to the social world is that of the naturalistic observer. Some of its proponents seem to go about their work as if they were sociological social psychologists. Certainly most of them are aware that their constructions are only constructions, that is interpretations of the actors' world. Their methodology is basically a self-conscious participant observation. In the research process itself, they contend, the only possible strategy is to take the role of the other. For example, in Goffman's *Asylums* (1961), the way we come to know and understand the nature of the institutional pressures on patients is not by a detailed analysis of the outside determinants of action, although these are obviously critical, but by an almost intuitive reconstruction of the patients' definition of the situation. Now Goffman may possibly be wrong about the way in which psychiatrists, social workers and nurses go about constructing and typifying neurosis and psychosis. He may also be wrong in his conceptualisation of the way in which patients accept the official definitions of their mental illness, but, if he is wrong, he is not wrong because he did not follow adequate research and sampling procedures.

The standard objection to this approach in the social sciences is that it is not scientific, that it smacks of some form of interpretive humanism which is more suitable to literary criticism or aesthetics, but not sociology. No matter how plausible and convincing a Goffman (1961) or a Becker (1963) may be, it is argued that their work is mainly an account or description which is not supported by consensually validated research procedures. It is a romantic humanism in which identity and the negotiation of identity are substituted for the hard brute facts of everyday life. In this respect it cannot, so the argument goes, help us to understand the reality of deviance nor the operation of legal and social sanctions. It cannot help us to understand the real institutional forces at work in society. It cannot help us to tease out the structural and class determinants of action. But it would seem to me that it is precisely at the level of everyday understanding of action that the symbolic interactionist makes a contribution to the explication of the subjective dimension of social structure. If deviance is socially constructed, then it makes sense to investigate the way in which this social construction is mirrored in the consciousness of the target group.

I am aware that there are countless objections to an approach which seems to be rooted in social psychology, and the sociology of interpersonal relationships, rather than in a hard-headed structural stance. In addition there is a distinct possibility, as one critic trenchantly comments, that symbolic interactionism is oblivious to the true nature of society and to the actuality of deviance, conflict and inequality. He asks:

> What effect, for instance, does the fact of being a negro have on the smooth interaction between individuals in defining the situation? Would the possession of a black skin be merely to add one further factor on to those of which account must be taken when defining the situations? Or would the colour of the skin be the sole or at least the decisive factor in determining the performance of the individuals? In brief, can symbolic interactionism retain its validity in a society in which some men are more equal, or more free, than others? (Shaskolsky, as quoted in Meltzer, Petras and Reynolds, 1977, p. 102)

How can we reject the claim that symbolic interactionism is a form of obscurantist humanism or bourgeois romanticism? I do not think we can. However, I suppose it cannot come to grips with history and social structure because, by definition, it does not pretend to be macro-sociological — it is *inherently* micro-sociological. It deals with interpersonal conduct so that its domain is fundamentally at the social psychological level. Indeed, it might be that it does the perspective a disservice to force it into a position for which it is not manifestly designed. What arguments can we produce in defence of symbolic interactionism as a viable sociological perspective and not simply a form of social psychology? More pertinently, how useful is symbolic interactionism for the understanding and analysis of social control phenomena like the law and political power? As an example, I have adapted Lindesmith and Strauss's discussion (1968, pp. 299-302) of the administration of criminal law in the United States.

Symbolic Interactionism and the Study of Law

Formal System of Criminal Law

In theory these involve rights and obligations explicit in the constitution as well as the definitions of criminality contained in various enactments by Congress and State governments. Moreover, it contains associated notions of justice and equality before the law. From the point of view of the individual, the formal system may or may not be significant. It becomes significant only when he or she is presumed to have broken the law. Now this could mean anything from a driving offence to murder, but what is important is that it seems highly unlikely that the individual would define the law in terms of a negotiating process. For all practical purposes the law is there as a 'given' — *it is taken for granted.* It is something that exists monolithically in historical time. Yet such an acceptance of its existence must depend on a series of patterned negotiations with 'significant others'. The notion of legal omnipotence is transmitted as part and parcel of the socialisation process.

Structure of the Legal System

The abstraction of the legal system as a set of formally constituted rules is translated into the actual personnel and procedures which underpin the system. Being caught up in the legal system means that an individual comes into contact with officials who define themselves as role-players who have the right to articulate the values and expectations of this system. These officials are believed to be the official definers of the law. Accordingly, they are also the definers of deviance.

Having broken the law, machinery is set in motion which categorises and labels the offence. The offence itself eventually defines the deviant or criminal. However, the actual labelling process is dependent on a long set of negotiations between various role-players. Legal procedures are (in theory) not static, but subject to constant interpretation and re-interpretation. So, in principle, a criminal or deviant identity should not be conferred until a conviction is obtained. In practice, the labelling begins from the very moment that the individual comes into contact with officials as a suspected person. This is well documented in Cicourel's *The Social Organization of Juvenile Justice* (1968).

Structural Location

It is self-evident that the participants in this process will define the situation differently. In Lindesmith and Strauss's words (1968, pp. 301-2), 'The accused who is sentenced to a twenty year term sees the process in a radically different way from the judge who pronounces the sentence. Similarly, the judge, prosecutors, defence lawyers and policemen all see it from different perspectives.' The counter-argument to this is that different perspectives are not simply a function of the definition of the situation, but are rooted in real forces at work in the legal system. Hence, the accused will have the dice loaded against him if it is obvious to the law-enforcement officers that he belongs to a minority which regularly produce deviants. Although it is tempting to talk about the negotiation of identities in this context, it is more appropriate to see it in terms of the imposition of identity. The question remains whether or not such an imposition will eventually lead to the accused completely accepting the definitions of the definers. What identity is available to a person who has been sentenced to a twenty-year stint in a maximum-security prison?

Negotiations do not imply that social actors are equal when they confront each other in the legal process. To make such claims would be to accept at face value the official view of criminal justice. There is no equality between the accused and the prosecutor, between the judge and the accused. Negotiations are conducted in terms which do not permit us to construe the power of the accused as being equivalent to the power of the judge. Negotiations are therefore not symmetrical. However, this is qualified by the probability that in some courts the defence may be more powerful than the prosecution, because of the accused's access to the decision-making process. At a more prosaic level it is unlikely that the highly formalised and ritualised relationships in a criminal court can ever be described in terms of reciprocal negotiation. Inter-personal relationships of an informal kind are relegated to contacts between the defence lawyer and his client outside the context of the formal system.

Informal Negotiations

I suppose the hub of the symbolic interactionist position about social structure is contained in their view that society is a 'negotiated order'. But such a negotiated order must depend on literally hundreds of interaction episodes in which participants relate to each other in everyday life . . . It is precisely this notion of the informal episode which underpins institutions and structures. It is at the informal level that contacts are made between role-players or functionaries who talk to each other in settings outside the formal legal framework, that is they interact in a situation in which routine and formality are at a minimum. Lawyers talk to judges, clients talk to lawyers, policemen have drinks with informers and so forth. For the symbolic interactionist this is the bedrock of negotiation which feeds back into the more formal apparatus of the legal system. Bargains are struck, deals are made, perhaps favours are distributed, and political pressures are applied. Put differently, it is at the informal level that we can see the ubiquity of power relationships and the dominance of interest commitments. Negotiations are conducted which are then translated into the formal institutional level.

It is not only the informal episode which modifies institutionalised interaction but also their incorporation into the appropriate stylistic categories. Dramaturgical models suggest that most forms of interaction tend to be dramatic. By this is meant that participants usually act in front of audiences who monitor their performances. Dramaturgical theorists claim that the 'on stage' imperative holds true at both the micro and macro levels. There are a number of strands to this claim.

First, at the sociological level, social structure is seen in terms of patterns of reciprocal orientations or forms. These forms are similar in kind to the sociological grammar discussed by Simmel and which have their counterpoint in various types of exchange theory. It is claimed that dramatic form is essentially *the* sociological mode, and, by implication, also the social psychological mode. This means that, although we use terms from the theatre like roles, performances, scenes, actors, props and so forth, we are not saying that social structure is merely analogous to stage drama — what is being said is that the theatre is a microcosm of social structure. Thus the terms borrowed from the theatre are ones we have put into a spatio-temporal context; they are terms we have socially constructed or invented. We use them to highlight social behaviour within the confines of an artificial construction, namely the stage. This means that when Mead, Goffman, Burke, Duncan and others reintroduce these terms into social thought, they are really translating from a complementary social language.

Secondly, if this is so, then this would seem to imply that some of the older models employed in sociology and social psychology are non-social in that they derive from other universes of discourse, from other levels of analysis. Accordingly, when we examine the organic and mechanical analogies, the thing that strikes us is that their origins are fundamentally non-sociological. So it is the contention of proponents of the dramaturgical mode that the failure of these models is directly attributable to their inability to come to grips with interaction as negotiated meaning (where meaning is defined as scene-situation or context bound). Moreover, the limits of negotiation are circumscribed by the interference of audience factors such as reference groups, peers, or interaction partners. Social control is always exercised by audiences and performances are always partly under the influence of these audiences.

Of course, it could be said that in place of some of the more mechanistic models we are merely substituting an alternative which itself is in danger of being reified and over-worked. The symbolic interactionist position can often degenerate into pure tautology unless one is very careful, but of course this is true of sociology in general.

Thirdly, to argue that social interaction is dramatic does not necessarily mean that one has demonstrated the validity of the dramatic mode in macro-processes. Both the dramaturgical mode, and symbolic interactionism in general, stress the crucial relevance of language and communication as constituting an essential aspect of social order and conflict. The case for extending the parameters of theatrical models of social interaction to macro-processes is made very strongly by Duncan. Traditionally Duncan claims language and communication have been treated as if they were media through which other interests, forces, powers, motives, needs and ideologies were expressed. He argues that while the study of interests is vitally important for social theory, it is wrong to conceive of the medium through which these interests are demonstrated as being neutral or as being a mere mechanism. Hence the dramatic mode makes its cardinal claim that symbols themselves are partly constitutive of social reality. Duncan writes in an almost apocalyptic vein:

> the great social revolution of our day has been in communication, the means whereby those in power create and control the images or names that legitimate their power. Political ideologies are created; their terrible power to goad men into wounding, torturing and killing others are not simply mechanical reactions to interests. They are symbolic forms, they are names, and whoever creates and controls these names, controls our lives. As any revolutionary handbook tells us, the first step in the seizure of power is the control of all symbols of power and communication. (Duncan, 1968, p. 33)

It is in this respect that symbolic interactionism might be said to move away from a purely micro approach to the social world, but it seems to do so by erecting the dramatic symbol as an overarching determinism which negates to some degree the posited voluntarism implicit in aspects of Mead's original position. What is certainly true is that it has a certain force when we examine some of the paraphernalia that go with ritual and legal systems as well as providing some kind of focus for an understanding of ideological forms.

From the perspective of the individual caught up in the legal process it makes a good deal of sense for him to see his predicament in theatrical terms. Certainly the whole process is articulated dramatically. The trial is suffused with dramatic ritual. Moral and legal categories are bandied around by various legal practitioners in such a way that it frequently appears to the outsider as some kind of spectacle put on for the benefit of vast public audiences. However, I do not want to make too much of this.

Conclusion: The Problem of Negotiation

What I want to do now is to examine briefly some of the possible implications of considering legal processes from the point of view of symbolic interactionism. Some of these implications have already been spelt out, namely symbolic interactionism's apparent commitment to negotiability and the symbolic construction of social objects. The reality that is caught in this perspective is one in which human beings constantly have to establish and re-establish the conditions of their existence. Hence, legal processes are seen as being subject to the test of re-interpretation and re-negotiation. There is nothing immutable in social structure or in legal institutions. They depend on a *temporary consensus* among humans to define power, authority, crime, deviance, guilt and justice in a way that is appropriate to the purpose at hand. Put more strongly, symbolic interactionism argues for a symbolic relativism in which law and deviance are expressions of volatile definitions of the situation. However, symbolic interactionists are not so naive as to claim that the definition of the situation is dependent on some random set of negotiations between human actors. Negotiations imply some kind of power relationship, some kind of already existing structure and procedure in which bargains can be struck. But, in contrast to strongly structural accounts of legal processes, symbolic interactionists claim that, in the final analysis, it is at the level of interaction that the law itself is constructed and subverted. In other words, instead of regarding the legal system as being externally imposed upon human masses by an external authority, or by their belief in the naturalness of institutional constraints, symbolic interactionists stress the essential openness and fluidity of all social interaction, this despite the obviousness of situations in which there does not appear to be much leeway for negotiation.

So it is perhaps the concept of negotiation which is most problematic for symbolic interactionist accounts of law. There is a temptation to see negotiation as *the* fundamental property of all legal and structural processes. In principle, this means that nothing cannot be subverted by the strong presentation of an argument in an apparently closed situation. What this suggests is that the law is ultimately a codification of talk, and that talk itself is subject to the influence of procedures which allow for the real possibility of changing the procedures themselves. For example, while the rules of the game in a trial are supposed to be validated by the statutes of parliament, precedents and the consensual understandings of the participants, there is no way in which this can be said to represent an accurate picture of the law in action. The concept of negotiation is introduced in order to account for the competing definitions used by the various parties who play roles in a stereotyped situation. In the typical mainstream sociological description of these situations, what is usually averred is that role-players will play their parts according to some notion of a master script which leaves not much room for alternative outcomes. By emphasising negotiation, symbolic interactionists claim that even the most rigidly specified situations are under the possible control of *all* participants to the interaction. But we may ask how can negotiation take place when social control factors are those which seem to have the full authority of the state behind them? True, one may bribe a policeman, threaten a judge, lie to a solicitor, but this does not mean that the procedures themselves can be reconstituted. Negotiation may work for this or that individual, but does this imply that the whole legal system itself can be talked or argued into a new consensual equilibrium?

However, in defence of the symbolic interactionist argument, we could say that there is no truth in the accusation of its astructural bias. For most symbolic interactionists, the reality of social structures is not at issue. What is at issue are the interpretive procedures whereby human beings represent that structure to themselves. And it is in this context that they pay so much attention to the ambiguities and imprecisions of all symbolic discourse, especially that discourse that has to do with the ascription of motive and guilt. In this context, while there are difficulties associated with labelling theory, there can be no doubt that its judicious use can make us sensitive to the ways in which some people are often forced to accept definitions of their behaviour that profoundly influence their future deviant careers.

Such an acceptance of other people's definitions indicate that these people are often in a position to negotiate from a position of strength, but this does not mean that negotiation inevitably results in a victory for the powerful. On the contrary, because all labels are socially constructed (class determined?) there is a probability that deviants, victims, clients and so on may contribute to their own negotiated identities. If there is any merit to the symbolic interactionist perspective, it is precisely at this level, namely in its highlighting of the ambiguity of social life as manifested in talk and argument. In this sense the law can be seen as a negotiated order subject to the control of a multiplicity of competing 'definitions of the situation' that are mediated by human actors who find it impossible not to question the immutability of the 'taken-for-granted-world'.

Bibliography

Akers, R.L. 'Problems in the Sociology of Deviance: Social Definition and Behaviour', *Social Forces*, vol. 46 (1968), pp. 455-65
Becker, H.S. *Outsiders* (Free Press, New York, 1963)
Brittan, A. *The Privatised World* (Routledge and Kegan Paul, London, 1977)
Burke, K. *A Grammar of Motives* (University of California, 1969)

Cicourel, A.V. *The Social Organization of Juvenile Justice* (Wiley, New York, 1968)
Cooley, C.H. *Human Nature and the Social Order* (Schocken, New York, 1964)
Dewey, T. *Experience and Nature* (W.W. Norton, New York, 1929)
Duncan, H.D. *Symbols in Society* (Oxford University Press, New York, 1968)
Goffman, E. *Asylums* (Doubleday, New York, 1961)
______ *The Presentation of Self in Everyday Life* (Doubleday, New York, 1969)
Husserl, E. *Ideas: Pure Phenomenology* (Allen and Unwin, London, 1931)
James, W. *Pragmatism* (Longmans, New York, 1949)
Lemert, E.M. *Human Deviance, Social Problems, and Social Control* (Prentice-Hall, Englewood Cliffs, New Jersey, 1972)
Lindesmith, A.R. and Strauss, A.L. *Social Psychology* (Holt, Rinehart and Winston, New York, 1968)
Mead, G.H. *Mind, Self and Society* (University of Chicago Press, Chicago, 1967)
Meltzer, B.M., Petras, J.W. and Reynolds, L.T. *Symbolic Interactionism* (Routledge and Kegan Paul, London, 1977)
Morris, M.B. *An Excursion into Creative Sociology* (Basil Blackwell, Oxford, 1977)
Schutz, A. *The Phenomenology of the Social World* (Heinemann, London, 1972)
Simmel, G. *The Sociology of George Simmel* (The Free Press, New York, 1950)
Thomas, W.I. *The Child in America* (Knopf, New York, 1932)

10 Law from a Phenomenological Perspective

Maria Łoś

Introduction

The boundaries of phenomenological sociology are hard to grasp. Its tasks, scope and methodological principles are defined in various ways by different representatives, as well as by critics of this perspective. Yet despite great differences among the various currents in phenomenological sociology, they all seem to protest against some common enemies and to reject some forms of sociological enterprise as being contrary to their epistemological commitments. They certainly reject:

(i) the behavioural orientation in sociology (as they are primarily interested in the subjective experience and construction of meanings);
(ii) the deterministic vision of the relationship between man and society (as opposed to the dialectical one);
(iii) the separation of the observer (a sociologist) and the object of the observation, as if they belong to different worlds;
(iv) the obligatory nature of the common presuppositions usually taken for granted by ordinary people, or by social scientists;
(v) the quantitative approach to qualitative phenomena (since they believe that the main task of sociology is not to count or to measure, but to grasp the meanings, or even the essences of social phenomena);
(vi) the notion that views reality as existing in an abstract realm, awaiting passively to be discovered (rather, reality is being constituted and reconstructed by the conscious processes of perception).

As far as methodology is concerned, a basic disparity exists between those who believe in the validity of transcendental reduction in studies of society (the ideas of Husserl, 1962), and those who do not. *Transcendental reduction* assumes a purification of subjectivity which leads to the attainment by the observer of the state of anonymous consciousness (transcendental ego), whereby he has access to absolute, apodictic knowledge. According to Husserl, transcendental phenomenological reduction consists of bracketing off the outside world (the world external to oneself) and concentrating instead in the living of one's experiences of the world so that pure consciousness, in which the world presents itself to the reflecting ego, can be attained. Those phenomenologists who are not satisfied with general postulates have usually been sceptical about the virtues of an orthodox application of Husserl's ideas in the field of sociology. In particular, phenomenologists who attempt to accomplish concrete sociological tasks usually abandon the ambition of achieving transcendental insight into the essence of things. They do this, to some extent for practical reasons, but also — more importantly — because they believe that it does not make very much sense to bracket the existence of the shared social world if we want to study its content. The social world would become meaningless if we stopped believing that it is similarly experienced and interpreted within a similar context by some of our fellow-men. Meanings are socially constructed; they cannot be discovered by a negation of the existence of *alter ego,* for without it, a social world itself would not be possible.

Schutz (1962, 1964, 1966) initiated the sociological inquiry into the subjective 'naive' attitude and everyday knowledge of average people in their 'life-world', that is, the common-sense, taken-for-granted, everyday reality. The peculiar form of cognitive style assumed by people in their everyday lives implies — in contradistinction to the 'epoch' of phenomenological transcendental reduction — a suspension of every doubt concerning the existence of the outer world and its objects. Schutz chose to assume a cognitive style of the average people, in order to see the world through their eyes. However, he hopes to discover not only what they see, but also what actually they no longer see, since this forms an invisible, obvious, taken-for-granted background to all their activities. He believes that people are conscious in a passive, natural way, which can easily be proved by the fact that they become alert and puzzled as soon as anticipated patterns do not occur, or when they assume different forms.

It is clear that Schutz did not believe that the understanding of social life could be achieved by the abstract, detached, transcendental ego, which operates within the cognitive style in a way that is completely alien, and indeed opposite, to that typical of members of society in their inter-subjective, shared with others, 'paramount' reality. In view of this, Schutz passed over transcendental reduction when he suspended the unquestioning, 'naive' attitude, and attempted to face directly those very features of the social life which are commonly treated by people as obvious and as not deserving any systematic attention. Such a procedure is basically compatible with the main directives of the phenomenological perspective (as defined by Husserl), since the sources of knowledge and the significant starting point of inquiry are located in pre-scientific reality of everyday life, as also is its language — free of any assumptions except those accepted within the studied world. According to Schutz, the cognitive interest of the researcher — as opposed to the practical interests of people in their everyday life — and his detachment from his biographical situation, are supposed to guarantee the objective nature of the 'thought constructs' of second order which he builds up on the basis of 'common-sense constructs' found in everyday reality, by systematising and elaborating them according to the rules of logic.

Diversity of Tasks

It would be a gross distortion to assume that the scope of possible phenomenological inquiries into society is limited merely to intuitive studies of the subjective experience of different persons or communities. It seems that much more has been, and still can be, achieved by systematic efforts to introduce this perspective into sociology.

Study of the Basis of Social Life

Phenomenological sociology seems to be exceptionally well equipped to study the basic premisses and the unique features of human associations. It should be able to establish the necessary conditions for the existence of human societies, for natural attitudes and for a shared life-world.

Schutz (1962, 1964, 1966) criticised those social scientists who simply take for granted the existence of societies, groups, institutions, patterns of communication among people, and so forth. His attempts to investigate why and how they are possible were focused on studies of the nature of human consciousness, of inter-personal communications, and of the basic mechanisms of social order. It seems that the primary task of phenomenological sociology should consist of the elaboration and testing of such general, fundamental concepts which could be utilised further in more advanced studies of concrete forms of societies.

At this level of abstraction, the use of imagination, guided by the rules of *phenomenological reduction,* seems to be most suitable (so-called 'imaginative variation'). In such an exercise, a researcher tries to imagine the existence of society without various features or elements which appear to constitute important parts of what he perceives as society. Consequently, he should be able to select those elements which seem to be necessary and constitute the core meaning of society. If they cease to exist, the existence of society would no longer be possible.

Naturally, such an approach has often been criticised (by critics both inside and outside phenomenology) as too abstract and detached from empirically-accessible reality. It seems, however, that it may be quite useful if treated as a starting point and a frame of reference for further sociological work (also in the area of sociology of law).

Phenomenological Sociology of Knowledge

It seems quite obvious that what people do is, at least to some extent, guided by what they know. And what they know is not exactly what is written in sophisticated books which contain what is usually treated as knowledge. Phenomenological sociology may thus fulfil an important task by studying the structure and content of everyday common knowledge and its links with the pragmatic goals and projects of the people involved.

Very important contributions in this area have been made by Schutz (1962, 1964, 1966), Berger and Luckmann (1966), as well as other phenomenologists. Many studies in the area of ethnomethodology and socio-linguistics are also of a great relevance for this kind of sociology of knowledge. The notion of 'humanistic coefficient' (defined by Znaniecki (1976) in 1934, as a requirement to study the meaning and use of the given cultural phenomena in a concrete social context as a condition of understanding it) has helped to grasp the real consequences of people's beliefs, perceptions, assumptions about reality, superstitions and collective illusions. The Weberian methods of organising certain elements of reality into logically precise conceptions by revealing (or constructing) their internal rationality (ideal types) — refined by Schutz — have proved to be very useful in studying stereotypes and habits which guide the perceptions and predictions of people in their everyday life. They constitute a convenient cognitive tool which helps people to come to terms with reality and to make it more predictable.

This type of inquiry has been criticised as very trivial, due to its concentration on very mundane or tedious aspects of popular knowledge which are scientifically uninteresting and irrelevant (see Gorman, 1977; Grahl and Piccone, 1973; Molina, 1969; Piccone, 1968, 1971; and many other writers, especially those representing transcendental phenomenology, existential phenomenology, and the Marxist orientation). Yet it is often overlooked that, by discovering what is commonly-known or automatically assumed, one is also able to reveal what is unknown or treated as questionable. For example, for many needy people the language and the logic of the legal regulations connected with social benefits for the poor may be too difficult to understand. Under such circumstances they have no clear idea what sort of claims they can make, nor are they able to predict the outcome when they apply for financial aid. Studies of the legal regulations, of the relevant legal agencies and of the inflow, as well as the outcome of the applications may provide a quite satisfactory picture of the functioning of the institution of supplementary benefits. Yet, studies of the structure and distribution of knowledge in this area may reveal the strain caused by the existence of uncertainty, even in those cases when the applicants were, in the end, successful. Ignorance in a particular area is normally associated with feelings of unpredictability and powerlessness.

The lack of knowledge or its relative vagueness may be — as Schutz suggested — due to its perceived irrelevance to the interests and life goals of the individual. Yet it may also be caused by the sheer inaccessibility of information or by some generalised attitude (fear, for instance) which makes it difficult for people to demand or even to face the truth. Social ignorance in certain areas, or the awareness of unpredictability in the interaction with certain people or institutions, may precisely be one of the key factors in the successful management and control over a society or a group. Its predominating influence may also be significantly strengthened by positive knowledge, and especially by those unreflectively taken-for-granted categories and stereotypes. The question of the social distribution of knowledge, if linked with the interests of the power elite and with the nature of political system, thus becomes a fundamental issue for any comprehensive sociological inquiry.

In the area of law the actual accessibility of knowledge is regulated by many, generally recognised, factors, such as the consistency of law, clarity of language, selectivity of legal information and propaganda, and so forth. However, one immediately discovers further complications while studying a significant role which legal fictions play as the major pillars of both law and the overall political systems (for a broader discussion of legal fictions see Fuller, 1967). Many questions can be raised concerning the awareness of legal fiction by the members of various groups (especially those of a less technical nature). They may not know about them at all; they may be familiar with their normative content but do not realise their fictitious character; they may finally perceive them in accordance with their true nature. In the latter case, they may disapprove of them and demand that the law should not be treated as a smoke screen (they may, for instance, organise protests against hidden racial or sex discrimination). They may disapprove of them, but may not actually be bothered by the specific cases of fiction (as they may believe, for example, that 'the laws are made to suit the rich anyway', or that the powerful 'they' can interpret the law as they wish, and 'if they are after you they will no doubt get you'). The fiction may also be such an obvious element of the political reality in a given country that to complain, for instance, that the constitution is not enforced, would mean that one actually assumed that the constitution was a serious document, which could be a most unrealistic expectation indeed.

The political and legal fictions are maintained exactly because people recognise them as such, and they behave according to this common *knowledge:* 'A fiction taken seriously, that is "believed", becomes dangerous and loses its utility. A fiction becomes wholly safe only when it is used with a complete consciousness of its falsity' (Fuller, 1967, pp. 9-10). It would really be disastrous if people suddenly started to behave as if they believed in fiction. Yet this unspoken understanding has received, so far, surprisingly little attention by the researchers.

Study of the Everyday 'Life-World'

Connected directly with the previous task of phenomenological sociology is the task of studying the direct reality experienced by the members of various groups (including elites), classes or societies. In this case, attention is focused on the subjective experience of the people involved in their everday pursuits, and the mechanisms by which their experience is programmed and organised. Such studies should eventually help to answer the basic questions of consensus, conformity and continuity which constitute an essential aspect of social order.

As mentioned above, this task can be achieved by *philosophical reduction* which consists mainly of the suspension of the unquestioning, 'naive' attitude, and which allows the penetration of the unreflective part of the consciousness of studied groups. Such a task can be performed by an insider playing (intellectually) a stranger. It relies on the personal intuitive evidence and ability of the sociologist to reflect upon life, as well as to organise the outcomes in a coherent manner.

Many critiques (mainly by non-phenomenologists) have been raised against this prevailing interpretation of the aim of phenomenological sociology. For instance, it has been argued that the study of natural attitude tends to stress consensus and reciprocity of perspectives, while in reality there exist conflicts, oppression and manipulation. Attacks on the tediousness and irrelevance of the focus on the mundane have been paralleled by charges of neglect of the existence of power, as well as of the economic and political organisation of society. However, it must be understood that what appears as consensus, conformity and taken-for-granted wisdom is not politically neutral. It has been moulded and conditioned by political and cultural forces. And yet, on the other hand, it constitutes the most solid fabric of society which tends to resist manipulation and pressure towards change. A penetrating insight into this basic fabric of social consciousness should certainly facilitate a much more adequate understanding of the social structure of a given society.

It is sometimes argued that phenomenology offers an uncritical apologia of the taken-for-granted *status quo.* Indeed, the work of Schutz (1962, 1966, 1970) gives exactly such an impression. However, it should be clear that the taken-for-granted aspects of reality are not necessarily approved and welcomed by the people, as it is commonly believed. For example, in many prisons, prisoners take it for granted that their mail is checked and censored, but it would be rather naive to assume that they approve of it. Most probably there is always a part of the taken-for-granted reality which — if reflected upon — would be *approved* and supported. This part would be most likely associated with the moral and religious values, highly internalised by the members of a given group.

Another part would probably be considered as *pragmatically useful* although of neutral value in the light of the accepted normative order. This would include all those convenient arrangements and practical routines which make life easier, if observed by the members of the community. A great many of these practical arrangements are obviously of a legal nature, although this is rarely realised by people in their normal, everyday activities. Only when these routines are disturbed by somebody's non-conformity is an appeal to the legal status of the regulation involved likely to be made.

There is, however, still another part of the taken-for-granted reality which, although *unacceptable,* is generally perceived by the people as being outside their influence. In extreme cases, the whole socio-political system may belong to this category. Taking for granted of the unacceptable may occur in various ways. It may take place when people accept imposed 'rules of the game' in order to survive (in some countries, for instance, it may be absolutely obvious and, in fact, taken for granted that one does not criticise the authorities in public; thus behaviour contrary to this expectation provokes astonishment or suspicion).

Another way of neutralising the unacceptable consists of various rationalisations which help to protect one's dignity and integrity in the face of irresistible pressure. There are many honourable ways of ruling out a temptation of dissent (it may be, for instance, taken for granted that any attempt to change the situation would bring a cruel reprisal on innocent people, or would result in further restrictions of freedom). The legalistic attitude aimed at by most legal systems consists in automatic conformity with legal norms, even if they conflict with one's convictions, for the sake of the stability of social order which is protected by the legal system as a whole.

A still different character shows the defence mechanisms which help to neutralise the oppressiveness of the situation. Uncritically accepted false images, fictions or convenient scapegoats prevent people from facing their frightful plight. It is no accident that in times of political or economic crises, law and order campaigns are quite often successful in shifting people's attention and fears from the real difficulties to the threat posed by crime and so-called deviant subcultures (see Hall *et al.,* 1978).

Comparative studies of the structure of the taken-for-granted reality in different societies might probably produce very interesting results. It would at least prove that the mundane reality of everyday life does not exist independently of the overall structure and organisation of society.

Study of the 'Life-World' in a Broader Context

The task of studying the subjective 'life-world' in the broader subjective and objective context follows logically from the last field of inquiry. This kind of approach should help to elucidate the causes of differences in the structure and content of the 'life-worlds' of different groups or societies. The differences discovered should pose some questions which cannot be answered without reference to the complex organisation of a given society, the relationships among various groups (or classes) within it and their relations to the material resources of the society.

In order to shed some light on the problem under discussion it may be useful to analyse hypothetical differences among the 'life-worlds' of people living under different political conditions. It is most likely, for instance, that these differences would be rather striking if we compare the countries with the centralised, totalitarian control system and those characterised by a pluralistic system of control and 'hegemony' rule (as defined by Gramsci).

One can speculate that the pragmatic level of the taken-for-granted knowledge would be rather disintegrated in the countries of the first kind (totalitarian). A grossly limited ability to predict in the most prosaic, mundane areas of life results in the constant preoccupation with everday problems, which prevents people from having a fuller involvement in other areas. Unpredictability of the legal system and the questionable nature of legal rights is directly conducive to such a situation.

It may be expected that this pragmatic level of the everyday routine tends to be much more integrated and smoothly organised in the countries of the second kind (ruled by 'hegemony'). Satisfaction with the organisation of the society which is generated on this level is supposed to incline people to accept the whole system.

The approval level of the taken-for-granted morality is — in the first case — shaken by official attempts to redefine traditional values, or to link them with new ideological values which lead to the emergence of completely new normative phenomena. As a result, many traditional values are compromised (for instance, patriotism, when it is linked with the fascist ideology), while new ones do not become legitimised. This contributes to the atmosphere of a moral void and of general mistrust, and is reinforced by an impossibility to abide by laws which are marked with ambivalence and double standards.

In countries ruled by the 'hegemony' principle, moral traditions are cultivated in order to preserve a generalised attitude of trust in the good will and common sense of the government, and of fellow citizens. The image of the legal system appears to reinforce this basic moral hierarchy and trust in the just moral order.

The unacceptable, but realistically taken-for-granted part of the life-world is, in the first case, characterised by the highly encouraged shift from morality towards realistic instrumentality (opportunism), supported by the whole range of rationalisations and rituals, as well as by habitualised double-talk. The unacceptable, when it is perceived as unavoidable, becomes a part of the 'normal', automatically anticipated, and an immediately recognised reality. Radical alternatives are treated as too dangerous even to think of, and therefore impossible.

The unacceptable in the second case tends to be seen through the common-sense philosophy of scarce resources, overpopulation, imperfect human nature, unhappy international developments, or mistakes in domestic policies. Radical alternatives are treated as utopian or as outrageous.

The above *example* is based on a very unsatisfactory distinction between the two types of societies. A more advanced analysis could be achieved only through attempts at a synthesis of the outcomes of the phenomenological approach (including the unanswered questions which it generates) with more macrostructural attempts at analysis of the social structure and the economy. Yet the most successful attempt at reconciliation of phenomenology and Marxism (for example, those by Merleau-Ponty, 1974; Paci, 1972; Piccone, 1968 and 1971; and Sartre, 1963 and 1966) represents a rather different level of analysis, and are concerned mainly with the unmasking and liberating mission of these two directions of thought (above all, with their critique of ideology).

Liberation of Human Consciousness

This final task of phenomenological sociology, although not particularly modest, has been emphasised by many phenomenologists (above all, by Husserl, 1970; Merleau-Ponty, 1974; O'Neill, 1972; Paci, 1972). According to their claims, phenomenological studies of the social world can facilitate the process of the unmasking of the reification and mystification of social phenomena. Naturally it includes also the demystification of sociological concepts and the unmasking of the role sociology has played in supporting and legitimising dominant cultures and dominant ideological fictions. It also includes a scrutiny of sociological techniques and sources of data — for instance, official statistics (see Cicourel, 1964, 1968).

Studies aimed at the demystification of social consciousness can be, for instance, guided by the vision of social construction of reality offered by Berger and Luckmann (1966). One can attempt to disclose systematically the process of the reification and institutionalisation of various social ideas and interests; the processes of their legitimisation, when moral validity is given to the institutional order, and, finally, their incorporation into the general world view (or symbolic universe) perceived as given and constant. These processes are probably facilitated by the common human need of social order and of fear of chaos. Yet the processes of the institutionalisation of the particular form of social order are not so spontaneous, egalitarian and 'innocent' as many phenomenologists would have it.

Those phenomenologists who recognise the fallacy of the apologia of the taken-for-granted reality stress the need for the constant unmasking of alienating institutions and the demystification of manipulation. They emphasise the importance of the creation of social conditions for continuous human self-discovery and self-liberation, as well as the need to prevent people from voluntarily giving up their subjectivity and authenticity. It implies the opening up of the horizon of society beyond the mystified limits and restraints. However, it seems rather obvious — contrary to the beliefs of some 'radically minded' phenomenologists — that the collective search for freedom and purity of consciousness does not automatically lead to the elimination of power, domination, inequality and exploitation, even if it succeeds in unmasking their mystified nature.

Phenomenological Critique of the Sociology of Law (Dangers and Prospects)

Sociology of law is, at the present stage of its development, very loose and fragmented, and does not offer any consistent theoretical framework. It is not surprising, since its subject is so broad and multiform that it seems impossible to formulate any theoretical statements which would adequately apply to so unrealistically defined a field. Practically everything in society has some relevance from the point of view of the law. If, for instance, sociologists of law study divorce, why should they not study marriage, which is, after all, one of the most prominent legal institutions? If they study unlawful dismissals why should they not inquire into normal work processes which are regulated by law? Legal aspects permeate modern social life so entirely that it is almost unthinkable to study any social phenomena without bringing legal aspects into the picture. On the other hand, it seems rather unreasonable to try to isolate all these legal threads and treat them as a separate field of inquiry ruled by its own logic.

Certainly an important task for which the phenomenological perspective may be helpful is a careful and penetrating scrutiny of the subject-matter of the sociology of law and its basic taken-for-granted concepts. One may suspect that, for instance, market legal regulations and laws connected with psychiatric treatment may not have enough in common to treat them as a homogeneous field of study. One may also have some doubts whether the concentration on legal professions as a separate subject-matter is sufficiently justified, as law is, in fact, enforced and executed in everyday reality by the representatives of so many other professional categories (various experts, different kinds of controllers, teachers, social workers, managers, trade union officials, internal revenue office employees and so forth). By focusing on only some forms of law, certain agencies and selected professions, the sociology of law reinforces a false image of the scope of the law and is likely to help to sustain the fiction of separation of law and politics.

Compartmentalisation of the social sciences seems incompatible with the basic rules of the phenomenological approach. People in their everyday life do not isolate artificially one aspect of reality from another. If, for instance, they feel oppressed, they see various aspects of oppression intermingled, and their perception of the legal regulations involved is inseparable from other elements of the experienced situation. To some extent, of course, it changes when ordinary people adopt the concepts used by the mass media and by the politicians. Their response to complex situations may thus be narrowed down by the available formal vocabulary and they would almost automatically exclaim that 'there should be a law to forbid this', or 'the courts of law do not punish criminals any more, they breed them'. Ready concepts (law, crime and so on) are often used uncritically, as if they had precisely defined meanings, and a more or less homogeneous nature. This disjoined, compartmentalised experience indicates a common inability to grasp social reality in a more total and meaningful way. Sociologists should be made aware of the role sociology and its numerous sub-disciplines have played in promoting these artificially narrowed categories which structure the processes of the perception of social reality.

Sociologists of law tend to take some legal norms or institutions as their starting point and treat them as being of a primarily legal nature. However, it may be argued that their legal form is of secondary importance, even if it is pragmatically indispensable. The legal regulations of labour relations, housing, taxation, immigration, and many other areas, are determined by the decisions and the guidelines of a purely political nature. One cannot remove these legal devices from the more general context of the political process without losing access to their initial meaning and purpose. Furthermore, one cannot understand the nature of the political process without achieving an insight into the intentions and interests of the political and economic elite, as well as into the perceptions, expectations and interests of many other groups in society. Certainly 'law' and its different concrete forms may mean various things to different people. For the politicians it may be a convenient tool for the implementation of their ideological choices of policies, or for disguising their ideological concessions. For many employees of the legal agencies it may appear as an autotelic system: it is to be enforced for its own sake. For many ordinary people, it may have some superior — symbolic or instrumental — value or, otherwise, it may be seen as legalised injustice.

In sum, law in action cannot be studied in isolation from the political and social processes of which it is a part. Nor can it be understood without reference to the interests, intentions and perceptions of the various groups involved. None the less, whether these groups are seen as classes, as social strata, or as, for instance, professional categories, depends very much on the vision of social structure held by the researcher. The only guidelines provided by phenomenology refer to the group boundaries defined by the scope of shared 'life-world'. Yet in order to understand the forces behind the structure of societal differentiation according to common experience (which leads to the shared symbolic community), one has to be able to grasp the basic features of organisation of the economy, the historical past and the international relationships of a given society. Naturally, these basic features never reveal themselves to the researcher in an unequivocal way. In his attempt to break through appearances and mystified notions, he is bound to make some arbitrary decisions about the valid criteria for uncovering the 'real nature' of the studied phenomena.

Bibliography

Berger, P.L., Berger, B. and Kellner, H. *The Homeless Mind* (Penguin, Harmondsworth, 1974)

Berger, P.L. and Luckmann, T. *The Social Construction of Reality* (Doubleday, New York, 1966)

Cicourel, A.V. *Method and Measurement in Sociology* (Free Press, New York, 1964)

______ *The Social Organization of Juvenile Justice* (Wiley, New York, 1968)

Fuller, L.L. *Legal Fictions* (Stanford University Press, Stanford, California, 1967)

Gorman, R. *The Dual Vision* (Routledge and Kegan Paul, London, 1977)

Grahl, B. and Piccone, P. (eds.) *Towards a New Marxism* (Telos Press, St Louis, 1973)

Hall, S., Critcher, C., Jefferson, T., Clarke, J. and Roberts, B. *Policing the Crisis* (Macmillan Press, London, 1978)

Husserl, E. *Ideas*, rev. edn (Allen and Unwin, London, 1962)

——— *Phenomenology and the Crisis of Philosophy* (Harper and Row, New York, 1965)
——— *The Crisis of European Sciences and Transcendental Phenomenology* (Northwestern University Press, Evanston, 1970)
Lassman, P. 'Phenomenological Perspectives in Sociology' in J. Rex (ed.), *Approaches to Sociology* (Routledge and Kegan Paul, London, 1974), pp. 125-44
Lukacs, G. *History and Class Consciousness* (Merlin Press, London, 1971)
Merleau-Ponty, M. *Adventures of the Dialectic* (Heinemann, London, 1974)
Molina, F.R. (ed.) *The Sources of Existentialism as Philosophy* (Prentice-Hall, Englewood Cliffs, New Jersey, 1969)
O'Neill, J.C. *Sociology as a Skin-Trade* (Heinemann, London, 1972)
Paci, D. *The Function of the Sciences and the Meaning of Man* (Northwestern University Press, Evanston, 1972)
Phillipson, M. *Sociological Aspects of Crime and Delinquency* (Routledge and Kegan Paul, London, 1971)
Phillipson, M. *et al. New Directions in Sociology* (Collier-Macmillan, London, 1972)
Piccone, P. 'Dialectical Logic Today', *Telos,* vol. 2 (1968), pp. 38-83
——— 'Phenomenological Marxism' *Telos,* vol. 9 (1971)
Psathas, G. (ed.) *Phenomenological Sociology. Issues and Applications* (Wiley, New York, 1973)
Sartre, J.P. *Search for a Method* (Knopf, New York, 1963)
——— *Being and Nothingness* (Washington Square Press, New York, 1966)
Schutz, A. *Collected Papers,* vol. I: *Social Reality,* edited by M. Natanson (Nijhoff, The Hague, 1962)
——— *Collected Papers,* vol. II: *Studies in Social Theory,* edited by A. Brodersen (1964)
——— *Collected Papers,* vol. III: *Studies in Phenomenological Philosophy,* edited by Ilse Schutz (1966)
——— *On Phenomenology and Social Relations,* edited by H.R. Wagner (University of Chicago Press, Chicago and London, 1970)
Schutz, A. and Luckman, T. *The Structure of the Life-World* (Heinemann Educational Books, London, 1974)
Smart, B. *Sociology, Phenomenology and Marxian Analysis* (Routledge and Kegan Paul, London, 1976)
Znaniecki, F. *The Method of Sociology* (Farrar and Rinehart, New York, 1976)

11 Ethnomethodological Approaches to Socio-Legal Studies

J. Maxwell Atkinson

Introduction

Ethnomethodology is such a relatively new development within sociology that, had this volume appeared ten years ago, it is fairly unlikely that it would have qualified as having been deserving of a special chapter. If it had been included, however, it would have been a good deal easier to outline its concerns with the study of legal phenomena then than it is now. Thus, it could have been noted that the first published research of the founder of ethnomethodology was based on observations of homicide trials (Garfinkel, 1949) and that it had been during his subsequent involvement with the celebrated Chicago jury project that he had actually coined the word 'ethnomethodology' (on the origins of which, see Garfinkel, 1974). Similarly, it was also the case that several of the researchers whose earlier work was influential in establishing the viability of this emerging tradition had, at various times during the 1960s, been affiliated to the Berkeley Center for Studies in Law and Society (see, for example, Cicourel, 1968; Sacks, 1972a; Sudnow, 1965). A number of other studies from that period also focused on a range of legal contexts, such as police arrest practices on Skid Row (Bittner, 1967), traffic courts (Pollner, 1974, 1979), a public assistance agency (Zimmerman, 1969) and a half-way house for ex-convicts (Wieder, 1974). Given that pre-publication drafts of many of these were already available ten years ago, it would at that time have been relatively easy to have summarised 'the work so far' with a view to outlining its relevance for the study of law.

Since then, however, research influenced by these earlier studies in ethnomethodology has developed and diversified to a point where it no longer makes much sense to treat the range of approaches now being pursued as if they represented an identical or unified theoretical orientation. At one end of the spectrum, for example, the work has become much more philosophical and further removed from the analysis of empirical data (see, for example, Blum *et al.,* 1974). By contrast, the development of research in conversational analysis has been made possible by paying increasingly close attention to the details of naturally occurring interactions that can be captured and preserved for study by using audio- and video-recording technology (see, for example, Sacks, Schegloff and Jefferson, 1974). To do justice to the range and complexity of the work that has in various ways been inspired by ethnomethodology is therefore hardly possible within the confines of a single chapter, and what follows is accordingly both highly selective and generalised. It begins with an attempt to summarise some of the main issues associated with the study of social order that led Harold Garfinkel to propose the reorientation to sociological inquiry that has become known as 'ethnomethodology'. This is followed by a brief consideration of why researchers working within this evolving framework may have been particularly attracted towards interaction in legal settings as a focus for research. Subsequent sections deal briefly with studies in the production of official statistics, and in conversational analysis.

Ethnomethodology and the Problem of Social Order

For at least a century, sociologists have dreamed of producing descriptions and explanations of social phenomena that would exhibit some of the rigour and general applicability achieved by natural scientists. The suggestion that this has been a 'dream' is not intended to ironicise or ridicule the discipline for its failures, nor to propose that the aim of accumulating a corpus of systematic knowledge about social order is somehow mistaken or not worthwhile. Rather it is to draw attention to the fact that sociologists still have a great deal of trouble in convincing a more general public that their 'expert' claims about how the social world works should be taken any more seriously than those of anyone else. In addition, as is evidenced by the range of different perspectives represented in the present volume, sociologists also find it difficult to persuade each other about matters as basic as how social order should be conceptualised, researched, described and explained.

A curious feature of the various disputes that divide sociologists into rival theoretical camps is that the arguments revolve around a relatively small number of well-known and very obvious problems.

These are not just familiar to the professional theorists, but they are also already known by newcomers to the discipline who stop to think, or are asked by their teachers to think, about what problems there might be in trying to study social order 'scientifically'. Thus, first-year students are quickly able to point to the tension between objective appearances and subjective experiences of social phenomena, between socio-cultural determinism and individual choice as antecedents of action, to the problems posed by our already being members of the society we wish to study, to the difficulties of conducting controlled laboratory experiments, and so on. Students who stay the course will subsequently learn that such issues provide the central focus for most of the debates that make up advanced sociological theory. And, given that they will in the meantime have learnt that sociological research has much to report on such things as the family, class, education, social change, the law, they may also realise that sociology is a discipline that proceeds 'in spite of known problems'. In other words, neither an appreciation of the difficulties nor the knowledge that they seriously undermine particular studies has done much to deter sociologists from their hopes of being able to say important things about the major social problems of the day. A general theme in the emergence of ethnomethodology, however, has been the suggestion that an insistence on preserving such hopes may be the biggest obstacle in the way of coming to terms with the 'known problems'. And central among these are those associated with the analyst's membership of the society under study, and the relationship between common sense and professional methods of reasoning about social order.

Conflict and consensus theorists, symbolic interactionists, phenomenologists and the rest all claim to have identified the most appropriate model of social order and social action, as well as the most suitable research methods. Unfortunately, however, there are no widely accepted independent procedures for deciding between the competing versions. And, in the absence of these, the various theoretical approaches continue to coexist, a consequence of which is that they provide the 'data' for yet further speculation aimed at producing some new synthesis or reconciliation between the alternatives. On at least three issues, however, there is fairly widespread agreement between the majority of sociologists, irrespective of their particular theoretical orientation. The first is that (in spite of all the evidence to the contrary) sociology, or the favoured approach to it, is capable of producing descriptions and explanations of social phenomena that accurately represent or correspond with the actual events in the world to which the descriptions and explanations refer. A second point of agreement is the belief that professional sociological accounts of what goes on in the social world (and why it goes on) are of a different and superior order to the kinds of descriptions and explanations that are available to and routinely used by ordinary people in making sense of their everyday lives. And a third and closely related theme common to most sociology is the view that such everyday methods of practical reasoning are in some sense 'flawed', and hence are to be either avoided, or at least repaired, modified or otherwise cleaned up for the purposes of doing professional sociology.

Now it might be thought that to reject any or all of these long-standing assumptions would be to deny the possibility of pursuing any kind of sociological research at all. For if descriptions cannot be shown to be 'correct', if the distinctiveness of sociological accounts in comparison with common-sense ones cannot be demonstrated, and if sociologists are unable to escape from or improve on the everyday methods of reasoning over which they had command long before they ever encountered the discipline of sociology, then it is not altogether obvious what options remain other than the writing of journalistic reports, fiction, or political propaganda. However, the approach to social research developed by ethnomethodologists during the past twenty years or so is one which *neither* accepts those long-standing points of sociological consensus, *nor* recommends the abandonment of further attempts at the systematic investigation of social phenomena. At first sight, of course, such a position might seem somewhat paradoxical, and it is therefore perhaps unsurprising that its development involved a fundamental revision of sociology's traditional views on social order, of the sorts of questions to be asked about it, and of the kind of empirical research to be done.

Central to ethnomethodology's response to the more traditional conceptions of social order is the idea that they presuppose a social world which simply could not work, or at least could only work in a very different world to the one in which most of us live. Thus, were it the case that descriptions and explanations of social order and particular social phenomena could be empirically validated independently of contextual variation, then there would presumably not only be a much greater degree of certainty in human affairs than appears to be the case, but there would also be little scope for originality, diversity, innovation, conflict, or social change. The facts of any particular situation or event would never be in doubt, its causes would be identifiable with complete precision, and its consequences would be wholly predictable. In short, the dream of Auguste Comte (who invented the word 'sociology') of a society organised on an 'objective' or 'scientifically' warranted basis, and run by 'sociologist priests', would long since have become more than a dream. Sociology would by now have succeeded in identifying *the* 'correct' version of social order from the multiplicity of versions which are to be heard in the real world, and the discipline would presumably have achieved a greater degree of consistency and coherence than is suggested by the myriad of competing sociologies currently on offer.

The suggestion that traditional models of social order presuppose a world which could not work is not directed solely at those associated with positivistic approaches to sociology, as might seem to be implied by the above remarks. In other words, it might seem that the alternative views of social order proposed by interpretivist sociologies can be exempted from such a charge. For it is, of course, the case that positivism has been widely criticised by sociologists other than ethnomethodologists for having failed to give adequate attention to the 'meaningful' dimensions of social action, the understanding of actors' subjective orientations to action, the 'constructed' and 'negotiated' character of social reality. But, in the very way that interpretivist sociologies replace the excessively determined, certain and objective models of positivism with variously indeterminate, uncertain and differentially experienced conceptions of social reality, they too appear to be proposing models of social order which could not work. For they suggest a world in which the subjectively assessed meanings of actions and events would be so diverse and so utterly ambiguous that it is difficult to see how anyone would be able to adhere to a single one for long enough to be able to accomplish anything at all, or how any semblance of order would be possible.

Viewed in these terms, then, the two great sociological traditions of positivism and interpretivism can be viewed as having concentrated too exclusively on one *or* other of two recognisable dimensions of social reality, and have therefore failed to come up with a model of social order that would systematically accommodate *both.* In other words, an adequate theory of social order would presumably have to come to terms with the ways in which the social world is comprised of unique circumstances which are nevertheless recognisable as instances of generalised types, is simultaneously flexible *and* patterned, subjectively experienced *and* externally objective in appearance, uncertain *and* certain, indescribable *and* describable. The theory would thus have to be *neither* so inflexible and rigid that it lacks any sensitivity to the potentially infinite range of contextual variation in the real world, *nor* so flexible and loose that nothing at all is held to be general across different contexts. And the ethnomethodological interest in the methods of reasoning routinely used by societal members, both lay and professional, in finding *practical* solutions to the basic dilemmas that divide positivist and interpretivist sociologies is informed by the quest for just such a model of social order.

As far as most ethnomethodologists are concerned, then, the confusions of traditional sociology are inevitable so long as the search for descriptions and explanations of *the* realities underlying the common-sensically available appearances of social order is preferred to an examination of *how* such appearances are interactionally produced, managed, recognised and used *as if* they were the facts of the matter by societal members in living their everyday lives. In other words, objective appearances of social order are viewed by ethnomethodologists as being arrived at *via* the use of hitherto unexplicated methods of practical reasoning which professional sociologists, by virtue of their own societal membership, have used as a taken-for-granted resource in pursuing their specialist investigations. According to Garfinkel (1967), the major implication of this is that the resource should become the *topic* for sociological analysis, and that empirical research should thus be directed to explicating the methodic practices employed by members in the collaborative production of social order. The basic theoretical question was no longer to be the obstinately elusive one of *why* 'in principle' social order is as it is (or is claimed to be). Rather it was to become that of *how* 'for practical purposes' are particular manifestations of social order achieved? By combining the terms 'ethno' (meaning 'folk' or 'members') and 'methodology' (meaning 'methods of reasoning' or 'sense assembly procedures'), Garfinkel sought to capture the revised topic for research that was being proposed (on the origins of the word, see Garfinkel, 1974). In this respect, then, ethnomethodology refers neither to a theory nor a method in the conventional sociological sense. Rather it indicates a previously neglected domain for inquiry, a focus for serious intellectual puzzlement.

Had ethnomethodology been no more than another critique of traditional sociology and a promise of better things to come, it would no doubt have had little lasting impact on a discipline in which ambitious programmatic claims are commonplace. But, in contrast with most other purportedly new theoretical developments within sociology, ethnomethodology seems to have had a special appeal for empirically oriented sociologists, perhaps partly because Garfinkel was dealing with basic problems that researchers will inevitably have encountered, and partly because he appeared to be pointing to a novel and largely unexplored area for investigation. Those who took his work seriously were therefore likely to be more interested in pursuing empirical inquiries than in making a career out of continual theorising. An important consequence of this was that it led to the steady accumulation of a research literature. Thus, while the initial impact of ethnomethodology may have been as a theoretical challenge within sociology, the subsequent empirical studies have been more important in establishing its viability as a research programme with genuinely interdisciplinary relevance.

As was noted earlier, however, it is now somewhat misleading to talk as if there were a single homogeneous style of ethnomethodological research. That a diversity of approaches has developed is probably a result of the fact that the earlier writings were proposing so difficult a way forward. Thus, while there was considerable excitement and interest in what looked like a new domain for inquiry, it was not immediately obvious how it could be subjected to systematic empirical study without falling back into some of the old traps from which an escape was being sought. Garfinkel's stress on the importance for social organisation of taken-for-granted methods of practical reasoning meant that empirical research should be directed towards an examination of the ways in which tacit rules, background expectancies and common-sense theories were used by members in achieving orderliness in particular contexts. In pursuing such studies, however, researchers were to operate under a number of analytic constraints or injunctions entailed by such a programme, most of which related to the analyst's own status as a 'competent member', and the implications of this for the way he was already able (as a member) to observe, describe and explain any of the activities he might encounter. A general exhortation to view what seemed to be obvious, mundane and commonplace as 'anthropologically strange', then, was to be a constant reminder to analysts that obviousness was itself an orderly and methodic product of their members' interpretive competences. To ignore the mundane and commonplace would therefore be to fail to regard the explication of the members' methods of reasoning that rendered them 'obvious' as a topic for analysis, and would thereby involve relying on them as an unexplicated resource in much the same way as had been done for so long by traditional sociology. How work under such a constraint could actually be done, then, was a major challenge facing those who sought to conduct research within the framework of ethnomethodology.

A closely related and equally challenging constraint was entailed by the way in which Garfinkel's model of man involved a view of social actors as practical rule-using 'analysts', rather than as the pre-programmed rule-governed 'cultural dopes' depicted elsewhere in sociology. Thus, the professional analyst's major task was not to assert or stipulate what rules members 'really were following' or 'governed by', but to locate tacit rules which they might be 'orienting to' and using to recognise and produce orderliness in some setting. To find a way of making statements about rules and practices which could be warrantably said to be 'oriented to' by members, then, was another of the difficult challenges posed by ethnomethodology. For it demanded, among other things, that traditional sociological recommendations about the importance of studying actors' orientations to action and avoiding the imposition of observers' constructions were to be taken more seriously than in the past. That is, any solution which involved paying lip service to such matters as a prelude to stipulating observers' versions would be regarded as unacceptable.

To this point, then, an attempt has been made to outline in fairly general terms some of the issues that were important in the emergence of ethnomethodology. Such a discussion, however, leaves open the question of what possible relevance the approach might have for studying the law, and what follows therefore involves a more explicit focus on this. The matter is addressed first with reference to a general consideration of why legal settings may have been seen as a particularly attractive area for ethnomethodological investigation, and second with reference to some specific studies of how official rates of crime and suicide are produced. The chapter then concludes with a brief discussion of the potential of recent developments in conversational analysis for the study of interaction in legal settings.

Law as a Focus for Ethnomethodological Research

Before considering why a substantial proportion of the earlier studies in ethnomethodology were conducted in legal settings (for example, Bittner, 1967; Circourel, 1968; Garfinkel, 1949, 1956 and 1967; Pollner, 1974; Sacks, 1972a; Sudnow, 1965; Wieder, 1974; Zimmerman, 1969), at least one preliminary *caveat* is worth mentioning. For it is important to remember a factor that has been important in encouraging this type of specialisation by sociologists of most theoretical persuasions, and hence to beware of overstating the case about the attractiveness of the law as a focus for ethnomethodological interest. Thus, research funding and job opportunities have always been fairly readily available for studying the big social problems (such as crime and deviance) which worry governments, and sociologists have never been slow to boast about their abilities to deliver news on such matters. Given this relatively large research investment, then, it would probably have been more surprising had no ethnomethodologists found themselves working on projects concerned with deviance, crime and the law.

None the less, there are features of the everyday routines of persons caught up in the legal process that are of particular interest in the light of some of the central preoccupations of ethnomethodology. In his study of jury deliberations, for example, Garfinkel (1967, ch. 4) focuses on 'jury activities as a method of social inquiry' (1967, p. 104), and the immediate practical concerns of jurors are depicted as being very similar to those of social scientific researchers:

> In the course of their deliberations, jurors sort alternative depictions made by lawyers, witnesses and jurors of what happened and why between the statuses of relevant or irrelevant, justifiable or unjustifiable, correct or incorrect grounds for the choice of verdict. When jurors address such matters as dates, speeds, the plaintiff's injury and the like, what do the jurors' decisions specifically decide? In something like the jurors' own terms, and trying to capture the jurors' dialectic, jurors decide between what is fact and what is fancy; between what actually happened and what 'merely appeared' to happen; between what is put on and what is truth, regardless of detracting appearances; between what is credible and, very frequently for jurors, the opposite of credible, what is calculated and said by design. (Garfinkel, 1967, p. 105)

Within finite time limits, then, jurors have to find ways of arriving at a series of decisions which are not only very complex, but are also of just the sort that have provided a central and elusive problematic for generations of philosophers and social scientists. And they are also, of course, just the sorts of practical decisions that professional sociological researchers have to make in the course of producing orderly descriptions and explanations of some aspect of social reality.

As Garfinkel goes on to note:

> Jurors come to an agreement among themselves as to what actually happened. They decide 'the facts', i.e., among alternative claims about speeds of travel or extent of injury, jurors decide which may be used as the basis for further inferences and action. They do this by consulting the consistency of alternative claims with common sense models. These common sense models are models jurors use to depict, for example, what culturally known types of persons drive in what culturally known types of ways at what typical speeds at what types of intersections for what typical motives. The test runs that the matter that is meaningfully consistent may be correctly treated as the thing that actually occurred. If the interpretation makes good sense, then that's what happened. (1967, p. 106)

Persons involved in legal work, then, cannot enjoy the luxury of speculating about how truth claims can be validated, or whether it would even be possible to specify independent and decontextualised procedures for so doing. The local interactional business at hand is such that, *somehow or other,* participants have to make decisions about matters of fact and responsibility that are treated as definite 'for all practical purposes'. For the ethnomethodologist, that *somehow or other* provides the main focus for analytic attention, the challenge being to explicate the taken-for-granted reasoning practices used to produce such decisions and treat them as definite. Thus, the observation that people like jurors rely on various common-sense conceptions and *ad hoc* interpretive procedures is *not,* it should be stressed, a prelude to the production of 'sociologically informed' critiques or complaints to the effect that they must therefore be behaving improperly, failing to follow official legal instructions, or whatever. For to do so would be to propose the practicability of doing otherwise and/or the availability of alternative (but so far unidentified) methods of practical reasoning. And to do that would involve researchers in resorting to the sort of *a priori* stipulative theorising from which an escape is being sought.

While it may be the case that issues like 'what actually happened' and 'who is to blame' are explicitly oriented to as central concerns in the everyday work that takes place in legal settings, it should not be thought that such matters are unimportant to or absent from the processes through which participants produce orderliness elsewhere in the social world. For the question of 'what is actually happening here and now at this particular moment in this particular context' is one to which practical solutions have to be routinely and continually found in the course of going about the everyday business of living real world lives. How 'in principle' (that is in abstracted theoretical terms) one can be sure that a post on the pavement *really* is a 'bus stop', and that the thing coming towards it is properly describable as 'a bus', may pose deep and unanswerable dilemmas for the philosopher or theorist in the confines of his study. But, once on the street, he will no doubt find, like the vast majority of his fellow human beings, that such decisions pose few problems in practice. As a competent member, he is equipped with a methodology for deciding that, for the local practical purposes of getting from his study to the lecture theatre, this large moving object can be treated definitely and unequivocally as 'a bus which will probably stop somewhere near *this* post on *this* pavement'. That such mundane activities are regularly accomplished unproblematically, and typically treated as passing matters of fact deserving no special attention, suggests that there must be something methodic about the practices used to produce them. It also suggests that, while the problems of description, proof, verifiability and so forth may be tortuously difficult when considered in the abstract, there are practical ways of solving them in real world contexts.

Viewed in these terms, then, the fact that participants in legal settings are engaged in a continual process of analysing the actions and circumstances with which they are confronted in order to recognise and produce 'facticity' and 'orderliness' does not make 'legal conduct' uniquely different from any other. In at least two respects, however, there are some features of legal settings that mark them out as a potentially interesting area for specialist study. First, as has already been hinted at, the business of reaching definite (for all practical purposes) decisions about facts, truth, responsibility, and so on is an explicit, rather than implicit, abiding concern for persons involved in such settings. A second intriguing feature arises from the fact that, while there may be profound disagreements in jurisprudence about just what 'the law' is, one thing about which there is a reasonable consensus is that it involves a whole series of generalised rules that can be invoked in relation to particular instances. And relatedly, of course, the law also provides in its various specialised rules of evidence and procedure, a further set of generalised specifications about proper and improper methods for deciding whether a particular instance falls under the jurisdiction of some generalised definition. A close examination of procedural and evidential rules suggests that they can be viewed as the products of an evolving analysis of everyday practices for deciding matters of fact and resolving disputes, and as such may reveal interesting observations about the sorts of taken-for-granted assumptions that are of interest to ethnomethodologists.

This last point may be clarified somewhat with reference to an earlier discussion of procedural rules:

> Most rules of evidence are 'exclusionary' which means that they seek to prohibit the use in court of various conversational practices which may, in most everyday settings, be perfectly adequate and acceptable methods for discovering and deciding matters of fact, blame, responsibility, and so forth (e.g. statements of opinion, evidence of past conduct, hearsay, etc.). In other words, such rules of evidence can be seen to be oriented to specific features of mundane talk which are perceived as being in some way flawed or inadequate for certain purposes . . . Interestingly, however, attempts to specify rules of evidence and procedure, as well as the further ones for putting them into practice or recognising breaches of specific ones, are eventually confounded before arriving at anything like an ultimate solution by the very features of language use (and particularly its open-textured and context-dependent character) which occasioned the design of the rules in the first place. Thus, however thorough legal scholars are in their attempts to spell out the nature and scope of a rule, the demands of accuracy will sooner or later call for some confession such as 'everything depends on context', which Cross (1974, p. 200) makes in relation to the problem of how to recognise a 'leading question'. (Atkinson and Drew, 1979, pp. 8-9)

Again, it should be stressed that such remarks are not made with a view to criticising lawyers and legal scholars for not having achieved the impossible. Rather they are intended to point to areas of potential interest for ethnomethodological analysis.

Production of Official Categorisations

One of the substantive areas in which some of the above issues were pursued in more detail was the work involved in the production of official statistics (for example, Atkinson, 1971 and 1978; Cicourel, 1968; Kitsuse and Cicourel, 1963; Sudnow, 1965). These studies, the fieldwork for which relied heavily on participant observation, focused on the question of how the official categorisations of persons as, for example, 'criminal' (Sudnow, 1965), 'delinquent' (Cicourel, 1968), 'suspicious character' (Sacks, 1972a), and 'suicide' (Atkinson, 1978) are reached by the officials responsible for making such decisions. The interest such studies appear to have had for a wider sociological audience probably resulted from the fact that their findings provided a critical resource for those who were sceptical of more traditional quantitatively based 'positivist' approaches to the study of crime and deviance.

At least since Durkheim's (1898) classic treatise on suicide, the explanation of differences in the rates of deviant conduct had been seen as *the* paradigmatic aim of sociological research on such topics, and the long-term survival of such an orientation is exemplified in the following extracts from studies of suicide published more than half a century later:

> The problem is approached from the sociological angle, which means that the investigator has concentrated on the underlying reasons for differences in suicide rates. (Kruijt, 1965, p. 44)

> The foremost task of sociological studies of suicide is to explain differences in rates. (Gibbs, 1966, p. 228)

Equally succinct summaries of what was for decades taken to be the dominant approach to studying other types of deviance could readily be produced by the simple substitution for 'suicide' of 'crime', 'delinquency', 'drug addiction', 'mental illness', and so on. Thus, by suggesting that the production of official categorisations might be a topic worthy of serious study in its own right, ethnomethodologists were seen raising a potentially damaging question about what had traditionally provided researchers with their main data base. As if this were not challenging enough, the findings from these inquiries suggested that, by treating official categorisations as 'facts' to be explained, previous researchers might have done little more than rediscover the common-sense theories and assumptions that had been used by the officials to categorise the actions as 'crime', 'suicide' and so forth in the first place. As a result, these early studies in ethnomethodology came to be seen as offering a thorough-going critique of the very basis of the more established sociological approaches to deviance.

For example, in a very influential study of how delinquents are processed by official agencies, Cicourel (1968) showed how factors such as a child's class background and family circumstances were taken into account by the relevant personnel in deciding whether or not the case should be taken to court and, if so, whether or not a custodial order should be recommended. Thus, a word with the parents might be considered adequate for children whose parents lived together and were deemed to be 'respectable', while cases involving children from broken homes and/or low-income families were more likely to be taken further through the officially available mechanisms. In making their decisions, then, the officials were consulting common-sense models of 'the typical delinquent', and theories of delinquency causation and motivation. Accordingly, it was hardly surprising that large numbers of working-class children from broken homes were finding their way into the official statistics. Researchers who used samples derived from official sources, or from inmates of custodial institutions, would therefore inevitably 'discover' a statistical correlation between 'variables' like broken homes and delinquency rates. By viewing such 'variables' as *causes* of delinquency, however, researchers had not only presupposed that an infant social science was already capable of validating ambitious and far-reaching explanatory theories, but had also missed the point that more or less identical theories to those 'expert' ones were commonly available to, and used by, the officials in producing 'the facts'.

Very similar findings have resulted from studies of how official definitions of suicide are applied. Thus, while Durkheim and others had sought to distinguish between their proposed 'scientific' definitions of suicide and common-sense conceptions, their comparisons of regional variations in the rates ignored *both* the local legal definitions *and* the everyday categorisation procedures used to apply them by the thousands of anonymous officials concerned. Research into the work of coroners and their officers, however, has shown that neither purportedly 'scientific' nor legal definitions may have much bearing on the way that officials analyse and interpret sudden deaths. Indeed, it does not even appear to be necessary for a coroner to know what the official legal definition of suicide is for him to be routinely able to categorise deaths as such, and to do so for many years without a murmur of complaint from official authorities or the public at large (Atkinson, 1978, pp. 90-3). Here again, the ethnomethodologist would not treat this as evidence that such an official is somehow incompetent at his work, and hence is yet another likely target for sociologically based criticism. Rather the lesson is taken that it may be more sensible to look to places *other than* the legal definitions and procedures if one is to come anywhere near an understanding of what practices might constitute such competence.

Studies of official categorisations of suicide on both sides of the Atlantic (for example, Atkinson, 1978; Douglas, 1967) have suggested that coroners and their officers employ methods of investigation that are very similar to those traditionally used by professional social scientists. The initial scene of a death proposes a preliminary hypothesis (for example, that this was a suicide, accident, or whatever), which then makes relevant a search for some types of evidence rather than others. In the course of the inquiries, the original hypothesis will be progressively confirmed or disconfirmed in the light of discovered relics (notes, bank accounts and so on), post-mortem examinations, statements by witnesses, etc. In deciding *that* a person committed suicide, the officials look for evidence as to *why* a person might have done such a thing, and whether or not a possible 'cause' or 'motive' is found can be criterial in categorising the death.

Just as the theories used by officials in categorising delinquents were very similar to the 'scientific' ones of professional criminology, so too do those used by coroners and their officers closely approximate those which feature in the research literature of suicidology. Thus, sociological research has stressed the importance of social isolation as a causal variable, while psychiatry has laid greater emphasis on psychological problems in general, and depression in particular. The 'newsworthy' character of such theoretical claims, however, may become somewhat dubious if it is the case that officials have already used such accounts in producing the samples and materials (for example, coroners' records of suicide cases) used as data by the professional researchers. And there is much evidence to suggest that they do, an example of which is the following exchange between a researcher and a coroner's officer:

R: In the light of your quite long experience of this kind of work, did you come to any sorts of conclusions about the kinds of reasons why people commit suicide? Did you come up with any theories of suicide?

CO: Well, I did, but they're entirely personal and — um — I think basically it's the inability of the individual to come to grips with a situation. *He finds himself totally isolated from his fellows, from his family, from his friends* . . . He can't see any

> way out of his dilemma and the only path open to him is through suicide, *generally brought about by or preceded by acute depression.* (Atkinson, 1978, p. 170 author's italics)

This coroner's officer's 'entirely personal' theory, then, includes the major explanatory propositions from sociological and psychiatric research into suicide. And, in combination with other evidence from studies of the death registration procedures, it supports the earlier suggestion that research which treats official categorisations as 'facts to be explained' may end up by rediscovering the common-sense theories used in producing 'the facts'.

Ethnomethodological studies of official categorisation procedures are sometimes regarded as being merely negative critiques of the way sociologists have traditionally used officially derived data for research purposes. They are also sometimes read as recommendations to the effect that previous methodological procedures should be reformed or improved, so that in future 'more careful' or 'more accurate' studies could be based on the analysis of official statistics. These are not, however, the implications that ethnomethodologists take from their work on official categorisations. Rather they see them as confirmations of the promise of treating methods of reasoning, hitherto taken for granted, as the *topic* for inquiry, and of the essentially uninteresting and un-newsworthy character of professional research that merely relies on them as an unexplicated resource. Accordingly, traditional approaches to the social and behavioural sciences are viewed as interesting only in so far as they, like the analyses of coroners and others, testify to the methodic ways in which human beings are readily able to construct plausible descriptions of social action and social order. Thus, if the production of ambitious and plausible-sounding theories (whether of crime, suicide, or society as a whole) is such an easily and routinely accomplishable task, then to adopt the construction of such theories as a professional enterprise hardly seems enough of a challenge to justify a specialised discipline such as sociology. But what does emerge as being much more of a challenge is the attempt to identify and explicate the workings of the methodic ways in which members collaborate to produce sense, facticity and orderliness.

Developments in Conversational Analysis

Just as categorisation practices featured as a central topic in the studies of how official statistics are produced, so also were they a major focus in the emergence of what has become the most productive empirical sequel to the earlier writings in ethnomethodology, namely the style of conversational analysis developed by Harvey Sacks, Emanuel Schegloff and Gail Jefferson. Thus, for his doctoral research, Sacks studied a series of tape-recorded telephone calls to a suicide prevention agency (Sacks, 1966 and 1972b). A problem that was found to be recurrently oriented by both parties to such calls was found to be that of how the caller had come to categorise himself or herself as having 'no one to turn to' (other than the suicide prevention agency). In the course of this study, Sacks provided a detailed demonstration of just how systematic the search procedures leading to such categorisation could be, and his attempt to describe the operation of 'membership categorisation devices' was to have an important influence on the early studies in conversational analysis. At around the same time, Schegloff was also working on recorded telephone conversations (Schegloff, 1967), and published another influential paper on the procedures used by interactants in selecting categorisations of physical locations (Schegloff, 1972). Schegloff's early studies were also to prove important for the direction that much subsequent research in conversational analysis was to take, in that it focused more specifically on how the sequential ordering of utterances in relation to one another provides a crucial basis for the interpretation and production of actions (Schegloff, 1968).

The initial work in conversational analysis was innovatory in several important respects, particularly in so far as it provided a workable solution to some of the more problematic features of the ethnographic methods on which many of the other studies in ethnomethodology, including those on official categorisation practices, had been based (for a more detailed discussion of these difficulties, see Atkinson and Drew, 1979, pp. 22-33). Thus, the new style of research involved a strategy of collecting and analysing data in a form (recordings and transcripts thereof) to which readers and hearers can have more direct access. Indeed, it is probably the first and only type of social scientific research that insists on giving its audience equal access to *all* the data being analysed, and which thereby does not require recipients either to make guesses about how some features came to be described rather than others, or to rely on the analyst's claims about how the selections were made. Instead, they are provided with an opportunity of inspecting the analyst's interpretations of what appears to be going on with reference to *the same materials* as those to which the analyst's claims refer. In contrast with what is possible in the case of ethnographies and other forms of social research, conversational analysts are therefore able to present their claims about how participants are displaying their orientations to each other's actions in a way which is much more *open for inspection and scrutiny by their audiences.*

Implicit in the foregoing is another feature of the conversational analytic approach, which has to do with how hearers of tape-recorded sequences of naturally occurring interactions are able to make a sense of what they hear. This is clearly dependent on our own members' competence to monitor and analyse talk, and in this respect it is useful to recall Garfinkel's observation to the effect that life goes on in a relatively orderly fashion in spite of the fact that it is impossible to 'say what one means in so many words'. Any attempt to do so is likely to lead quickly to the discovery that descriptions are indefinitely extendible (on which see Garfinkel, 1967; Sacks, 1963) and/or that trying to describe what is intended by an utterance currently in progress will almost invariably be treated as an accountable, if not bizarre, thing to do. In short, speakers rarely include in their utterances explicit instructions such as 'hear what I am about to say/what I just said as a greeting, invitation, apology, accusation . . . etc.' Rather we rely on others to make out what we meant from whatever we said, and with each utterance display the products of our analysis of what we took the other party to be meaning. And, when troubles, doubts or misunderstandings arise, there are methodic procedures available for repairing the trouble (Schegloff, Jefferson and Sacks, 1977).

By 'eavesdropping' on tape-recorded interactions, then, an analyst is able to examine repeatedly and in detail the ways in which the participants are displaying their understandings of each other's utterances. As Schegloff and Sacks observe at the start of their study of conversational closings:

> We have proceeded under the assumption (an assumption borne out by our research) that in so far as the materials we worked with exhibited orderliness, they did so not only to us, indeed not in the first place for us, but for the co-participants who had produced them. If the materials (records of natural conversations) were orderly, they were so because they had been methodically produced

> by members of the society for one another, and it was a feature of the conversations that we treated as data that they were produced so as to allow the display by the co-participants to each other of their orderliness, and to allow the participants to display to each other their analysis, appreciation and use of that orderliness. Accordingly, our analysis has sought to explicate the ways in which the materials are produced by members in orderly ways that exhibit their orderliness and have their orderliness appreciated and used, and have that appreciation displayed and treated as a basis for subsequent action. (Sacks and Schegloff, 1973, p. 290)

Research conducted within this evolving framework has generated a growing corpus of empirical research reports, primarily on aspects of the organisation of conversational interaction (for example, Atkinson and Heritage, 1981; Psathas, 1979; Schenkein, 1978 and forthcoming; *Sociology,* 1978; Sudnow, 1972). Developments have been greatly facilitated by the pioneering work on turn-taking by Sacks, Schegloff and Jefferson (1974), and by Jefferson's continuing refinement of a transcription system that is capable of capturing a range of detail, while at the same time remaining accessible to readers unfamiliar with systems involving specialised phonetic symbols. The research literature is, for the most part, made up of papers which report sequential regularities that have been found to be recurrent in the context of particular actions (such as openings, closings, assessments, proposals, offers, invitations, accusations, agreements, disagreements, corrections and so on) being done by participants. And the ensuing explications of how such actions are routinely recognised and produced is leading to what is beginning to look like an increasingly coherent corpus of findings about the systematics of everyday conversational interaction.

However, in contrast with many other styles of sociological research, including some of the earlier studies in ethnomethodology, conversational analytic findings are quite extraordinarily difficult to summarise in a few paragraphs. This is probably partly because the explications tend to relate so closely to the data that attempted summaries are unlikely to be able to do justice to the original analyses without also reproducing the relevant transcribed extracts. Moreover, it is often the case that such research reports are already written as economically as is possible, and hence are highly resistant to yet further abbreviation. This may well be one reason why this style of work is one of the few areas of specialism in contemporary sociology that has failed to spawn a plethora of generalised introductory texts. One consequence of this, of course, is that anyone curious to learn more about the work has no choice but to turn directly to the original studies themselves.

It may seem from the foregoing that conversational analysis has taken ethnomethodology in a direction that is far removed from a concern with studying matters of legal interest. But there are various grounds for supposing that this is by no means the case. It is fairly obvious, for example, that a very great deal of the work that takes place in legal settings is accomplished through processes of verbal interaction, and as such must have considerable potential as an area for this kind of research (providing appropriate access can be gained for the collection of tape-recorded data). It may also be noted that a number of the actions which have begun to be examined by conversational analysts (such as proposals, offers, accusations, promises and the like) are also ones which are highly relevant to central legal concerns, both civil and criminal. And, as has been discussed at greater length elsewhere (Atkinson and Drew, 1979), this raises a range of interesting and researchable questions about how far the ways such interactional tasks are done in legal settings resemble or depart from the practices used in conversational settings.

If features of the legal processes themselves recommend that they become a focus for conversational analytic research, so too do certain recent developments that are taking place within this evolving tradition. Thus, a growing number of researchers are beginning to turn their attention to the study of interactions in various specialised or institutional settings, such as therapy sessions, classroom interaction, doctor-patient consultations, news interviews, political meetings, debates and so on. It is therefore consistent with such a trend that legal interactions are also being subjected to such investigations, and preliminary studies are already available on calls to the police (Eglin, 1979; Sharrock and Turner, 1978), police interrogation of suspects (Atkinson, Heritage and Watson, 1979), plea bargaining (Lynch, 1981; Maynard, 1980), and court hearings (Atkinson and Drew, 1979; Dunstan, 1980a, b). These last-mentioned examples derive from a more broadly conceived interdisciplinary project on procedures for adjudication and dispute settlement, which also involves lawyers and psychologists.[2] It is being specifically designed to examine various matters of legal interest, such as the operation of 'formal' and 'informal' procedures, and to this end tape-recordings from a range of different types of court hearing are being collected. For the most part, these developments are very recent ones, and it is difficult to predict accurately which other areas of the law will become a focus for conversational analytic research. One very likely candidate, however, is lawyer-client interaction. And, with regard to 'methodological' developments, an increased utilisation of video-recording technology can be confidently expected in the near future.

Notes

1. Parts of this paper draw heavily on materials published earlier in Atkinson (1978) and Atkinson and Drew (1979), both of which include more extended discussions of ethnomethodology and conversational analysis, as well as preliminary empirical investigations of legal settings.

2. This project is one of several that make up the overall research programme at the SSRC Centre for Socio-Legal Studies, Wolfson College, Oxford.

Bibliography

Atkinson, J.M. 'Societal Reactions to Deviance: The Role of Coroners' Definitions' in S. Cohen (ed.), *Images of Deviance* (Penguin, Harmonsworth, 1971), pp. 165-191

______ *Discovering Suicide: Studies in the Social Organization of Sudden Death* (Macmillan, London, 1978)

Atkinson, J.M. and Drew, P. *Order in Court: The Organisation of Verbal Interaction in Judicial Settings* (Macmillan, London, 1979)

Atkinson, J.M., Heritage, J.C., and Watson, D.R. 'Suspect's Rights and the Standardisation of Interrogation Procedures', evidence submitted to the Royal Commission on Criminal Procedure (1979)

Atkinson, J.M., Heritage, J.C. (eds.) *Structures of Social Action: Studies in Conversational Analysis* (Macmillan, London, 1981)

Bittner, E. 'The Police on Skid Row: A Study of Peace Keeping', *American Sociological Review*, vol. 32 (1967), pp. 699-715

Blum, A., McHugh, P., Raffel, S., and Foss, D.C. *On the Beginning of Social Inquiry* (Routledge and Kegan Paul, London, 1974)

Cicourel, A.V. *The Social Organization of Juvenile Justice* (Wiley, New York, 1968)

Cross, R. *Evidence* (Butterworths, London, 1974)

Douglas, J.D. *The Social Meanings of Suicide* (Princeton University Press, Princeton, 1967)

Dunstan, R. 'Contexts for Coercion', *British Journal of Law and Society* vol. 7 (1980), pp. 61-77

______ 'Informal Formality: A Practical Solution to Some Interactional Problems', paper presented at the Baldy Center for Socio-Legal Studies Joint Conference, Buffalo, 1980

Durkheim, E. *Le Suicide* (Alcan, Paris, 1898)

Eglin, P. 'Calling the Police: Some Aspects of the Interactional Organization of Complaints in Crime Reporting', *Analytic Sociology*, vol. 2, no. 2 (1979), (microfiche)

Garfinkel, H. 'Research Note on Inter- and Intra-Racial Homicides', *Social Forces*, vol. 27 (May 1949), pp. 212-17

______ 'Conditions of Successful Degradation Ceremonies', *American Journal of*

Sociology, vol. 64 (1956), pp. 420-4
—— *Studies in Ethnomethodology* (Prentice Hall, Englewood Cliffs, New Jersey, 1967)
—— 'The Origins of the Term 'Ethnomethodology' in R. Turner (ed.), *Ethnomethodology* (Penguin, Harmondsworth, 1974), pp. 15-18
Gibbs, J.P. 'Suicide' in R.K. Merton and R.A. Nisbet (eds.), *Contemporary Social Problems* (Harcourt Brace and World, New York, 1966), pp. 281-321
Goldthorpe, J.H. 'A Revolution in Sociology?' *Sociology,* vol. 7 (1973), pp. 449-62
Kitsuse, J.I. and Cicourel, A.V. 'A Note on the Uses of Official Statistics', *Social Problems,* vol. 11 (1963), pp. 131-9
Kruijt, C.S. 'Suicide: A Sociological and Statistical Investigation', *Sociologica Nederlandica,* vol. 3 (1965), pp. 1-14
Kuhn, T. *The Structure of Scientific Revolutions* (Chicago University Press, Chicago, 1962)
Lynch M. 'Disclosure and Argument in Plea Bargaining Sessions: The Topicality of Plea Bargaining' in J.M. Atkinson and J.C. Heritage (eds.), *Structures of Social Action* (Macmillan, London, 1981)
Maynard, D.W. 'A Conversational System for Plea Bargaining', paper presented at the Law and Society Association/ISA Research Committee on the Sociology of Law Joint Meeting, Madison, USA. (1980)
Pollner, M. 'Mundane Reasoning', *Philosophy of the Social Sciences,* vol. 4 (1974), pp. 35-54
—— 'Explicative Transactions: Making and Managing Meaning in Traffic Court', in G. Psathas (ed.), *Everyday Language: Studies in Ethnomethodology* (Irvington, New York, 1979), pp. 227-55
Psathas, G. (ed.) *Everyday Language: Studies in Ethnomethodology* (Irvington, New York, 1979)
Sacks, H. 'Sociological Description', *Berkeley Journal of Sociology,* vol. 8 (1963), pp. 1-16
—— 'Notes on Police Assessement of Moral Character' in D. Sudnow (ed.), *Studies in Social Interaction* (Free Press, New York, 1972a), pp. 280-93
—— 'An Initial Investigation of the Usability of Conversational Data for Doing Sociology' in D. Sudnow (ed.), *Studies in Social Interaction* (Free Press, New York, 1972b), pp. 31-74
—— 'The Search for Help: No one to Turn to', (unpublished PhD dissertation, University of California, Berkeley, 1966
Sacks, H. and Schegloff, E., 'Opening up Closings', *Semiotica,* vol. VIII, no. 4 (1973), pp. 289-327
Sacks, H., Schegloff E.A., and Jefferson, G. 'A Simplest Systematics for the Organization of Turn-taking for Conversation', *Language,* vol. 50 (1974), pp. 696-735
Schegloff, E.A. 'The First Five Seconds: The Order of Conversational Openings', unpublished PhD dissertation, University of California, Berkeley, 1967
—— 'Sequencing in Conversational Openings', *American Anthropologist,* vol. 70, no 4 (1968), pp. 1075-95
—— 'Notes on a Conversational Practice: Formulating Place' in D. Sudnow (ed.), *Studies in Social Interaction* (Free Press, New York, 1972), pp. 75-119
Schegloff, E.A., Jefferson G. and Sacks, H. 'The Preference for Self-correction in the Organization of Repair in Conversation', *Language,* vol. 53, (1977), pp. 361-82
Schenkein, J.N. (ed.) *Studies in the Organization of Conversational Interaction* (Academic Press, New York, 1978)
—— *Studies in the Organization of Conversational Interaction: Volume II* (Academic Press, New York, forthcoming)
Sharrock, W.W., and Turner, R. 'On a Conversational Environment for Equivocality', in J.N. Schenkein (ed.) *Studies in the Organization of Conversational Interaction* (Academic Press, New York, 1978), pp. 173-97

Sociology, Special Issue: 'Language Use and Practical Reasoning', vol. 12, no. 1 (1978)
Sudnow, D. 'Normal Crimes: Sociological Features of the Penal Code in a Public Defender's Office', *Social Problems* vol. 12 (1965), pp. 255-70
_____ *Studies in Social Interaction* (Free Press, New York, 1972)
Turner, R. (ed.) *Ethnomethodology* (Penguin, Harmondsworth, 1974)
Wieder, D.L. *Language and Social Reality: The Case of Telling the Convict Code* (Mouton, The Hague, 1974)
Zimmerman, D.H. 'Record-keeping and the Intake Process in a Public Welfare Agency' in S. Wheeler (ed.), *On Record* (Sage, New York, 1969)

Concluding Remarks: Sociological Theories and the Study of Law

Introduction

It is clear that the empirical studies in law which have accumulated in recent years have not been matched by an adequate number of theoretical studies. Provocative books, including the works of Black (1976), Friedman (1977) and Unger (1977) only partially fill the gap. Moreover, these books, (particularly Donald Black's), refer to empirical material mainly to support ideas which are *apriori* accepted, or which are based on traditional legal thought. They are not usually connected with current sociological perspectives. Thus, while they are often inspiring, these books do not indicate methods with which to prove or to disprove their arguments. As far as relationships between legal systems and sociological systems are concerned, they do not provide any definitive answers. They are not sufficiently inductive, nor consequently are they deductive; they do not draw their statements from sociological premisses. Thus, they make no attempt to connect adequately the knowledge about social phenomena which has been accumulated in the existing theories in sociology or social sciences in general with the particular topic of the law.

In 1973, the authors of *The New Criminology* defined 'theory' as 'a consistent and interrelated set of hypothetical concepts' (Taylor, Walton and Young, 1973, p. 158). Although this definition appears to be accepted amongst many social scientists in the United Kingdom, in terms of the study of law, a more detailed statement is required. In general one can distinguish between two types of theory: 'substantive theories' and 'reflexive theories' of a methodological character. Substantive theories which are concerned with social processes do not stipulate how to study the law, instead they are mainly concerned with the task of how to explain the functioning of legal phenomena. They try to apply general sociological rules which may be useful in the study of law and society. In this way they have real implications for the law. Reflexive theories mainly give some indication of how to study and to understand legal phenomena, although they may be unable to explain the operations of legal processes and the functioning of legal institutions.

In terms of the study of law, both types of theoretical approaches are complementary in that substantive theories require data which may be gleaned from studies of the law based on reflexive theories. However, in a sociology of law, it might be profitable not merely to utilise sets of concepts and hypothetical interrelationships which are contained in theories, but to take advantage of these principles and concepts to point out in the law or legal system features which are essential either as perceived or in practice.

It would be particularly interesting and fruitful in this chapter to view a specific area of law from the different sociological perspectives. This is too difficult for present purposes, and must be viewed as a project for the future. However, we shall try at the end to show the ways in which various perspectives could be utilised to explain one area of law, the law of contract, so that the scope of a multi-dimensional approach may be revealed. But first, we shall use some other examples to show how attempts can be made to study the law from different sociological perspectives.

Functionalism

According to this theoretical perspective, behaviour or social structure or indeed law should be studied in terms of both its manifest functions, which are the intended consequences of social actions, and their latent functions, which are neither intended nor recognised (Merton, 1957, p. 51). Generally speaking, legal science is concerned with manifest functions; it mainly takes into consideration the positive description of law. Functional models of society are initially valuable therefore in showing that law is a dependent social phenomenon (being shaped by outside forces), and that traditional legal science is limited by not recognising this. For social activities in general and laws in particular do not only have short-term and recognised (and anticipated) consequences, but also ones which are unrecognised and enduring. In functionalism, law is therefore to be seen not only as constructing social standards, but as being itself derived from its social context (Stone, 1965).

To use an example in the law of contract, a functional analysis of collective agreements between trade unions and employers might consider the contractual functions of the agreement, but, in addition, it would have to consider the latent, normative functions. It would analyse the ways in which people were bound by the agreement, *and* the ways in which norms were created.

Let us take a more complicated example. Various sociological studies have revealed that some educational and corrective institutions adopt certain types of so-called 'second life'. What was characteristic in the 'second life' was, when the research started in Warsaw, completely unknown. The educators and teachers in educational and corrective institutions under study had only fragmentary and incomplete knowledge about this strange phenomenon. More thorough sociological research later disclosed that where such 'second life' existed, the lives of those incarcerated in such institutions were roughly split into two forms. The first was an official life associated with school activities and behaviours controlled by official guardians. The second was a closed hidden life, governed by its own specific laws. The essence of this 'second life' consisted of the inmates' particular stratification which is basically reducible to 'people' (or 'Lords') and 'suckers' (or 'slaves'). The former are equals and differ only in the degree of acceptance of the patterns of behaviour relating to the 'second life' ritual. The latter are 'dirty' individuals (if they try to reject their status they are raped) with whom no social or physical contact (except instrumental-homosexual) should be maintained. The 'people' are independent and completely dominate the 'suckers'.

This unique picture of social stratification does not exist only in Poland but also flourishes extensively in the United States. Functional analysis suggests that a search for the 'concealed functions' of that type of stratification is quite fruitful. One may say that in the situation of the isolated institution, there is a constant feeling of stress and aggression and continual chaos. An informal community subjected to oppression also generates a certain type of order. Mutual aggression, as a result of constant clashes, finally — in order that the prisoner survives — produces generally accepted patterns of behaviour. Thus, a unique set of interrelations constituted by these mutual aggressions comes into being as a peculiar social order. Thus the 'second life' emerges as the result of the mutuality of aggressive acts as a stratified system of punishments and rewards. Then relegation into a lower position and occupying it is treated as a punishment and rising to a higher stratum and enjoying its privileges is a reward. These rewards are needed in order to survive the oppressive situation existing in the given institution. A functional analysis thus discloses that members of isolated institutions bring into being 'artificial stratification' which serves them to reorder their life-styles to meet this created social system. It seems to be more adequate to the life conditions existing in such institutions.

It is clear from the second example that a functionalist may tend to explain activities in terms of the need to maintain an existing social system. Thus, while this approach points out that law does not only have immediate and isolated consequences, but has long-term systematic ones also, it is an approach which has been criticised for its conservatism. The assumption may exist that because a social system has needs, these are necessarily being met within it. Opponents have argued that given the degree of conflict and changes that occur in society, functionalism takes the social system too much for granted. In terms of the study of law, this criticism need not apply in principle, for the value of the functionalist approach exists in its efforts to determine the effects on the whole system of some part of it. The problem remains, however, which functional alternative is to be selected if more than one is available.

Structuralism

Structuralism is one of the least explored theoretical approaches in the area of theoretical and legal studies based on empirical research. Potentially, however, it is a powerful explanatory tool facilitating the understanding of the legal relationships between various groups in society. It is thus, primarily, a descriptive method. According to structuralists, social reality consists of abstract networks of interrelationships, and cultural phenomena represent the attempts to embody those networks. Thus as a method, structuralism proceeds at a fairly abstract, even metaphysical level in an attempt to understand the facts of the social world. By helping to explain cultural phenomena, it interprets information of the entire system. Structuralists, then, try to accumulate this information; structuralism is a guide trying to understand the different observable data of social existence.

In a very preliminary way, it is possible to outline those fields of inquiry which may be regarded as appropriate targets for an inquiry by a structuralist. One of them is the very structure of the legal norm. It is not always understood that the norm has at least three essential elements. The first is a description of the situation. (If somebody borrowed a book, the norm refers to certain facts — the fact of lending the book). The second is a disposition or recommendation (if somebody borrowed the book, he is supposed to return it on time and the owner has a claim to have it). Additionally the norm provides a sanction for not returning it to the owner. Criminal law deals mainly with sanctions and situations, and usually omits recommendations or meta-norms which are hidden behind the given rule. Quite often norms seem to be ineffective when their different elements are dispersed in different fragments of the legal system. Only if one understands the legal norm as a unit of (1) a description of the situation, (2) a recommendation and (3) a sanction, is one able to put together these elements and reconstruct the norm to reveal its full and proper shape. (See Harris, 1979, for further discussions of the notion of the norm.)

The second line of possible inquiries based on a structuralist approach is connected with the normative scheme of a legal system, and asks the question why the substance of law takes the shape it does. The legal system as a whole (and its parts) prescribes in the given social system expected and desired behaviour. Thus the legal system assesses this type of behaviour which is demanded by the legal system. The legal system has several devices (the hierarchy of norms, interpretation of norms which unites them into a consistent whole, so-called legal reasoning and so on) to maintain the strength of the legal system as a whole. Quite often reasoning based on normative assumptions is in open contradiction to normal logic. Nevertheless, this reasoning is heuristic in order to keep divergent elements of the legal system together. The obligatory character of the law is an essential element of its normative structure. Thus a study of the criminal process might determine the structural features of various situations; it may also correlate these structural features with the structures in the social system by a study of the legal system's rules, definitions and devices for constructing reality: that is the structural contingencies involved in and influencing what is defined as legal (Young 1971, p. 26).

The third dimension which is apparently the most interesting in the possible use of structuralism is the study based on the factual operation of the law in social life. This large realm of research contains at least five elements. *The first* consists of normative assumptions (constitutions, declarations, specifications of general values and so forth) which indicate and prescribe how the given legal system should function. *The second* is composed of directives which explain how to implement these classic values into the social reality of the given system. These directives usually have the form of governmental recommendations. *The third* realm is constituted by various subcultures of the agencies of legal order. This is because the various social institutions and organisations have different ways of applying the law. Those ways are established as certain patterns of behaviour which are relatively long-lasting. *The fourth* element is shaped by public expectations connected with the law (knowledge of it, its understanding, evaluative attitudes towards it, possible help to utilise the law and so on). Finally, *the fifth* element of real structure of the legal system is directly connected with the actual operation of legal norms and legal institutions. Thus, it is obvious that the real structure of the legal system in action may be (and usually is) essentially different from its normative structure.

Interpretive Sociology and Phenomenology

Some scholars claim that interpretive sociology is the sociology of Weber. For him, the task of sociology was to understand and explain social action, by considering both the context of the situation and the subjective sense of the individual. Phenomenology is also the study of the subjective experiences and perceptions of individuals; the world and social phenomena, it is argued, is given meaning by lived experience. Accordingly it is a broad approach, it does not artificially bracket one aspect of reality from another, which in terms of the study of law would mean that considering the decisions and guidelines which determine legal norms and not just the norms themselves would be required.

It is not easy to find the real boundaries between 'interpretive sociology' and phenomenology in connection with the theoretical studies based on empirical research of the law. Phenomenology would recommend the rejection of those 'semi-normative glasses' which select for study by the theoretician and practitioner mainly those topics which are practically useful (punishment or reformatory action in criminal law or litigation in civil law and so on). These types of 'glasses' have a tendency to focus attention only on those parts of the legal system which have pragmatic or practical value. They do not make possible an entrance into the inner spectrum of legal reality as it is perceived by those who live inside it. Also, 'interpretive sociology' and phenomenology would stress the importance of the so-called 'living law' ('intuitive law'). This point of view regards as the essential elements ('atoms') of the legal system not legal norms as they are formulated in constitutions, statutes, enactments and so on, but it will mainly treat as law those phenomena which exist in the human psyche, phenomena according to which individuals have an attitude of claim or duty reciprocated by somebody else's duty or claim attitude. If somebody has his own subjective perception of the law then this subjective perception creates certain psychological and sociological consequences which might be taken into consideration. For example, if somebody treats himself as the sole owner of Oxford University then probably this subjective feeling of this particular person does not have too many consequences which may affect the possible behaviour of others. But if newly emerging social groups — 'a revolutionary class' — demand a reconstruction of the given legal order then these growing attitudes of — more or less — organised masses could lead to a revolution which may completely reshape the existing structure of official law.

For example, ignorance of possible social benefits can affect the application for financial aid by the needy. The study of the perception of the legal institutions involved may provide a more comprehensive picture of the whole legal system. The study of the direct reality experiences by various group members may help to answer basic questions relating to social and legal order. The 'taken for granted' is part and parcel of the overall structure and organisation of the whole society.

'Interpretive sociology' and phenomenology stress the importance of the anthropology of law as an additional perspective to understand the law. According to this point of view, the law should be seen not only as an objective phenomenon, not only as a subjective phenomenon, not as a 'liquid' element specific for the so-called primitive societies, nor as a formal framework for the developed societies. It is connected with the very basic structure of human existence — its need for integrity. From this point of view anthropology of law probably seems to be a more adequate concept to approach the law than the notion of sociology of law and the realm of socio-legal studies.

Ethnomethodology

The systematic socialisation of lawyers into the legal profession may change them — as a consequence of this process — into people who treat laws as reified objects, as 'hard' and final data and as arbitrary chosen instruments of social change and intervention. Due to this extensive socialisation process lawyers have a tendency to regard the phenomenon of law as something obvious, natural and taken for granted. This point of view drastically differs from what is represented by an average 'customer' of legal services. He, on the contrary, quite often is afraid of law, is sceptical about the efficiency and justice of legal institutions and often tries to find a refuge in the court only if this appears to him as the only possible defence. An ethnomethodologist intends to grasp this peculiar perspective of an insider and outsider of the obligatory legal system. In connection with that, ethnomethodologists suggest a new look at the so-called socio-legal 'hard data'. 'Hard data' in sociology have been treated for a long time as basic and final research material. Ethnomethodology is sceptical about this. It tries to show that 'hard data' appear as the result of many subjective evaluations and are regarded as such only after a complicated process of more or less conscious selections, approximations, defining mechanisms used by different established schemes and official patterns of various agencies which have the task to accumulate that data. If the members of certain agencies have some sort of preconception or methodological prejudices which incline them to observe only certain phenomena, then the reliability of the collected data is predetermined by the underlying assumptions, which are prefixed by the administative practice. Even such 'hard data' like suicide statistics appear to be biased as a result of different sorts of administrative behaviour.

The major thrust of ethnomethodological empirical research has been by analyses of speech exchange systems including the sequential organisation of turn-taking in conversation. In particular, these studies have been aimed at elucidating the everyday methods of practical reasoning that occur at the mundane, taken-for-granted level of naturally occurring conversation. Clearly the trial system in common law countries is premised on the principle that orality is paramount; interrogation of suspects and witnesses, judicial argument, rules of evidence and so forth, are at the heart of any legal system. Accordingly, problems of order in court, the organisation of verbal interaction in legal settings and the dichotomy between formal and informal judicial procedures, all of which involve specialised speech exchange systems, could be studied from an ethnomethodological perspective.

Symbolic interactionism

A variety of groupings come under the umbrella of 'symbolic interaction', but for all these groups, social structure is defined in terms of negotiated order. Thus, whether it be through a notion of reflexivity (Mead, 1934), through the idea that interaction should be viewed as performances (Goffman, 1959) or through the thesis that meanings are interpreted individually (Blumer, 1969), sociology is defined as the science of social interaction rather than social relations.

It is quite well known that law has not only different images but also that it has various sociological, psychological and economic functions. Some of these are informative, instrumental, educational, pragmatic, symbolic, restrictive, oppressive and policy-making. Symbolic functions of the law — being less recognisable than others — aim to give general guidance about how to behave. It is possible to list as examples of this type of legal expressions, constitutions, declarations, preambles and so forth. Sometimes these symbols are designed in order to give a real guidance (as information) for the behaviour of organs which are supposed to implement the law and also for the 'average legal citizen', but quite often they serve as disguises, hiding behind the elegant rhetoric and spectacular display of values, and with the aim of hiding the real intentions. Symbolic interactionism can single out various social systems and various social milieux in which the law plays symbolic functions together with — or instead of — other functions, such as reformatory, punitive or instrumental functions. In this respect, symbolic interactionism may correspond closely with functionalism, as a complementary perspective, but with a different methodology, which in the case of symbolic interactionists is basically a self-conscious participant observation. Symbolic interactionism may also co-operate in certain ways with exchange theory, especially when it describes the complicated system in which, in exchange for real goods or services, only the symbols of spurious values are offered.

Symbolic interactionist study of law, then, would approach the context of law broadly, even though it is primarily concerned at the 'micro' level of inter-personal conduct. It can place notions such as 'innocent until proved guilty' into a context whereby, through labelling theory, it reveals that juveniles are labelled delinquents before conviction (Cicourel, 1968). Not surprisingly therefore, symbolic interactionism has been utilised most with questions of deviance and societal construction of identities. If deviance is socially constructed, then it makes sense to investigate the way in which the social construction is mirrored in the consciousness of the target group.

An approach which views society in terms of negotiated order would be valuable in studying the actors of the legal process and some of their practices, including for example, plea bargaining (Baldwin and McConville, 1977), and the granting of immunity — the bedrock of negotiation which feeds back into the more formal apparatus of the legal system. Bargains are struck, deals are made, perhaps favours are distributed, and political pressures are applied. (Chapter 9).

Exchange Theory

The starting point for exchange theorists is that most social interaction can be conceptualised as the exchange of goods and services. In this way, it can be said that exchange theory is closely connected with the anthropological perspective which stresses the importance of the norm of reciprocity. According to this perspective, so-called primitive societies are based mainly, although not exclusively, on the rule of reciprocity. Anthropological studies have elucidated this point of view quite clearly. But the exchange theory can be applied also to explain the quite puzzling phenomenon of the efficiency of the socialist economy in certain areas. It is quite well known that the socio-economic order in socialism is almost completely prescribed by the structure of normative legal order which — according to its design and contrary to intentions — weighs down the economic processes in this system. Nevertheless, this system seems to be efficient in certain areas not due to the guidance of the instructions of this normative legal system but due to the peculiarly developed, informal, semi-legal structure which displaces, and is quite often contradictory to, the normative legal system. Various informal arrangements among directors of the formally linked factories, based on the exchange of help, mutual profits, understanding of mutually 'difficult' situations, different types of blackmail, private and institutional bribes, establishes informally accepted and operational structural patterns of co-ordinated behaviour. (This phenomenon is well described by Kurczewski and Frieske, 1977.) The application of exchange theory indicates that the establishment of a scheme of reciprocity may provide an opportunity to avoid the petrified and frozen legal structures which can lead, in some areas of social life, to the smoothing of the economic processes. This could be described as the 'positive' application of exchange theory. Its 'negative' consequences are connected with the systematic corrosion of the legal system which is constantly under attack from behaviour which undercuts its prestige. Exchange theory does not attempt to explain why the law is the way it is, but rather to describe the character of different legal arrangements, including the pay-offs of the exchanges between those involved. Thus, the exchange theory approach could also be utilised to study the practice of plea bargaining. It could also analyse the granting of immunity to witnesses.

Marxism

Use of the Marxist theoretical approach is now widespread in Britain. One can point to at least three relevant reasons for this. First, after methodological scrutiny (contradictions of dialects, appeal to emotional forces, tending to produce a religious comprehensive *Weltaushaung* and so on) Marxism appears as a 'positivistic' approach which simplifies social reality in a significant way. It thereby presents a suggestive model of social reality and its changes. Secondly, Marxism seems to be especially illuminating when it is connected with functionalism: then it is able to single out those hidden forces which act as 'invisible pressure groups', active agents of manipulation which are undetectable at the first glance, and which 'trigger' off manifest social changes. The theoretical perspective of Marxism combined with concrete analysis of law, then, considers not only the form of law, but also the specific effects of legal intervention in social, economic and political relations. Marxism may be useful also when it undertakes the task of forecasting those results which may be generated by conscious social economic changes. Since many economic activities are subject to forms of legislative intervention, Marxism may be illuminating in disclosing those forces which operate behind these interventions. Thirdly, Marxism attacks vehemently all other theoretical perspectives that pretend to elucidate the various factors of social change. Thus, criticism launched by Marxism can be constructive: it could disclose the weaknesses of those theoretical approaches which are under attack.

Therefore, one may say that the main contribution of a Marxist approach to the study of law is its unmasking character, to the extent to which it discloses the hidden forces which shape the visible picture of the law, and when it criticises the possible weaknesses of other theoretical standpoints.

Frankfurt School

Behind its idiosyncratic terminology, the 'critical theory' of the Frankfurt School (like Marxism) belongs to those theoretical approaches which are mainly substantive — it does not say how to study the law, but it intends to elucidate its relation to the society. Nevertheless, in its general form, 'critical theory' is normative in nature, being both policy oriented and practical in its concern with fundamental changes in society. It confronts existing social reality with the norms and ideals that are claimed to be realised. Briefly it says three things. First, the law plays an essential role in the process of keeping together diverse elements in order to reinforce the existing establishments. Secondly, the law becomes in societies 'reified' in this sense, that it is perceived by the social justice administration apparatus and also to some extent by the 'average legal citizen' as a stable, natural, sacred authority which comes from above and has a natural hiding force. Finally, in their attempts to develop a comprehensive theory of present society, the Frankfurt School argues (a) that the principle of exchange penetrates all human relationships, and (b) that public administrative power is increasing. Both these factors result in the absolute supremacy of society over the individual. The theory thus says that the law is supported by the authoritarian attitude which regards 'law and order' (as they are perceived by this attitude) as the fundamental, binding element of the existing social structure. In this sense the Frankfurt School stresses domination as the main function of the law. (It might be an interesting question to analyse the similarities and differences of the concept of 'domination' — as it is perceived by several members of the Frankfurt School and by A. Gramsci, who tried to develop this notion using as a general framework his analysis of the Marxist point of view.) The Frankfurt School suggests accordingly that the sociology of law should, to a greater extent, take up the problems of a theory of state, emphasising the study of politico-legal steering mechanisms in socio-economic processes.

The Frankfurt School offers insights, then, which, derived from the various sources, can be utilised to study law. Habermas, for example, argues that the development of normative structures is the real pacemaker of social evolution. Rottleuthner describes Habermas's increasing concern with socio-legal questions as a 'remarkable trend' (Rottleuthner, Chapter 6). Indeed, his model of communicative ethics can be applied (as Rottleuthner has observed) to courtroom interaction, the structure of conflict resolution through the application of legal or moral rules, and structures of action including the differentiation between action, role, norm or principle such as strategic action in economic relations.

Conclusions and Observations

Within social science, there is profound disagreement between the various approaches. Some would claim that the recent trend in sociology of law has been generally moving away from the study of a given social structure and is drifting towards more empirical and interpretive analyses of social interaction (for example, Blumer, 1969; Cicourel, 1964, 1968; Skolnick, 1966; Sudnow, 1965; Turner, 1974). The above review of theories may appear to gloss over these problems, but the intention of this summary, as well as the collection of reviewed theories, has been to demonstrate that certain perspectives can offer, to a greater or lesser extent, innovative insights for the study of law. It is obvious that existing theories are in competition with each other as to which is the 'best' one. On the other hand, it seems reasonable to believe that a single theory cannot answer all the questions involved in the study of law. This would imply that there is only one version of the study of law that is valid and available. In fact, there is not a standard or comprehensive theory. Instead, there is a multiplicity of approaches which range from the substantive theory to the reflexive theory of a methodological character.

The law of contract is broad enough to be studied from virtually any of the perspectives discussed above, and it has indeed been the subject of various studies (including Beale and Dugdale, 1975; Kurczewski and Frieske, 1977; Macauley, 1963, 1977). At the heart of contract is the principle of the bargain and the exchange. This notion is fundamental not only to exchange theory, but also to Marxism and the Frankfurt School, albeit with different emphases. The Frankfurt School might be concerned with a study of politico-legal steering mechanisms involved in socio-economic processes, Marxists might consider the forces operating behind the law as well as the effect of the law on social, economic and political relations, while exchange theorists could consider the ways in which contracts actually operated, including the character of the informal arrangements between parties that may be integral to the contractual relationship. Clearly, the three approaches overlap.

A structuralist approach would be concerned with the more abstract networks of interrelationships that, it is argued, make up social reality. In particular, a structuralist might inquire into the normative scheme of a contract and ask why it takes its specific form, what devices it uses, if any, to maintain itself; in short, the structural contingencies involved in and influencing what is defined as contractual. Thus, a structuralist could analyse the factual operation of the contract in social life — the normative assumptions, the directives and the agencies set up by the contract, the public response to the law and the actual operation of the contract. In many cases, there may be a gap between the rhetoric of the contract and the practice of its operation. A functionalist could also consider the social context in which the individual contract is framed as well as its impact on social standards. In more general terms, a functionalist might try to locate the law of contract within the social system as a whole.

The stages of a breakdown in the contract relationship would be of interest to the remaining sociological approaches. Aspects of the procedures for dealing with disputes could be the subject of analysis by phenomenologists, ethnomethodologists or symbolic interactionists. For these, the world is given meaning by lived experience. A phenomenologist would be concerned with subjective perceptions of individuals; an ethnomethodologist might consider the speech exchange systems of courts and tribunals established to deal with contractual disputes; while symbolic interactionists could analyse the symbolic functions of contracts, the machinery, the actors and their practices which feed back into the formal apparatus of the contract.

The importance of communication is stressed in several theories; to symbolic interactionists and conversational analysts (ethnomethodologists), language is of crucial importance, while Habermas developed a normative theory of communicative ethics which makes assertions regarding speech acts. Phenomenologists are concerned with everyday common knowledge as are many ethnomethodologists. Loś has argued that a more advanced analysis of different societies could be achieved only through the attempts at a synthesis of the phenomenological approach with a critically oriented analysis of social structure and economy (Chapter 10), while Brittan has observed that most symbolic interactionists adopt a phenomenological stance (Chapter 9). We have outlined the links of functionalism to other approaches earlier.

A multi-dimensional approach tries to combine several perspectives simultaneously. It is to some extent an eclectic approach. But it is not aways possible to utilise. Indeed, some approaches are in direct conflict with others. Thus Habermas would probably reject the empirical analysis of linguistics. Symbolic interactionists reject the doctrine of functionalists (as do others).

However, the complementary nature of different perspectives in the analysis of law can be further observed by considering the approaches suitable for the analysis of certain legal topics. The practice of plea bargaining, for example, has been referred to already, as has the problem of language and communication in the law. More broadly, courtroom interaction is a subject which could be viewed from several perspectives, both the reflexive theories of a methodological nature, such as structuralism, and the substantive theories, including that of the Frankfurt School. The personnel and actors involved in the legal process and its institutions, the jury, and analyses of rules, norms and actions are other examples from a list of infinite topics associated with the study of law that could be approached from sociological perspectives.

Bibliography

Baldwin, J. and McConville, M. *Negotiated Justice* (Martin Robertson, London, 1977)

Beale, H. and Dugdale, T. 'Contracts between Businessmen: Planning and the use of Contractual Remedies', *British Journal of Law and Society*, vol. 2, no. 1 (1975), pp. 45-60

Black, D. *The Behavior of Law* (Academic Press, London, 1976)

Blumer, H. *Symbolic Interactionism: Perspective and Method* (Prentice-Hall, Englewood Cliffs, New Jersey, 1969)

Cicourel, A.V. *Method and Measurement in Sociology* (Free Press, New York, 1964)

______ *The Social Organisation of Juvenile Justice* (Wiley, New York, 1968; see rev. ed., 1976)

Ehrlich, E. *Fundamental Principles of the Sociology of Law* (translated by W.L. Moll, Harvard University Press, New York, 1936)

Friedman, L.M. *Law and Society* (Prentice-Hall, Englewood Cliffs, New Jersey, 1977)

Goffman, E. *The Presentation of Self in Everyday Life* (Doubleday, New York, 1959)

Harris, J.W. *Law and Legal Science* (Clarendon Press, Oxford, 1979)

Kurczewski, J. and Frieske, K. 'Some Problems in the Legal Regulation of the Activities of Economic Institutions' *Law and Society Review*, vol. 11, no. 3 (1977), pp. 489-505

Macauley, S. 'Non-Contractual Relations in Business: A Preliminary Study', *American Sociological Review*, vol. 28, no. 1 (1963), pp. 55-69

______ 'Elegant Models, Empirical Pictures and the Complexities of Contract', *Law and Society Review*, vol. 11, no. 3 (1977), pp. 507-28

Mayhew, L. and Reiss, A.J. 'The Social Organization of Legal Contacts', *American Sociological Review*, vol. 34 (1969), pp. 309-18

Mead, G.H. *Mind, Self and Society* (University of Chicago Press, Chicago, 1934)

Merton, R.K. *Social Theory and Social Structure* (Free Press, New York, 1957)

Nader, L. and Metzger, D. 'Conflict Resolution in Two Mexican Communities' in D.

Black and M. Mileski (eds.), *The Social Organization of Law* (Seminar Press, London, 1973), pp. 95-105
Parsons, T. *The Social System* (Free Press of Glencoe, Illinois, 1951)
Skolnick, J. *Justice Without Trial* (Wiley, New York, 1966)
Stone J. *Social Dimensions of Law and Justice* (Stanford University Press, Stanford, 1965)
Sudnow, D. 'Normal Crimes: Sociological Features of the Penal Code in a Public Defender's Office', *Social Problems,* vol. 12 (1965), pp. 255-70
Taylor, I., Walton, P. and Young, J. *The New Criminology* (Routledge and Kegan Paul, London, 1973)
Turner, R. (ed.) *Ethnomethodology* (Penguin, Harmondsworth, 1974)
Unger, R.M. *Law in Modern Society* (Free Press, New York, 1977)
Young, M.F.D. (ed.) *Knowledge and Control: New Directions for the Sociology of Education* (Collier-Macmillan, London, 1971)

Notes on Contributors

S.L. Andreski is Professor of Sociology at the University of Reading. He has written numerous books including *Military Organisation and Society* (Routledge and Kegan Paul, London, 1954), *Elements of Comparative Sociology* (Weidenfeld and Nicolson, London, 1964), *Parasitism and Subversion: The Case of Latin America* (Weidenfeld and Nicolson, London, 1966), *The African Predicament: A Study of Pathology of Modernisation* (Michael Joseph, London, 1968), *Social Sciences as Sorcery* (André Deutsch, London, 1972), *The Prospects of a Revolution in the U.S.A.* (Tom Stacey, Littlehampton, 1973), and *Cultural Pollution* (André Deutsch, London, forthcoming). He has also edited a number of books.

J. Maxwell Atkinson is Senior Research Fellow in Sociology at the Centre for Socio-Legal Studies and Research Fellow of Wolfson College, Oxford. Dr Atkinson is author of *Discovering Suicide: Studies in the Social Organization of Sudden Death* (Macmillan, London, 1978) and, with Paul Drew, of *Order in Court: The Organisation of Verbal Interaction in Judicial Settings* (Macmillan, London, 1979), and has been a member of the editorial board of *Sociology* and *Language and Communication.*

Arthur Brittan is Senior Lecturer in Sociology at the University of York. He is the author of *Meanings and Situations* (Routledge and Kegan Paul, London, 1973) and *The Privatised World* (Routledge and Kegan Paul, London, 1977). He is also the general editor of *Monographs in Social Theory* for Routledge and Kegan Paul.

J.W. Harris is Lecturer in Law at the University of Oxford and Fellow of Keble College. Dr Harris is the author of *Variation of Trusts* (Stevens, 1975), *Law and Legal Science* (Clarendon Press, Oxford, 1979) and *Legal Philosophies* (Butterworths, 1980).

Anthony Heath is Lecturer in Sociology at the University of Oxford and Fellow of Jesus College. Dr Heath is author of *Rational Choice and Social Exchange* (Cambridge University Press, Cambridge, 1976) and, with A.H. Halsey and J.M. Ridge, *Origins and Destinations: Family, Class and Education in Britain* (Clarendon Press, Oxford, 1980).

Alan Hunt is Assistant Dean (Law) of the Faculty of Business Studies and Management at Middlesex Polytechnic. Dr Hunt's books include

Class and Class Structure (Lawrence and Wishart, London, 1977), *The Sociological Movement in Law* (Macmillan, London, 1978), *Marxism and Democracy* (Lawrence and Wishart, London, 1979), and, with M. Cain, *Marx and Engels on Law* (Academic Press, London, 1979), and *Law and the Social Order* (Macmillan, London, 1980).

Edmund Leach was formerly Provost of King's College, Cambridge. Sir Edmund has written numerous books including *Rethinking Anthropology* (The Athlone Press, London, 1961) and *Culture and Communication* (Cambridge University Press, Cambridge, 1976).

Maria Łoś was formerly Research Fellow in Socio-Legal Studies at the Centre for Criminological Studies at the University of Sheffield. She is the author of two books in Polish, and, with Adam Podgórecki, of *Multi-Dimensional Sociology* (Routledge and Kegan Paul, London, 1979).

Adam Podgórecki is Professor of Sociology and Anthropology at Carleton University, Ottawa, Canada. Prior to this, he was Special Research Fellow at the Centre for Socio-Legal Studies, Oxford. He has written many books in Polish. His books in English include *Law and Society* (Routledge and Kegan Paul, London, 1974), and with W. Kaupen, J. Van Houtte, P. Vinke and B. Kutchinsky, *Knowledge and Opinion about Law* (Martin Robertson, London, 1973), and *Practical Social Sciences* (Routledge and Kegan Paul, London, 1975). He has also edited a book, *Sociotechnics* (Mouton, The Hague, 1975).

Hubert Rottleuthner is Professor of Sociology of Law at the Free University of Berlin, West Germany. His books include *Richtirliches Handeln* (Athenaum, Frankfurt am Main, 1973), *Rechtswissenschaft als Socialwissenschaft* (Fischer, Frankfurt am Main, 1973) and *Rechtstheorie und Rechtssoziologie* (Alber, Frankfurt am Main, 1981). He has edited *Probleme der Marxistischen Rechtstheorie* (Suhrkamp, Frankfurt am Main, 1975) and Professor Rottleuthner is joint editor of the new German journal on the sociology of law, *Zeitschrift für Rechtssoziologie.*

David Schiff is Lecturer in Law at the London School of Economics. He has written numerous articles on jurisprudence and sociology of law, including 'Socio-Legal Theory: Social Structure and Law', in the *Modern Law Review,* vol. 39, no. 3 (1976); he is currently writing on the works of Timasheff.

Christopher Whelan is Research Officer in Law at the Centre for Socio-Legal Studies, Wolfson College, Oxford. Dr Whelan has written articles on socio-legal studies, law and economics, and labour law.

Philip Wilkinson is Research Officer in Sociology of Law at the

Centre for Socio-Legal Studies, Wolfson College Oxford. He has co-authored with Clive Grace, *Sociological Inquiry and Legal Phenomena* (Collier-Macmillan, London, 1978), and *Negotiating the Law* (Routledge and Kegan Paul, London, 1978). He has written several articles on socio-legal studies and sociological theory.

Author Index

Subject Index